G000114200

From Question to Quest

From Question to Quest:
Literary-Philosophical Enquiries into the Challenges of Life

By

Marian F. Sia and Santiago Sia

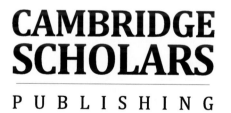

From Question to Quest: Literary-Philosophical Enquiries into the Challenges of Life,
by Marian F. Sia and Santiago Sia

This book first published 2010

Cambridge Scholars Publishing

12 Back Chapman Street, Newcastle upon Tyne, NE6 2XX, UK

British Library Cataloguing in Publication Data
A catalogue record for this book is available from the British Library

Copyright © 2010 by Marian F. Sia and Santiago Sia

All rights for this book reserved. No part of this book may be reproduced, stored in a retrieval system,
or transmitted, in any form or by any means, electronic, mechanical, photocopying, recording or
otherwise, without the prior permission of the copyright owner.

ISBN (10): 1-4438-2159-4, ISBN (13): 978-1-4438-2159-9

To

our students
who have shared our questions
and
joined in our quests

OTHER BOOKS

BY MARIAN F. SIA AND SANTIAGO SIA

From Suffering to God: Exploring Our Images of God in the Light of Suffering
The Fountain Arethuse: a Novel Set in the University Town of Leuven

BY SANTIAGO SIA

God in Process Thought: a Study in Charles Hartshorne's Concept of God
Process Thought and the Christian Doctrine of God
Charles Hartshorne's Concept of God: Philosophical and Theological Response.
(with André Cloots) *Framing a Vision of the World: Essays in Philosophy, Religion and Science*
Religion, Reason and God: Essays in the Philosophies of Charles Hartshorne and A.N. Whitehead
Philosophy in Context: Dharma Endowment Lectures 2005
(with Ferdinand Santos), *Personal Identity, the Self and Ethics*
Ethical Contexts and Theoretical Issues: Essays in Ethical Thinking

TABLE OF CONTENTS

FOREWORD

Matthew Arnold once left us shivering on Dover beach, the tide of faith receding and in the darkness of ignorance and violence. It was a bleak image from the middle years of the nineteenth century which has haunted the thoughts and imaginations of both modernity and postmodernity. But we might imagine another moment of standing on the shore before a blue expanse of ocean, a moment of contemplation and of thinking about that which remains but an idea, a question—what would it be to plunge into that immensity? Try it and see: the wading deeper, the moment when we cast ourselves upon the deepening waters, the exhilaration of the first strokes, the image of the bottom far below, the balance between the effort of swimming and the supporting, beautiful, dangerous, immense water.

To read this book is to experience that moment of the plunge, a moment of faith when we move from thinking in anticipation to thinking in the act of doing, from the questioner to the quester. Stanley Fish once admonished our intellectual endeavours with the warning that "Being Interdisciplinary Is So Very Hard to Do." Indeed, he said, within the "existing authoritative lines and boundaries" of our academies a genuine interdisciplinarity is finally impossible for it "merely redomiciles us in enclosures that do not advertise themselves as such."[1] He certainly had a point in the context of the banal incentives of contemporary policies within our higher education systems, but still this book offers a bright, serious and lively challenge to Fish's admonishings. We may attempt the separate disciplines of philosophy, the study of literature or theology, but finally to plunge into the complexities of language and textuality is to find that we can explore the meanings offered by life in a form of thinking which is only possible in daring acts of doing by conversations with the texts of philosophy, theology and literature and by conversations from within the fluidities of literature and the processes of thought.

The process thought of Alfred North Whitehead and of Charles Hartshorne lie close to the surface of this text. Their thinking celebrates the interdependencies and interrelationships of the world conceived as a social organism, a world in which God is both and at once affected and affecting

---

[1] Stanley Fish, *There's No Such Thing as Free Speech and it's a Good Thing Too.* (Oxford: Oxford University Press, 1994), p. 237.

and a world which is characterised by becoming and the challenges of change. Such thinking saturates the chapters which follow here, chapters which constitute a journey in which "the quest for the answer becomes the answer itself", known in that daring, exhilarating moment when we cease merely to think in anticipation and become one with the living ocean itself.

Here we are led in thinking not merely by direct guidance but also in the company of the great poets and writers—the Shakespeare, the Ovid, the Keats and others who immortalise in poetry, and also the imaginary conversations of the writers' own fictions and fictive texts in growing, living sentences. As readers, accordingly, we find ourselves as members of a great community, the community of interpreters, and thinkers—doing it, finally ourselves. Such are the signs of the great teacher who leads us and then has the courage to leave us as we begin to swim on our own, courageously and joyfully. We can do it ourselves, and the quest is one in which we are all participants in a shared life, seeking wisdom, the good, and finally deliverance.

This is truly a work of imaginative thinking. It confronts the great questions in a world in which we are all too often content with avoiding them in our obsession with particularity. It listens attentively to the great masters of philosophy and literature which have gone before, but knows that we can never truly think until we have summoned the courage to think for ourselves. The greatest writers know the importance of self-limitation, just as process thought acknowledges the self-limitation of God, for only then can life be fully shared—for those who participate in it not a sentence, but truly a quest for meaning.

I really enjoyed reading this book!

—Professor David Jasper
Professor of Literature and Theology, University of Glasgow
Changyang Chair Professor, Renmin University of China

PREFACE

The completion of any task, particularly if it has been a lengthy process, always brings about some wholesome relief. But it also provides one with a welcome opportunity to glance back and to record one's indebtedness to those who have made it possible and worthwhile. We are more than happy to do that here.

This book, which continues our collaboration in earlier publications, is the result not just of our research but also of our teaching. While conducting research work, particularly in our respective disciplines, can be a lonely pursuit, teaching those subjects certainly is not. We have interacted with so many students, of varying ages, in several countries and on diverse occasions. To them all—the book is dedicated to them—we express our thanks for stimulating us with their questions and for keeping us on track in the quest for answers. Our pursuit has always taken place in specific contexts. To the different academic institutions and their respective libraries which provided those valuable contexts, our sincerest thanks. Among these were: Terenure College, Dublin, Ireland; Loyola Marymount University, Los Angeles, USA; Katholieke Universiteit Leuven, Belgium; Newman College, Birmingham, England; and Milltown Institute, Dublin, Ireland.

We remain indebted to our respective families for the learning and nurturing environment which they have continued to provide for us—to all of them our heartfelt gratitude.

We are grateful to Prof David Jasper, whose work in literature and theology is internationally known, for kindly accepting our invitation to write the Foreword to this book. We also appreciate very much the endorsement of our book by Prof Jan Van der Veken, whose own work has been influential with so many scholars and students. We want to thank Aliman Sears for enriching our reflections on a particular challenge in life with his own insights and for giving us permission to include the resulting essay.

The publication of this book represents a stage in the academic career of one of us: his retirement as Dean of Philosophy at Milltown Institute. President Mary McAleese's message to mark the occasion is included in this book. To her and to Dr. Martin McAleese our sincerest thanks for the honour and for their good wishes.

We would also like to acknowledge with thanks the cooperation of editors/publishers who have given their permission to include in the present book sections/chapters from previously published work: "Before Another Dawn" (poem), "Reflections on Job's and Hopkins' Question (Chapter 1), "Literary Meditations on Death and Christian Hope" (Chapter 2) from *From Suffering to God: Exploring our Images of God in the Light of Suffering* (St. Martin's Press/Macmillan, 1994); "Concretizing Concrete Experience," (Chapter 3) and Aliman Sears, "Suffering and Surrender in the Midst of Divine Persuasion," (Chapter 5) in Darren J.N. Middleton (ed.), *God, Literature and Process Thought* (Ashgate, 2002).

Many individuals—and this is by no means a complete list—deserve our gratitude: Charles Hartshorne, John Füllenbach, John Gaskin, Mel Bertolozzi, Barbara Rico, Tony Amadeo, Janez Juhant, Timothy O'Connor, Maura Grant, Linda Hand, David Walker as well as all the staff at Cambridge Scholars Publishing.

INTRODUCTION

Life and its Challenges

Writing about life and its challenges is truly a daunting task. Many would regard it not merely as an ambitious but even a preposterous undertaking. After all, the complexity of life and its myriad of challenges, constantly confronting each of us at every stage and at different levels, have led many to claim—rightly—that life is after all a real mystery. We are perplexed by life no matter what aspect of it we are investigating. On the other hand, the seemingly endless list of publications which purport to guide people on how to deal with life's challenges would lead others—understandably it would seem—to express reservation about yet another work which deals with this topic.

Our aim in this book is a less ambitious one since we certainly do not regard this work as offering a manual, as it were, that would enable one to tackle, or at least cope with, the challenges of life. That would be beyond our competence. And given the complexity of life, we are well aware of the extent of the difficulty facing anyone who wishes to write about it. Our own personal and professional experiences, including our dealings with others, would attest to that. And yet, there is some justification for saying that if there is any topic on which every one of us—including ourselves— is equipped to say something, it is life itself. After all, it is the one centre from which everything that we are and do radiates. Life and its challenges—admittedly not on the same scale—are familiar to all of us insofar as we are living human beings. It is therefore a topic on which we can "touch base" as it were since we are on recognisable territory. That is the aim of this book. Our hope, in sharing our enquiries into specific themes, is to reach out to others and possibly facilitate their own reflections as they turn their attention to their own lives.

From Question to Quest

The main title of this book is intended to convey the approach we have taken. In facing up to life and its challenges, questions inevitably arise. A number of contexts or sets of experiences provide the setting. The kind of setting in turn produces specific questions—some fundamental, others trivial, but always seeking some kind of answer.

As teachers in our respective disciplines (literature and philosophy) but also as mentors in the educative process, we have been exposed to a barrage of questions—coming from our charges of all ages and from ourselves—not only about the subject-matter of our teaching but also, and more significantly so, about life itself. It is particularly refreshing when a question seeking knowledge of a certain item turns out to be a question yearning for wisdom. It is satisfying when an inquisitive mind on track for information treks into the larger terrain of which the original question is merely a launch pad. It is exciting, even if it is also puzzling, when the question or questions result in a quest. This is as true about our dealings with others as with our own journey in life.

The transition from question to quest—touched upon several times in the book—can be described as a rather natural transition. That is to say, as human beings, characterised as rational beings, it is common for us all to move from the stage of asking questions to looking for answers. There is something about human beings which somehow pushes us in that direction. Admittedly, sometimes that quest is rather mundane, dictated by immediate concerns or more pressing factors. And it is not a progression that we all have the luxury to indulge in. But it seems to us nonetheless that it is imbedded in our very humanity in such a way that at some stage in people's lives—given appropriate circumstances—even the so-called simple questions can trigger off the more fundamental ones which in turn lead us to a quest, not just for the immediate answers but also for the more searching ones.[1] The ordinary query that prompted a simple question can, at times, turn out to be a more protracted and fundamental quest.

Literary-Philosophical Enquiries

We believe that David Jasper's observations regarding the value of literature for theological reflections apply just as much for philosophical ones. As he puts it, "In literature we glimpse, at times, the fulfilment of our nature, cast in the imaginative genius of great art, and continuing to persuade us of the value and ultimate truth of the theological enterprise as a seeking for utterance of the divine mystery as it is known and felt in our

---

[1] Jan Van der Veken, writing on the importance of the quest, quotes one of his students after a lecture course: "To think about such problems makes life worth living." Cf. "My Way from Being to Becoming," in André Cloots and Santiago Sia, *Framing a Vision of the World: Essays in Philosophy, Science and Religion* Louvain Philosophical Studies 14 (Leuven University Press, 1999), p. 285.

experience."[2] Thus, we have drawn on our academic resources in these enquiries. It is well-known that literature and philosophy focus on life—and on other matters, of course. For that reason they have much to offer in this task. But in turning to them, we have avoided compartmentalising these disciplines since our main interest was not to write separate reflections in these academic subjects. Since we believe in their intimate connection—a certain continuity between literature and philosophy, as discussed more fully in the Appendix[3]—we wanted to enlist their aid in this joint venture into specific themes associated with life's challenges. It is for this reason that what the book offers is a set of *literary-philosophical* enquiries. It is the one set of quests—stimulated, deepened and widened by literature *and* philosophy as well as developed in a literary *and* philosophical way. Again, the source is no other than our own shared humanity and our experience of its challenges. Needless to say, given the enormity of the topic, we have focused only on selected themes prompted by our own interests and concerns.

The book is composed of different chapters. They were written at different times and for different occasions or for diverse audiences—which will account for a certain variation in the style of writing. There is some inevitable repetition, which we have kept to a minimum and did so only in the interest of preserving the original context of these enquiries. We have, however, edited and structured them, not just for the sake of coherence and consistency, but also because we wanted to show that the continuity of the topic "question and quest" is rooted in a common base, humanity. We have also arranged them in a certain order which reflects a rather temporal sequence—from life to death and in-between, as it were. At the same time, we have separated them as "distinct questions and specific quests" because the contexts from which they arise are really more aptly described as "a series of events".[4] Life, which prompts the question and leads to a quest, is not "experienced" as a continuous whole even if it is lived as such.

In Chapter One " Is Life a Sentence?: the Quest for Meaning" (based on a paper for the International Conference on the Art of Life, Celje, Slovenia, organised by the University of Ljubljana) we take up one, if not the

---

[2] David Jasper, *The Study of Literature and Religion: an Introduction.* Studies in Literature and Religion (Macmillan Press, 1989), p. 138. See also his, *The Sacred Desert: Religion, Literature, Art and Culture* (Blackwell Publishing, 2004).

[3] Some readers may wish to read this essay first before the actual chapters of the book.

[4] For a philosophical discussion and justification of this claim, cf. Ferdinand Santos and Santiago Sia, *Personal Identity, the Self and Ethics* (Palgrave Macmillan, 2007).

most fundamental, question *about* life, that is to say, whether there is meaning to life. Taking our cue from language and grammar, we enquire into the possibility of finding meaning in life. Suggesting that, just as the meaning of a sentence (and a series of sentences) can be properly read and correctly interpreted by inserting the correct punctuation marks, we should engage in certain activities in the course of our lives (likened to the different punctuation marks) to enable us to read life's message.

Chapter Two "Education—for What?: the Quest for Wisdom" takes up the quest for meaning further in the context of the educative process. Reflecting on the need to educate ourselves and others, we propose that the route we ought to take in our quest is the one that leads, not just to knowledge, but more importantly to wisdom. The question and the quest, in this particular context, enable us to explore the issues that arise because of the nature of the educand—a human person, and not just a knowledgeable and skilled worker.

The focus of Chapter Three "What Ought I to Do?: the Quest for the Good" is a fundamental ethical question. The quest for wisdom entails knowing what the right action to take is. We show that in raising the question, the quest for the good brings us to key issues which include not just knowing what is involved in judging the ethical status of an action but also, and more significantly so, why the question arises in the first place. It is essentially a *human* question and quest.

In Chapter Four "The Need for Another—Why?: the Quest for Community" our enquiry brings up a significant aspect of our humanity; namely, our social nature. Inasmuch as the question regarding the ethical status of our actions leads us to examining who we are as individuals, this chapter opens up another route to our human nature. We probe into our felt needs, enquire as to what is involved, and then "converse" with Martin Buber to help us understand our quest for community.

That question and quest guide us to Chapter Five "How Should We Interact with One Another?: the Quest for Power" (based on a paper prepared for the VII International Symposium in Philosophy, Koçaeli University, Izmit, Turkey). It is, of course, a complex question, and we have chosen to concentrate on a specific kind of interacting with one another; namely, the exercise of power. Here an alternative conception of power, based on Charles Hartshorne's philosophy, is put forward with a view to showing its implications on how we should interact with one another, including with nature and with God.

As we face life's challenges, we realise that one of the greatest challenges to any claim that it has meaning (the topic of Chapter One) is the reality of suffering (and the consequent problem of evil). Our enquiry in

Chapter Six "Seeing God in All Things—even in Suffering?: the Quest for a Rationale" takes the shape of analysing the "questioning" that both Job and Hopkins underwent as they demanded a rationale from God for their suffering. We then ask what we can learn from the quests of these two characters.

The reality and inevitability of death poses a significant challenge: can life be meaningful when, as various poets have expressed it so graphically, death cuts it short, at times so cruelly or so suddenly? How should we view it? As we pursue these questions, in the quest for deliverance from its threat, in Chapter Seven "O, Death, Where is Thy Sting?": the Quest for Deliverance", we turn to Henry Vaughan to provide us with some light in this dark passage. As we reflect further and seek meaning, we turn to John Donne and George Herbert who, in their poems, meditate on the Christian understanding of the death and resurrection of Jesus.

The last chapter is, in a sense, the ultimate question that challenges our human existence: what is our final destination? Chapter Eight "You still shall Live—for Evermore?: the Quest for Immortality" analyses Shakespeare's preoccupation with this theme.. He was obsessed with time, death and mortality, which can be seen primarily in the sonnets addressed to the young man and in the Dark Lady sonnets. It troubled him greatly that beauty is prey to, and subject to, temporality and mortality. We follow him in his quest for the right strategy to counter this challenge. We then pursue the matter further by engaging the philosophy of Charles Hartshorne who offers a particular interpretation of immortality.

By way of a Postscript, titled "Where Does it All End?: the Quest for Answers", we ask the reader to accompany a number of fictional characters from our novels, who have embarked on their own particular quests in life and to note what they have learned about the quest for answers about life.

Appendix A: "Literature and Philosophy: a Whiteheadian Nexus" develops A.N. Whitehead's insights into the relationship—Whitehead has introduced the term "nexus" to describe the relatedness of reality—between these two academic disciplines. It informs and underpins the methodology followed in this work.

Appendix B: "Suffering and Surrender in the Midst of Divine Persuasion: a Discussion of the Sias' Approach to the Challenge of Suffering and Evil" by Aliman Sears presents his reflections on one of the greatest challenges to life. Basing his essay on the published works of the authors, he puts forward an interdisciplinary and comparative interpretation and commentary that has been influenced by process philosophical thinking.

President Mary McAleese's "Message", conveying her good wishes on the retirement of one of the authors as Dean of Philosophy, brings our book of enquiries to a close—literally and figuratively. Yet she indicates that the conclusion of such a task is merely a chapter in the larger book of life and a phase in the continuing quest for answers to its challenges.

CHAPTER ONE

IS LIFE A SENTENCE?:
THE QUEST FOR MEANING

Sentence or Sentences

At a recent interview the question was posed to one of us as to what the most important fact that he had learned about life was. His immediate reply was that "Life is a series of sentences. We need to find the time to punctuate it properly to be able to read its message. Otherwise, life becomes a sentence." He added that this comment would probably not be regarded as a fact, but that there are innumerable cases that would justify the claim.

It may strike one that such a comment is merely a play on words; and philosophy, which informs it, is certainly not immune to this criticism. Moreover, to many people it certainly would not sound convincing. For various reasons, they find life meaningless; and the attempt to argue otherwise is futile. Such reactions would certainly be understandable.

Yet it seems to us that something deeply rooted in our nature as human beings grounds this comment. In one form or another our human situation unsettles us, and it is this which leads to the desire, and even a quest, for meaningfulness. If this observation is indeed correct, then that desire is translated in this context into the question as to whether life is after all a sentence passed on us. Admittedly but regrettably, that would seem to be the case as experienced by some.

The contrary claim that is being made in the reply at the interview is that life's message could be compared to a series of sentences.[1] For it to be properly read—drawing on what one learns from grammar—it needs the correct punctuation marks. We need, as it were, to punctuate it properly for its meaning to become clearer to us. This is another assertion that needs unpacking, of course. We propose to do that here. There is a further

---

[1] We are using "sentences" in the loose sense, and are therefore including questions, exclamations, imperatives and so on.

assumption in this claim; namely, that life *does contain* a message, a given one, and that the onus is on human beings to make the effort and to take the time to discover the punctuating moments that will facilitate us in our quest for meaningfulness. It is an assumption that would also need to be addressed.

A Poetic Reflective Moment

But first, let us read this poem, titled "Before Another Dawn":[2]

that awe-some sunrise here—
ever noticed it, Lord?
how the light streams out,
penetrating every nook,
passing out new cheer,
dissipating old fear
as the sun slowly rises!

> *well, it is like that, Lord.*
> *I mean, we human beings*
> *are searching for that sun in our lives—*
> *to put meaning into our daily lives,*
> *to bring cheer to us all.*

if we don't grasp it—
this meaning, that is—
nothing will look bright to us
nothing will ex-sist for us.

take away the sun—
you know what happens.
we turn to substitutes;
> *lighting candles*
> *switching on electricity*

> *and we are contented—*
> *at least for a time,*

---

[2] Reprinted from Marian F. Sia and Santiago Sia, *From Suffering to God: Exploring our Images of God in the Light of Suffering* (Macmillan, 1994), pp. xi-xii.

knowing the sun will re-rise
re-brightening
our world.

and so we are given courage
to face another morn.

yes, Lord, that's what we are searching for
meaning
real meaning
to lace together all the seemingly
in sig
ni
fi cant
de
tails
to re-make them into a whole.

for otherwise, we shall reach out for
evanescent substitutes.

as we g r o p e about
we feel restless
dis con nect ed

lonely.

but
could it be that restlessness,
frustration,
loneliness
are woven so intimately into the cloth of life
that if we dare pull them out
we would be ruining the whole weave of an intricate pattern?

are they really the shady colours
balancing the light and loud-coloured ones?

tell that to us, Lord, when things are bright—
we'll agree perfectly with you.

but explain that to us
when these shades really dampen us
and we'll just wonder—
in unbelief, perhaps.

Ah, men!

The Quest for Meaning

This quest for meaning in life—which we believe is rooted in our human make-up and expressed in the poem above—takes us in different directions. For some, religion provides the right setting; and the answers that the different religious traditions teach enable them to appreciate their present situation and the goal ahead of them. St. Augustine articulates this quite well—albeit in a slightly different context—in his famous statement that our hearts are restless until they rest in God. For an increasing number of people, however, a more acceptable road is that mapped out by psychology, the human sciences or even science itself. One can see this trend in the popularity of these disciplines, often as an alternative or even as an antithesis to religion. Others find greater satisfaction, and hence some meaning, in the more immediate and tangible results of their desire for a better kind of life as they pursue wealth,[3] health and fame[4]. There is nothing new here, but somehow as countries become more developed or sophisticated, an increasing number of people seem to turn in this direction. Despite these seemingly unconnected routes being taken, however, there is at least a certain common starting ground; namely, that all of us are *questing* for an answer. In fact, even the rather negative position adopted by those who reject any meaningfulness to life[5] or the attempt to discover it can be said to be itself some kind of answer—and that in turn implies a certain direction taken in life.

---

[3] The present global economic situation has left many in the developed countries disenchanted with such a direction.

[4] The lives of the famous are quite instructive in this respect.

[5] A particularly poignant image that has left a lasting impression on us regarding meaninglessness is that of a clock that has its numerals, but had lost its hands and still keeps on ticking.

The Philosophical Route

Since the claim being made here is that all of us, no matter what station in life we occupy, are in varying degrees engaged in this quest, what then has philosophy to contribute to our understanding of this human situation and of this human pursuit? What kind of route does it open up for us? Is the philosophical route not rather the privilege of a few? So why take a philosophical route on this quest?

Centuries ago the Greek philosopher Aristotle had commented on a similar situation. In his *Nicomachean Ethics,* he raises the question as to what it is that every human being is aiming for ("the object of life", as he calls it). He defines it as "good", not in the ethical sense but more in a biological or psychological sense since he bases himself on his observations of the general behaviour of reality. Referring more specifically to the human situation, Aristotle observes that all human beings aim towards a common good (or goal), leading him to maintain that there is agreement on the universality of the human search for happiness, *eudaimonia*. He notes, on the other hand, that people differ on what they consider to be the form of happiness they want. Aristotle lists wealth, fame, pleasure, and virtue as goals that some people set for themselves. Critiquing these as being inadequate—for Aristotle, these are goods rather than the good—he argues that each of these is really a means rather than the ultimate goal or end that human beings desire for its own sake. His own standpoint leads him to consider *eudaimonia* to be the full development of human rationality: contemplation, not in the religious sense, but thinking for the sake of thinking.

Aristotle's own answer to the question which he poses would hardly meet with much approval—in fact, some would view it rather cynically. He has nevertheless shown—and the reason for our reference to him on this point—that the quest itself is more solidly grounded because it is universal. And as he puts it, this is because of the kind of beings that we are. The search for happiness is rooted in our very humanity. It is useful to be reminded of that point as we turn our attention to the quest for meaning in life.

There is of course a link between the quest for meaning in life and the desire for ultimate happiness. Not only do both arise from our human nature, but it can also be demonstrated that achievement, or even the recognition, of the meaningfulness of life can be so uplifting that it results in more than transitory satisfaction. It could also be argued that attainment of happiness is only possible when one not only derives complete satisfaction but also grasps its full sense. It should be added too that meaningfulness therefore should not be given a restricted intellectual interpretation. While the distinction between *eudaimonia* and meaningfulness is probably less crucial, it would be helpful nonetheless to point out that meaningfulness involves not just seeing the sense *in* life but *of* life itself. It specifically focuses on more than an appreciation of what life has to offer but more significantly *that* it matters.

Philosophy—the route being pursued here—has long been associated with the pursuit of wisdom and with the search for truth. Since it implies a protracted and systematic activity, there seems to be a perception that only a few can really be engaged in it. Some philosophers themselves, including Plato and Aristotle, have perpetuated that misperception. Plato insists that only a handful of souls manage to emerge from the cave of darkness into the light, a rich image of the philosophical pursuit. Aristotle, for his part, maintains that philosophising connotes leisure, and hence is only possible for those who can afford it. Given this situation, turning to philosophy can hardly be helpful in our quest for meaning, which it has been claimed is widespread.

And yet, while conceding that philosophy as understood by these two philosophers and others is a specific concern of a few, a role undertaken by a handful and a task fulfilled only by those naturally gifted or properly trained, the pursuit of wisdom and the search for truth are far from being restricted to these individuals or to this grouping. These are human activities, whether we refer to them as philosophy or by another name is not as important. The knowledge and skills imparted by philosophical training can facilitate that pursuit but it does not initiate it. Nor can wisdom or the truth be attained only in philosophy as understood in this specific way.

The love of wisdom—the etymology of philosophy—is actually rooted in our common humanity. In one way or the other, all human beings are engaged in philosophical thinking, albeit at different levels. In fact, many of the issues discussed and developed further in academic philosophy stem from everyday concerns; and many of the philosophical findings, even when at times they seem rather far-fetched, can enhance everyday life.[6] The urge to pursue fundamental questions about life and reality is neither the prerogative nor the privilege of those who have dedicated themselves professionally to this task. Nor is philosophy limited to the academic investigations of those who do wish to delve deeper into fundamental questions and the answers given by past and present practitioners of this discipline. Strictly philosophical debates such as occur in scholarly conferences or recounted in scholarly publications have their place and significance,

---

[6] This search for wisdom is the theme of our novel, *The Fountain Arethuse.*

but they should not restrict our understanding of the nature and use of philosophical thinking.

To clarify this point, perhaps one should make the distinction between the study of philosophy and the act of philosophising. In some form or the other, it is actually the act of philosophising, that every human being engages in, rather than in philosophy itself. But it is that same act that leads to and is the basis of the study of philosophy. The more formal and structured form of this act—which is what concerns students and teachers of philosophy—is what is sometimes regarded as "philosophy". Needless to say, this is an essential development. After all, the pursuit of the questions asked and the answers given need to be carried out at a particular level that very few would have the luxury or the leisure to do so. Moreover, we can benefit from reading the works of those who have carried out the act of philosophising in great depth and to a large extent. Nonetheless, this more academic and formal pursuit should not ignore the basis of philosophical thinking itself.

Accordingly, in our quest for the meaningfulness of life, philosophy can be helpful, precisely because the desire for meaning needs to be pursued much more intensely and thoroughly if we are not to be satisfied with merely superficial answers. Admittedly, philosophers understand and practice philosophy differently—and this can result in much confusion—but philosophy, with its insistence on raising fundamental questions, analysing the issues and pursuing any answer to its logical conclusion, can prod us on towards a viewpoint that can stand the test of careful and rigorous scrutiny by human reason. While it cannot and should not guarantee indisputable conclusions, philosophy nevertheless can abet the task of arriving at a more consistent, coherent and adequate answer. After all, asking whether life is meaningful is more than just asking what one would like to do for the day. To give an answer to that fundamental question is definitely unlike merely enumerating the options that one can choose for the day's activity. Pursuing the meaning of life implies a thoroughness that befits our very humanity itself and challenges it. And for this task philosophy is particularly well-suited.

Philosophy and Language

Just as philosophy has been associated with wisdom and truth, so has it also, particularly in contemporary times, been linked with language. In fact, at times philosophy is interpreted as the analysis of language. One hears of philosophy's function to be the clarification of issues that have become clouded in the hope of dissolving, as it were, the problems that baffle philosophical minds. However, while this can be of invaluable assistance in arriving at truth or achieving wisdom, philosophy can and should go beyond—*pace* some philosophers—merely analysing language. Here we will try to do both.

In the present context, the connection between philosophy and language is particularly appropriate since the initial comment in this enquiry focused on life as a series of sentences and the correct punctuation to enable one to read its meaning. The grammar of language—more particularly, punctuation marks—will therefore serve as a valuable metaphor for this exercise. Taking up once again what was asserted at the start, the claim that is being made here is that we need to insert the proper punctuating marks—that is to say, to engage in certain kinds of human acts in life—to allow life's meaning to come across to us as readers—that is to say, as participants of life. Again, we need to be reminded that the assumption in the present context is that life does have a meaning and that our task is to make the effort to read it or discover it. That meaning is lost if we do not make the effort; and it becomes distorted when we insert the wrong punctuation marks—meaning, neglect certain essential human activities.

To assume that life does have meaning is not to ignore that this very fundamental issue itself should be of concern to us here. So taking up this point now, it needs to be said that what is implied by this assumption is that we will not know the answer *until* we are actually engaged in the very task of searching for it. In other words, it is *in and through* our efforts to discover meaning that we learn *that* life has meaning. This point is quite different from saying that we create meaning, as some existentialist philosophers were prone to assert, as if there is no other meaning except the one of our subjectivist creation.[7] Rather, just as a series of words can simply be a grouping of words with no coherent sense unless and until we punctuate them properly so that they become meaningful sentences, so does life present itself to us. It is of course possible that the grouping of words is merely that: words strung together, not even qualifying as clauses, much less sentences. But generally we will not know that to be the case until we take the trouble to place certain punctuation marks even if only tentatively. We could of course also be accused of reading meaning or sense into the assembled words. But that would in fact confirm the point

---

[7] Albert Camus, an existentialist thinker, cites the situation of Sisyphus, condemned to roll a boulder up a hill, only to have it roll down again after reaching the top. Sisyphus has to keep repeating this activity forever. For Camus, the human situation is a similar absurdity, but human beings can create values that will give them some purposes in life.

that it is in and through our effort that meaning is discovered. In short, the attempt is in a way also a disclosure.

Turning to Grammar

Punctuation marks, an integral feature of the grammar of any language,[8] enable us to read a group of words in ways that convey a definite sense and elicit a specific response from us.[9] Punctuation marks break up words, sentences and even paragraphs to facilitate our grasp of the message. They are marks which we add to the words of the text to enable us to get the meaning. Without them the text would be merely a collection or even an undecipherable jumble of words.[10]

For example, a particular grouping of words, which we would normally refer to as a sentence and ends in a full stop (or period) indicates a statement of fact, a description, a declaration and other similar claims. A question mark elicits a different response, this time from the reader or, in conversation, from the other party. At times, it may be what is termed a rhetorical question and thus no specific answer is expected or given. What is common is that a message that is followed by this punctuation mark, unlike a full stop, raises a point or makes a query. It asks rather than states. In contrast, a message that ends in an exclamation point comes across more strongly: it is intended to express the speaker's feelings, or to alert the reader.

Other punctuating marks play other roles in eliciting grammatical sense. Quotation marks enclose the message and disclose a source; they can also show that a certain significance is being given to the quoted message in relation to the primary text. A colon (or a semi-colon) halts the message, thus indicating that there is more to come: a further explanation or an illustration. Commas, on the other hand, merely provide a pause in the message, a "breather" as it were. They are essential in delineating the grouping of words, thus bringing out the sense not only of the group of words but also of the entire message. A dash is another kind of pause— more as an aside but one that is regarded as relevant to the point being made.

---

[8] The present context here is the English language (although there are differences even in that language, i.e. British and American English).

[9] No attempt is made here to provide an exhaustive list of punctuation marks.

[10] An interesting book in this regard is *Eats, Shoots & Leaves*. A particularly useful example which the author provides is: "A woman, without her man, is nothing." and "A woman: without her, man is nothing." Lyne Truss, *Eats, Shoots & Leaves: The Zero Tolerance Approach to Punctuation* (Profile Books, 2003), p. 9.

Punctuation marks can also be the basis of agreement or differences in-asmuch as we can agree on their appropriateness or inappropriateness as we seek to interpret the sense of the sentences or the entire message itself. They can be said to set the parameters of how we read (or are meant to read) the text. For this reason, care must be exercised by whoever inserts these marks to forestall any misinterpretation. The author or editor of a text needs to check the extent that a particular punctuation mark serves a purpose, and clarifies or confuses the meaning of the text.

Punctuating Life's Text

On a number of occasions life has been compared to a book—we even make references to the book of life. It has been said that various events in one's life are like the chapters of a book. Death is sometimes portrayed as the last chapter in one's book of life, with the reminder that often, as in a book, the conclusion is written on the basis of the contents of the preced-ing pages.[11]

Along these lines, but with a different focus, reading the meaning of life's message can be likened to the writing of the book. In the present context, instead of the composition of the book of life, it is the significance of the punctuation marks that we put on the text that we wish to stress. For it is also in the editing of our life's sentences and not just in the authoring of them, as it were, that life's message is communicated to us. Sometimes we compose the sentences, more often we receive them—and it is in the interaction between the active and the passive side of life, so to speak, that life's message can be read, interpreted and lived. At the same time, how we break up the text of our lives into meaningful phrases, clauses and sen-tences is what enables us to discover the meaning of life itself.

Taking our cue then from grammar, one could say that we need to make the effort—just as much as we need to be given opportunities—to place the appropriate full stops, question marks, exclamation points as well as the colons, the commas and the dashes in the proper moments, stages and cycles of our lives. For only then can we understand and appreciate what life is to us. We need to insert punctuating moments in the sentences that we compose in life as we carry on with our daily routine, engage in specific activities or celebrate certain events. Those sentences may be our responses to what life offers to us, or they could be creations of ours as we

---

[11] Existentialist philosophers are at times cited as maintaining that how we die—although not in the physical sense—is shaped by the choices that we have made in life.

make our own contributions to life itself as it moves on, affecting us and others. Just as in our use of language, there is a received as well as a composed side to the over-all communication.

Transliterated into the context of life, the full stops (or periods) of life are the moments when we do come to the end of one activity, event, or phase and then move on to the next. These moments spell decisions made, activities completed, or simply points accepted. To some extent, these are the general markers in our lives as we press on from day to day. Sometimes these are just routine; others are more significant but not sufficiently so for us to regard them as "out of the ordinary" such that they are life-changing moments. They are merely momentary stops indeed.

But life, too, has its ups and not just downs: when we are surprised, uplifted and even thrilled. These exclamation points of our lives are moments that enable us to see life as a gift, to see beyond the routine. They make us stand still—and it is a pause that is indeed pregnant. At times, these special situations make it all worthwhile for us to continue; and, since they stand out, they somehow throw light on our lives, enabling us to appreciate what we have been given or what we have achieved. Living is no longer merely "existing" but, as the earlier poem expressed it: "ex-sisting".

It will not come as a surprise that philosophical thinking would be associated with a particular punctuation mark—and that is the question mark. As had already been noted above, philosophy is equated with the pursuit of wisdom; and it is generally held that the beginning of wisdom starts with the questions we raise regarding ourselves and our world. The question marks of life are the moments when we, just like the symbol of this punctuation, "curl back" because we are reflecting *(reflexere)* on our experience of various aspects of life—both humdrum and profound. Daily life presents situations when we ask, query or challenge. Unlike full stop moments, these moments make us step back and not merely move on. There are even occasions when we raise fundamental questions about life itself: asking about its significance, its purpose and its destiny. These questioning moments are sometimes the result of terrible or tragic situations; in some cases, they come about because of our inability to see what is in store for us or whether there is any point in continuing.[12] At other times, because we wonder, we ponder.

At our times, we pause, not because we are reflecting or questioning but because we expect further information, explanation or illustration of what we have just experienced. These colon moments of expectation stand

---

[12] The existence of evil and of suffering is one such occasion. Cf. Chapter Six. In our book, *From Suffering to God*, Part II, we develop this point and its challenge to our concept of God.

between the past and the future, between what has just been or what is to come. And when what was expected has come to pass, we begin to appreciate what has happened because we have been provided with further information, explanation or illustration. Sometimes these colon moments simply take place unexpectedly; at other times, we ought to make them happen.

But there is another punctuation mark that can be said to facilitate our search for meaning; namely, the comma. The association of philosophy with the comma is not obvious in the way that the question mark is. But there is something about reflection—integral to the philosophical activity—that invites the comparison. For just as in grammar where, to decipher the meaning of a sentence or a text, appropriate commas can be useful, so in life appropriate pauses—which create an atmosphere of reflection—do enable us to establish balance, maintain priorities and sharpen a focus. [13] These comma moments can aid us in making sense of the seemingly endless series of activities that we are engaged in or the various pursuits that we are trying to fulfil—when we take the time to see how the particulars are to be understood in the context of the general, or when we "take a moment" to view the details as they come together in the light of the overall scheme of things. These moments enable us to see connections, small enough (like the symbol of the comma) to enable us to continue with everyday life but important enough to leave an impression on us. Comma moments are not just inserted as "breathers", as it were (although they can be useful in that way), but because they serve the important function of providing "sense". And as we see the sense of the various groupings, they can open up the bigger picture. It seems that as we take—and make—the time to add these comma moments in our lives, we provide ourselves with a greater opportunity to see not just the "senses" of the various happenings in our lives but even more importantly, the "sense of it all". In this respect, there is something quite instructive in the actual mark of the comma itself. The comma, unlike the period (or full stop), is a dot that curls downwards towards the left. It does more than just bring out the meaning of the sentence. It does this by connecting us, as it were, with the past—the group of words that have been separated by the comma. In life too, we need to be reminded that the question of where we are heading is partly answered by considering where we have come from.[14]

---

[13] Our hope, of course, is that reading this book is one such comma moment.

[14] A particularly helpful way of understanding and defending this point is provided by Charles Hartshorne's metaphysical category of creative synthesis. Cf. his *Creative Synthesis and Philosophic Method* (SCM Press, 1970). There are other editions of this book. See also, Chapter Five of the present book.

Text and Context

So far, the claim that has been made is that to draw out the meaning of a series of sentences in a text, the proper punctuation marks have to be inserted. This is a task both for the writer if he or she wants to ensure that the meaning is correctly understood and—in the absence of such marks—for the reader to insert the appropriate ones to elicit an intelligible interpretation. It should be added now that such a quest for meaning, particularly on the part of the reader—which is our point of comparison—is often aided by making use of various resources to complement one's individual efforts.

One such valuable resource to understanding the sentences in a text and their meaning is knowledge of the context of the sentences. In fact, a sentence that has been lifted from the paragraph or the section (or even a greater context like a chapter) does not always convey as full a sense as it is meant to. Awareness of the general theme of the text as well as of the background (including that of the writer), connotations, varying interpretations, culture and so on can heighten and deepen the reader's sensitivities to such an extent that the reader can confront not only the explicit but also the implicit meaning of the text and of the words which make up the text. The same claim can be made—if life is being likened to a text—about discovering the meaning of life. The quest for meaning can be greatly enhanced by taking life's contexts into account. This is because this task is not simply a matter of inserting punctuating moments, as it were, by the individual but also of interpreting the meaning of those moments and eventually appreciating them.

The task of interpreting a text—as is well illustrated in literature—is much more than merely providing one's own understanding of it.[15] While this can be and often is done, one nonetheless risks arriving at subjective conclusions. This is also the case with our quest for meaning in life. It is important that our individual efforts should also avail of the collective wisdom of humankind and the extensive experiences of others. After all, if it is true that the quest for meaning is a common human activity, then there is something that we can learn from one another.

The term "context" is sometimes interpreted differently by other philosophers, particularly by those influenced by Wittgenstein's philosophy. What it does not mean here is that the act of philosophising is fenced in by one's subjective experiences such that one finds it impossible to transcend

---

[15] In literary theory, it should be noted that there are various approaches to the study of the text.

them. Rather, we take it to mean—and use the term accordingly—that the act of philosophising takes place in the concreteness of life. These are specific life-situations, "contexts". But they are not completely subjective nor are they entirely particular instances, such that one does not see any resemblance to other situations. The concreteness of life serves as the starting points for our reflections. But "context" as used here also refers to some kind of a unifying vision or at least the need to recognise its significance. The specific life-situations on which the act of philosophising is based serve as pointers because it is through these specific situations that we become somewhat aware of a larger picture. In fact, we can only recognise them as specific because there seems to be a broader background against which they are set.

Whitehead's analogy of "seeing the wood by means of the trees" can be helpful here.[16] It is the trees that we initially encounter, but it is also they which enable us to become aware of the wood. In seeing the wood, we have gone beyond merely noticing the trees. We may even see them in a different light because we see them against the backdrop of the wood. Similarly, the larger picture or the vision, that is opened up by the various contexts in which we philosophise, can enlighten us when we look again at the specific situations, including those that have set us off initially on our philosophical pursuits. T.S. Eliot puts it even more succinctly: "...we arrive where we started/And know the place for the first time."

"Context", as used here, thus refers to two distinct but related meanings: (1) the concreteness of our human experience as the basis for our philosophical reflections; and (2) a unifying vision that underlies our response to that experience. The question that inevitably arises is how something concrete (or detailed) can be reconciled with what is essentially abstract (or general). In insisting that philosophising is always carried out in context, are we therefore claiming that this activity is at all times both concrete and abstract? That would be a correct conclusion except that as these terms apply, they refer to different dimensions of the philosophical act. Insofar as philosophical thinking emerges out of the concreteness of life, it is concrete. It is based on and grounded in the day-to-day questions which need to be addressed as we live our lives and carry on our daily routine. But philosophical thinking, if it is not to be a superficial or an ad hoc response, must address those questions against a more general framework that helps to provide a sharper focus. This is the abstract dimension since it is general and comprehensive. There is something about human nature that is not fully satisfied with mere instances or selected examples.

---

[16] Cf. Chapter Two.

The human desire for some continuity, comprehensiveness, and unity in our understanding of reality, and in our attempts to make sense of it, is what we believe drives us to this quest for a more general vision.

Religion as Context

Despite some valid criticisms as well as misinterpretations, religion can be regarded as providing one such valuable context in this instance, particularly since the various religions do concern themselves—in their scriptures, teachings and practices—with, among others, the human quest for meaning in life. But because "religion" is understood in so many ways, it would be useful to explain its usage here and to develop the point further.

In the light of what has been said so far regarding the quest for meaning, Whitehead can be of help to us. While accepting that there are special occasions which can lead to religious consciousness, religion as far as he is concerned emerges from ordinary human experience.[17] He refers to religion as "the human search" or "the longing of the spirit" for something which transcends everything; but the search or the longing for it is deeply rooted in mundane matters, in everyday experience. This search or longing results in what he calls "solitariness".

Solitariness, however, is more than just the common experience of loneliness. Solitariness is the sense of separateness, the initial experience having been that of belongingness. It enables one to become aware of one's individuality, which is a further stage from one's previous preconscious experience of sociality and relatedness. Since religion itself, according to Whitehead, is a response to solitariness, it means that solitariness is actually "pre-religious", despite being a further stage in one's search for the transcendent. Strictly speaking then, religion is not to be equated with individuality. And unlike the sense of solitariness, religion is more than a stage. There has been an evolution in one's experience and not just a prolongation. In addition, there has been a development since there is an active element: religion after all is what one *does* with one's own solitariness. It is the response to one's search or longing. There is a pur-

---

[17] According to Whitehead, "experience" is one of the most deceitful words in philosophy. For a more extensive and technical discussion, see A.N. Whitehead, corrected version. *Process and Reality: a Reflection in Cosmology* ed. by David Ray Griffin and Donald W. Sherburne (N.Y. The Free Press, 1978), particularly Part III.

poseful consciousness in religion that is merely latent in solitariness but is developing as one becomes aware of one's individuality.

It is interesting that Whitehead should regard the human experience of longing and searching, which leads to solitariness, as the fundamental base from which religion can emerge. Some of the modern critics of religion had attacked it for preying, as it were, on such experiences. Freud, tracing religion back to the need for emotional comfort, especially relief from disasters, accidents, sickness, and other natural evils that surround us, accused religion of perpetuating human immaturity through its teachings and practices. He regarded religion as an infantile neurosis that ought to be cured before we can grow into mature, healthy adults. Once cured of such a sickness, human beings, he alleged, can achieve maturity as a race. It will then no longer be necessary to invent fanciful beings personalised by religion for us to be able to face this impersonal and at times brutal world of ours. Marx criticised religion for enslaving people through its preaching of acceptance of one's miserable lot in life and its championing the virtues of patience, humility and self-denial. Religion, he claimed, misleads us in not recognising the real causes of our alienation and suppresses our desire to improve the economic and political conditions of life. Both of these influential thinkers would hardly agree with Whitehead that true religion stems from the human experience of longing and searching. If anything, such an experience in their view is being misinterpreted and misled by religion.

But these experiences of life, as our pre-reflexive starting point, are part and parcel of human life itself. While agreeing with Freud that religion is based on emotional needs, Jung rightly criticised him for not taking into account that they are basic to human nature and that we cannot deny them without inducing neurosis. What is called for therefore is not the abandonment of religion as demanded by Freud. Rather, it is our response to those needs that is really in question. It will determine the kind of religion that we have in mind, as Whitehead clearly states. Our response to human longing or yearning for something more does not have to be, and should not be, in the form severely criticised by Freud and Marx.

Many religious practices and customs have arisen in response to specific life-situations. Religion cannot ignore deep-felt hunger or yearning for "something more" even if it is not always clear what that "something more" is or even if the expression of this desire is simplistic or unreflective.

Whitehead correctly underscores this point whereas Plato neglects it. In the Western world Plato led the way in freeing religion from the particularistic, anthropomorphic expressions of it as exemplified by the Greek divinities. He insisted that true religion is concerned with fundamental and comprehensive questions rather than with emotional concerns. His own theory of religion was grounded in his desire to understand the universal attributes of reality, far removed from the transient, ever-changing environment which surrounded him. But by sharply establishing a line of demarcation between the established interpretation of religion in his day—understandably so, given its crudities—and his own one, Plato unfortunately cut off an important link with concrete life. He wanted to construct a theory of religion that had left behind the world of sense experience. While there were good reasons for dissociating genuine religion from the so-called religious practices and beliefs of his time, Plato's hard-line attitude resulted in a rather intellectualised, and even elitist, version of religion. Whitehead's conception of religion, on the other hand, rightly shows that it is in the midst of everyday life, experienced in various fashions and expressed in concrete ways, that we begin to ask questions which take us beyond the particular situation that we find ourselves in and lead us to what he refers to as "solitariness". And our reaction, also part of human living, to that solitariness shapes religious thought. Our further attempts—our quest, as it were—to make sense of our experiences of and in life lead to something more general and more complex as we yield to the urge for something more. There is in human life what Whitehead calls "a noble discontent", which is "the gradual emergence into prominence of a sense of criticism, founded upon appreciations of beauty, and of intellectual distinction, and of duty."[18] Such a discontent distances us from particular experiences and inevitably prods us to seek conceptual expressions and rational support.

But in what way can religion and the religious context be of help in the quest for meaning? Some theists have regarded religion as adding *depth* to life. But the word sounds very much like a negative judgment over non-religious interpretations. It would also be quite difficult to show, given the complexities of validating the belief in a God, that religion really deepens our understanding of life.

A less contentious word is *vision.* This means then that despite admitting that the quest for meaning is a human one, the theist can still claim to be influenced by a vision not shared by secularists of what it means to be human. Because religion holds that creation stands in a relation with God, the theistic perspective is shaped by that conviction. It is in this very point where the scriptures, be they Christian, Jewish, Islamic, Hindu, or Buddhist, play a significant role. For the scriptures capture and express in writ-

---

[18] A.N.Whitehead, *Adventures of Ideas* (Cambridge University Press, 1942), p. 12.

ten form that religious vision. What they offer is this vision of creation standing in a certain relationship to God. There are insights and themes which bring out this understanding. The sacraments or the rituals and worship of the different religions also highlight this relatedness to God because these do not make sense apart from this belief. To a great extent, the sacraments are a celebration of the theist's awareness of being related to God.

For many, the religious context. i.e. this particular vision, can make a difference to our quest for meaning in life and to how we punctuate it for its message. It can enrich one's understanding of life, heighten one's appreciation of its challenges, and facilitate one's responses.

Concluding Comments

In this enquiry, we have been concerned with developing further the claim that if life is not to become "a sentence" on us, we can regard it more as "a series of sentences". However, if we do not wish them to become disjointed or a mere collection of words, then we should make the effort to punctuate them properly. The use of punctuation marks in grammar is particularly useful in clarifying and developing this claim. Moreover, again turning to the role of punctuation marks in grammar, we assert that it is only when we insert those "punctuating moments" that we discover whether life has any meaning at all. In our quest for meaning, the various contexts in life, religion being one of them, can be helpful just as knowledge of the context can facilitate the interpretation of a text—to which life is being likened.[19].

.

---

[19] Another particularly helpful context in deciphering life's meaning and addressing our questions and quests is education, to which we shall turn our attention in the next chapter

CHAPTER TWO

EDUCATION—FOR WHAT?: THE QUEST FOR WISDOM

Lessons from Nature

Nature has a way of providing us with appropriate sceneries to facilitate our reflections on various matters. Philosophers, theologians and jurists have observed how nature functions as they formulate different versions of the natural law to guide human conduct. Poets have described the natural world while artists imitated it as they expressed their thoughts in graphic and illuminating ways. Designers at times follow nature in setting the trends for next season's fashion.

Nature can be a guide too when we turn our minds to education.[1] For an answer to the question: what is it that we are engaged in as we teach, do research or attend courses? we can draw some help from a nature-inspired quotation from A.N. Whitehead's *The Aims of Education*.[2] Whitehead is generally regarded as one of the most eminent 20th century philosophers, who having taught mathematics at Cambridge University and later, science at London University then turned to pursue his philosophical interests at Harvard University. While the words from one of his books take us outdoors, to view nature, it is also an invitation to turn inwards, to look deeper into what nature can teach us about our educational task.

We are very familiar with the saying "do not mistake the trees for the wood" or "unable to see the wood for the trees". Whitehead specifically and intentionally sees a different connection between the two: it is *by means of* the trees that we see the wood. The imagery gives us a glimpse into our educational task by reminding us of the distinction between knowledge and wisdom, both of which feature in any discussion of the goals of

---

[1] Cf. The section on Hopkins in Chapter Six and the Postscript.

[2] The phrase is: "seeing the wood by means of the trees". Cf. A.N. Whitehead, *The Aims of Education and Other Reflections* (The Free Press Paperback Edition, 1967), p. 6.

education. And it seems that what Whitehead's phrase hints at is that, there is indeed a distinction between wisdom and knowledge, just as the wood is not the same as the trees, but that it is through knowledge that one gains wisdom, that it is in the trees and because of them that we can see the wood.

A Reflective Moment

But before proceeding, let us first accompany Richard in the early hours of the morning as he reflects on the statue known as the Fonske:

Everything seemed peaceful in Leuven, the atmosphere lending itself to wanderings. As he quietly closed behind him the entrance door to the apartment, he toyed with the idea of simply roaming around the Begijnhof. He looked around. The Begijnhof was absolutely quiet, but it was not well lit-up so he thought he would go out to the street instead. Maybe towards the town center. It was always a focal point.

First he made his way to Naamsestraat, a street that he had come to know quite well. During the day, it was busy with traffic, although the number of cars would be nothing in comparison to that in Los Angeles. The narrow streets here meant that when cars were also parked, a driver had to be extra careful not to hit them or the cyclists who seemed to be everywhere.

But tonight Naamsestraat was almost empty, the peace and quiet broken now and then only by a passing car or a staggering pedestrian. He crossed the street when he noticed one of those pedestrians who had had a drink too many approach him. Further up the street as he neared the Centrum, he heard a group of merry students who must have been celebrating or simply enjoying each other's company. It looked as if they had come from the Olde Markt. Richard smiled—student life, oh, the fun and the freedom despite all the pressures of reflections and exams. Sometimes it was a luxury to live that kind of life.

The Fons Sapientiae—affectionately dubbed the Fonske by the students—was still lit up and flowing. Richard wondered whether it was left that way throughout the night as well as during the day. It certainly was an imposing statue, particularly with the brightly illuminated Stadthuis in the background.

He paused. Somehow the sight of the young scholar, Leuven's first honorary citizen, pouring water into his opened head as he read a book, beckoned to him and kept his attention. The fountain, Jef Claerhout's creation, had been a gift of the university of Leuven to the town on the occasion of its 550th anniversary in 1975. There had been some debate regarding its significance, but the popular interpretation was that Fonske pours out wisdom: 'If the beer is out of the can, then wisdom is in the man.' Richard had passed by this place a number of times, but tonight it suddenly loomed large in his horizon. Why?

He folded his arms, hugging his coat to keep warm. Although the temperatures were not unusually low, he started feeling the cold once he stopped walking. Now he found himself directly in front of the fountain.

No doubt, the fountain represented what this university town was all about. The pursuit of knowledge. But how odd, he thought. Did the pursuit of knowledge mean reading volumes and volumes of information? Was it to be poured into one's head? Why was the open book covering the face of the scholar like a shield? From what was the scholar being shielded? Did the bent knee have any significance?

Richard kept staring at the statue in front of him. Why was he asking all these questions? Did he expect the statue to answer him or to come to life? But he could not shake off the idea that this fountain was symbolic of something. It represented what academic life was all about. All right, not everything about it. But it stood for what was essential. On the other hand, maybe he was seeing too much in it. It is funny how many times we give an interpretation to something that even its creator had not thought about. Was this the case now?

Richard sat down on the cement seat facing the fountain since he felt odd standing in front of it—he, a lonely figure before a stone creation at such an ungodly hour. There was something about its symbolic significance that kept bothering him and preventing him from moving on. Somehow he felt that it was saying something to him personally.

As he kept staring at the young scholar who remained unperturbed by this onlooker's questions, it dawned on him that there was a connection between his earlier conversations with his colleagues and his present musings. He had been concerned about the gap between the problem of evil and the philosophical way of dealing with it. Now it seemed that he was actually questioning the very idea of academic life itself, the life that he had dedicated himself to.

What was it really that he was meant to do as a teacher? Pour information into his students' head? Or ram knowledge down their throat, as it were? Did students enter university merely to acquire knowledge? Or to get a degree, which many of his students still believed was the passport to well-paid jobs? Sometimes he felt that that was what was being communicated to his students in America—that education was a marketable commodity, and that was why they insisted on value for their money. But what about the pursuit of wisdom? Had academia become too stultified, too objectified? Where did inspiration come in? Questions and more questions.

Richard recalled what Martin Buber said of his philosophy, that he did not really have a philosophy but a vision, and all he wanted was to encourage people to open their own windows so they too could see that vision. It was an image which encouraged Richard to be a teacher. Teaching was his chance to broaden people's minds as well as his own. That was what he wanted to do; but despite excellent course evaluations by his students, he always felt hampered by expectations, probably caused by the evaluation itself, that teaching had to be marketed, analysed and assessed just like any other product. Centuries ago, Richard recalled, the Athenian stranger in Plato's *Laws* had bemoaned the practice in Italy and Sicily of leaving the judgement of poets in the hands of the spectators. Such a practice spelled the destruction of the poets since they were in the habit of composing their poems to suit the taste of their judges. Similarly, Richard found himself pressurised into teaching according to the evaluation, designing his methods, his style, his syllabus, to ensure that he would score high in the evaluation questionnaire. His syllabus, readings (including specific pages), assignments, grading criteria were set out in great detail, leaving nothing unexplained because he did not want the risk of possible complaint. Nothing was left to the imagination. His lectures were systematic, clear and informative. He labored hard to provide study-guides. Class time was effectively used: 'every minute of it,' many of his students wrote.

But where was the excitement of discovery, the suspense of groping for the truth, the challenge of ambiguity? Did he communicate that to his students? If not, was it his fault as their teacher? He felt that he was losing the creativity and the spontaneity that mark the work of a true educator. He was afraid of being inventive because it might not be appreciated by his students, a reaction that would be noted no doubt in the evaluation, and ultimately by the administrators.

Perhaps it was his own fault, perhaps he should not have been too obsessed with the questions being asked of his students in the evaluation, but if one wanted tenure one had to tailor one's teaching to meet those expectations. He wanted to discuss his misgivings with others in the department, but as a young assistant professor he did not want to convey the idea that something was wrong with his teaching. Despite assurances that the comments rather than the percentages (both of which were fine in his case because he had learned to play by those rules) were what really mattered, he suspected, based on ample evidence, that the increasing need for quick and tangible evidence meant that the survey of percentages was a more handy way of assessing someone as a teacher.

And yet he had not been asked by the Rank and Tenure Committee for those evaluations which he had carefully filed. Had he played the wrong game after all? Had he misunderstood the whole situation?

His mind drifted to his students back in the USA. He missed them. No one in particular, but being with them in the classroom situation. There were many bright sparks among them. And their eager and lively undergraduate minds at times forced him to forget the whole darned evaluations and accompany them on their journey towards the truth, unfettered by the specific questions that would be asked of his course at the end, out of Plato's cave into the sunlight. He cared too about the not-so-bright students, whose talents lay somewhere else, and whose academic efforts needed stimulating. By him, their teacher. There were hurdles to be overcome. His experience, his understanding and his skills would be much appreciated—

not his concern about how his performance in the classroom would be subjected to scrutiny.

All of a sudden something startled Richard and put a momentary stop to his reflections. The fountain had been switched off. Funny, he thought. Just as he was being stimulated by the sight of the water, they had to turn the whole thing off.

The sight of the young scholar now frozen, as it were, in that pose, created a different impression on Richard. It was a cold statue now; no movement or life that the flowing water had given it. Like a human being that had ceased to open herself or himself up to the current of life—merely an object, rather than a person.

Richard was reminded of something again from Plato, of how ideas get some kind of life. For Plato ideas are static, frozen and lifeless, like that statue now in front of this twentieth-century philosopher. But just as ideas get their life and motion in a live intelligent being, so does this statue when water vivifies it. Richard asked: Have we perhaps forgotten this in academia? That the pursuit of wisdom is about life itself and not just information?

Three o'clock in the morning on the streets of Leuven. Strange how this town provoked one's mind—at such a time. He had gone for a walk to clear his mind. Now the fountain had filled it with more thoughts.

Perhaps he should move ahead. Anyway, it was getting colder. The Centrum was still bathed in the yellow light that was focused on the town hall, imposing on it a particular splendor.

But Richard's mind would not rest, even as he retraced his way back to the apartment. More questions kept surfacing. What was it that he was really searching for? Were these questions about academic life, his teaching and his academic research symptomatic of something deeper? He had come to Leuven to do scholarly work, but was he being given, unplanned and unforeseen, an opportunity to take a closer look at himself and even at life itself? He turned around to check the fountain. It was still now. There were no answers there. Would there be? he wondered.

The dawn was long in coming.[3]

Knowledge, Competence and Skills

At a time when we are being asked in college or university education in Europe to specifically state the knowledge, competence and skills that we expect from all our programmes—the so-called "learning outcomes" that somehow have become the objectives of education today—we need to look more closely, as Richard in the passage above was doing, at how all that relates to what we are doing in education, particularly in our present

---

[3] M.S. Sia, *The Fountain Arethuse: a Novel Set in the University Town of Leuven* (Book Guild, 1994), pp. 116-121.

context.[4] When the end products seem to have become more important than the process itself, then there is a need to take stock. When the success of educational endeavours is measured in terms of empirical evidence, the so-called "hard outputs", that the learning outcomes have been achieved—all of which justify the academic award—one begins to wonder to what extent are we committed to simply ensuring that we reach our targets. All along one would be forgiven for wondering whether education has become too oriented towards producing the right products—as indeed some in the printed media or in academic circles have already been alerting us to.

Those of us who have looked at education as the process that begins in wonder but ends in wisdom—no doubt, influenced by ancient Greek philosophy's conception of itself, as Richard was—can become disoriented and even aggrieved at the changed focus of education. And if one adds to that the claim that education itself, *educere*, is about "the leading out" of the learner from darkness to the light, then one begins to have misgivings about the emphasis on the actual results rather than on the attempts or the efforts of both the educator and the educand. And one will suspect that the destination has become more important than the journey, robbing all of the excitement, the ups and downs as one moves towards the light.

Nonetheless, there are good reasons for this shift not only because it is called for and even required by the authorities to whom, among others, our educational task is accountable but also because it is crucial that students are prepared by their academic institutions with appropriate knowledge, skills, and competence to enable them to meet the present demands of society. The task of educating our students today takes place in a society that is fast changing, complex, and diverse, features which present significant challenges to educators. Every society and every generation, of course, have their own set of characteristics and problems that require different responses from educators throughout history. But it seems that today's society, with the values that it upholds, poses a particular challenge to those of us who are involved in educating today's students.

We would strongly defend as the context of our academic work the marketplace (or if you prefer, the agora, just as it was in ancient Greece). The reasonable demand that we take account of the labour market or that we consult our stakeholders whenever we propose or review our academic programmes forces us to remain relevant and competitive. It is very much worth our while to keep the end-result in sight. We would also like to align ourselves with the view that life-long learning, which is what education is

---

[4] Cf. "Education, the Business Model, and the Bologna Process: a Philosophical Response," in S. Sia, *Ethical Contexts and Theoretical Issues: Essays in Ethical Thinking* (Cambridge Scholars Publishing, 2010), pp. 33-50.

really about, should be marked by recognisable stages. Each stage is a definite goal, and a goal is worth pursuing when there are tangible features. In insisting that we clearly identify the learning outcomes for each of these stages, we are recognising and acknowledging the achievements at each stage of the learning process. Knowledge, competence and skills are the trees in Whitehead's vision of education. Without them, there would be no wood. They are important to enable our students to take their rightful place in society. And it is our responsibility as educators to facilitate that process.

On the other hand, education is much more than that, the wood is not merely a collection of trees, the whole is more than just the constituent parts. And with all the call for a "knowledge-based economy" we are in danger of forgetting that point. We believe—and this is a conviction that comes from more than 30 years of being involved in education in Ireland, Britain, the USA, and in shorter stints in various other countries—that this wider vision of education is just as true for students in the sciences, business, engineering, and other professional schools as it is in the humanities. This is because we firmly believe that education, in whatever form or context, should ultimately be grounded in the development of the human person.[5] It is a belief that has been nurtured, tested and developed by our academic pursuits and contextualised, facilitated and deepened by our involvement with the various academic institutions throughout the world.

The Pursuit of Wisdom

Education for us—and we would hazard the assumption that many would agree—is first and foremost *the pursuit of wisdom*.[6] It is a view that requires some qualification as well as clarification. We have already remarked on the present tendency, one that is particularly evident in our market-driven and technological society, to associate education with the acquisition of knowledge and the development of skills. Let us repeat that this is not only understandable but also crucial if the education an institution provides is to be found appropriate and relevant. Nonetheless, some-

---

[5] See Chapter Three which argues that in our exploration of ethical cases, we need to develop our moral sense as human beings and not just as engineers or scientists. Whitehead also talks of the need for "the liberal spirit" in technical education and science, cf. his *Aims of Education*, pp. 43-59.

[6] This concern for the pursuit of wisdom within the context of academia has led to our writing the novel, *The Fountain Arethuse* from which we have drawn passages for this book. The novel is about the search of various fictitious academics and others for the source of wisdom.

thing is amiss if the entire focus of the educational task becomes narrowly directed at this consideration, important though it may be. Moreover, as Alfred Lord Tennyson puts, "Knowledge comes, but wisdom lingers." The pursuit of wisdom as the educational task, understood as *the active participation in our full development as human persons*, highlights certain essential features that do not always stand out with the other conceptions mentioned earlier. It is also something that needs to be repeatedly emphasised today, while taking into account contemporary needs, as we reflect on "what it is that we are doing when we are educating our students".

Because the term "wisdom" itself is understood in different ways, we should like to explain how it is understood in this context. Wisdom, as will have been noted from the earlier comments, is not just the acquisition of knowledge or the development of skills and talents although these are an integral part of the pursuit of wisdom itself. Nor is it, as is sometimes narrowly interpreted, the development of one's individuality, particularly when one associates it with the description of "a learned individual". These interpretations fail to take into serious account the fullness of our humanity—which is the basis of education. Wisdom ultimately is rooted in our nature as human beings and the various dimensions of our humanity: intellectual, emotional, ethical, spiritual, aesthetic, social, creative and others. The pursuit of wisdom is the attempt to recognise, integrate and develop all those dimensions. It is also an awareness that our identity as human persons is shaped by and nourished by the community to which we belong. In turn our own activities, decisions, and commitments have an effect on the community. Plato, Confucius, and Buber, among others, drew our attention to this understanding of wisdom when they wrote about the importance of the development of one's moral character in connection with the search for wisdom. Education towards wisdom is thus a holistic process because the goal and its foundation are themselves holistic.

If indeed the educational task consists in the pursuit of wisdom as described above, we regard the role of an educator (pursuing Richard's questions and reflections) as one who enhances, that is to say, *evokes, provokes, invokes, and convokes*, that process among the learners.[7] In and outside the classroom, in informal and formal contacts with the learners, in creative and scholarly activity, one should strive to keep that task in mind. For this reason, teaching is neither a "pouring of information" nor merely "an intellectual exercise". W. B. Yeats puts it in rather picturesque terms:

---

[7] These are stages in our methodology of teaching: *evoke* (gaining the interest of the students), *provoke* (critically reflecting on possible answers), *invoke* (drawing on the sources), and *convoke* (enabling them to think through and develop their answers—the acronym being: EPIC.

"Education is not about filling the pail but about lighting the fire." Nor should it be seen as primarily preparing learners for the exams that will lead to an award.[8] Rather, it is a journey or an exploration whereby the learners and the educator address the questions that they are asking, evaluate their significance and draw on various resources for possible answers.[9] Moreover, the process (of searching for answers) is just as important as any answers that they may arrive at because the very act itself of pursuing wisdom already enhances our development as human beings. The process is also important because hopefully it transforms us into better human beings because we have taken the time (inside and outside the classroom) to delve deeper into those questions and to face up to their implications. If wisdom is indeed the development of the whole person, then the spiritual dimension cannot be ignored. There is a transcendent side to the human person, and if we are to do the human person justice, then it becomes an important factor in the pursuit of wisdom. The various service activities and the active cultivation of an ethos, an integral part of the programme of education, further the pursuit of wisdom. Moreover, they contextualise that pursuit as we broaden our vision of what it means to be a human person in the diverse and multicultural community that we find ourselves in and serve today.

This understanding of one's role as an educator should thus inform and substantiate the objectives, content and the methodology of one's teaching. Because an educator has journeyed towards wisdom, and continues to do so, he/she can be an effective guide in the learners' pursuit of wisdom.[10] Moreover, that role can be complemented and supported by scholarly, creative and professional endeavours. The questions we ask and the answers we gather from various sources need to be pursued even further. They need to be investigated with rigour at a deeper level. What prompts scholarly and creative work is similar to that which motivates teaching: the

---

[8] The issues of autonomy as well as of pressure on students because of course assignments/examinations inevitably arise, given this emphasis on their personal development. Admittedly, there is always a tension. On the other hand, part of the educational process (and thus of the student's personal development) is to help students to cope with pressure and to organise their work accordingly. Moreover, in the workplace performance review is regularly carried out. What is crucial, in the light of the argumentation in this chapter, is that that aspect does not become the most important consideration.

[9] The humanities subjects particularly lend themselves to this task of linking the students' concrete experiences with the academic study.

[10] Whitehead talks of the importance of taking into account what he calls "the rhythm of education", *Aims of Education,* pp. 15-25 as well "the rhythmic claims of freedom and discipline" *Ibid.*, pp. 29-41.

pursuit of wisdom.[11] An educator—as Richard in the passage above believes—wants to share with others the excitement, as well as any discoveries, as he/she undertakes his/her own journey.

Learning Outcomes or Learner Outcome?

This leads us to make the claim that the need to identify and achieve
the learning outcomes at various stages should not make us forget the fundamental reason for this task; namely, the development of the person. So
perhaps we should be describing the "learner outcome", awkward though
that phrase may be. The question which we believe should be addressed by
academic institutions is: "what kind of a learner" do they want to leave
their trusteeship—inasmuch as these institutions have been entrusted with
their education? Rather than seek to attract certain individuals (to gain
greater prestige) academic institutions, if they are really intent on showing
their worth, should concentrate on the kind of graduates who have benefit-
ted from the education they have had the responsibility of providing. Lest
this be misunderstood, our point is not so much the compiling of graduate
data showing the jobs, careers, achievements or further opportunities of
their graduates, but rather supporting the kind of persons who have
"emerged from their portals" as it were. An ancient inscription over a library captures this point succinctly: *Intra sapiens, exi sapientior.*
So what does it mean to be a "wiser person" or for that matter a "wise
person"? Philosophers will inevitably turn to the answer provided by Socrates: one who knows that he/she does not know. To some ears those
words would sound strange; but there is, as is always the case with pithy
answers, more to that answer. But in this instance, we could draw on the
words of another wise person: Confucius. After all, while we should act
locally, we should think globally. Interestingly, China has become an important player. Aside from the market value of that vast country, China has
captured the attention of educators. Programmes are being devised to meet
China's needs, and learners are being encouraged to learn the languages
and culture of that country—if these learners are going to do business with
their Chinese counterparts.[12] But China can justifiably boast of a great
thinker whose views on education can be of tremendous value to us, particularly in the context of our topic. In the books associated with his

---

[11] According to Whitehead, "it is the function of the scholar to evoke into life wisdom and beauty which, apart from his magic, would remain lost in the past." *Ibid.*
p, 98.
[12] We are reflecting on our experience in Ireland and in the USA.

name,[13] Confucius describes a *chun-tzu* (a noble person, a superior person, a wise person). Originally, that term referred to a person who was noble by birth, but Confucius argued that nobility comes from one's effort. To be a noble person is within the reach of everyone, that it is due to one's constant and determined effort to develop oneself as a moral individual. And it is through education—"learning" as he puts it—that one succeeds in becoming a *chun-tzu*.

The notion of *chun-tzu* is very much equated with the development of the whole person—a goal that Confucius kept in mind as he discoursed on the importance of rites, music, knowledge, and participation in the life of society. Unlike another Chinese sage, Lao Tzu, who advised retreating from society and discarding all books and cultural baggage, Confucius taught that it is in everyday life, through interaction with one another, and with the development of the individual's talents and skills that we become better persons.[14] In turn, we turn out to be valuable citizens.[15] Confucius was concerned with the best society and the virtuous individual, and he saw an intimate connection between the two. A harmonious society promotes the ethical development of its citizens, but such a society is brought about by the moral activities of its citizens. Education, for Confucius, is a way of improving that connection in a practical way. This is why he insisted on the cultivation of virtues and decorum as the essence of education. For Confucius, hopefully also for us in the Western world, there is no greater "hard output" than that of facilitating that process and of achieving that goal.

Time and space separate us from Confucius. Yet there are certain guiding principles which somehow transcend those boundaries. More importantly, perhaps, despite obvious differences and tremendous changes, we are after all dealing with a shared human nature. And it is that human nature that we should not forget as we "re-view", as it were, education today.

---

[13] The two books which are particularly relevant here are *The Analects* and *The Great Learning*. The first book contains the conversations between the Master and the disciples.

[14] This point invites comparisons with Martin Buber's phrase: "the hallowing of the everyday" and with his emphasis on the I-Thou relationship. Cf. Chapter Four.

[15] When Confucius was asked by a disciple whether he should enter political life to serve his fellowmen, he replied that the student should develop himself first as a human being.

The Quest for Wisdom and Philosophy

Let us now turn our attention to the more specific role of philosophy in this context. We have already noted that in many ways, to engage in philosophical thinking is not just to delve into the thoughts of the great masters of this art. The quest for wisdom, despite its close association with philosophy inasmuch as etymologically that academic discipline means "the love of wisdom" is not the prerogative of those who have made its study a professional preoccupation. One can even argue that each of us, irrespective of our educational background, by the very fact of asking a question, of wanting to go further in our knowledge, is already taking a step further in our quest for wisdom. This is why we have always maintained—to the delight of our students—that there is no such thing as a "stupid question", perhaps an idle one or an irrelevant one. But insofar as we ask a question, we are looking for more. The question indicates that we had prior knowledge, no matter how vague or confused it may have been. So in raising the question as to what it is that we are engaged in as we teach, research or attend courses, we have already embarked on our journey towards greater wisdom. But we do need to pursue the question further: what contribution does the study of philosophy make to our common quest for wisdom?

Here perhaps is what marks the philosophical pursuit of wisdom: the recognition of the human urge to ask fundamental questions and of the need to embark on that pursuit for answers. Yet it can be frustrating since it can lead to more questions when at times all one wants are straightforward answers—the "bottom-line" as they say across the Atlantic or "yes or no" as those in the legal profession or the media keep on insisting. Worse, to be told by such an influential philosopher as Socrates that wisdom consists in knowing that one does not know is hardly an enticement to study philosophy.

What then would make us want to enlist the help of philosophical questioning in our quest for wisdom? The same Socrates did provide some kind of an answer: the unexamined life is not worth living, he is known as saying. We would like to put that answer differently: unquestioned assertions or beliefs have a way of leading us astray. Let us explain this point by sharing with you an experience. Years ago as a young student in Ireland (and that was *decades* ago!), one of the authors drove to the West. Inevitably he got lost since the signposts had been turned around—a rather intriguing fascination of some of the youth at that time. He found himself literally and not just symbolically going around in circles. Finally, he spotted a farmer leaning on a fence. From the moment he approached him, he could sense that he was eyeing him with more than the customary interest. After all, he was not your average Irishman! The farmer must have been wondering what ill wind had blown him to this part of the world. He explained his predicament. The farmer's seemingly bewildering reply has stuck with him ever since: "D'you see that road? Well, don't take that. And that one over there? No, the one further up. Well, now, you'd be foolish to take that!" His initial reaction to these instructions was one of frustration until it dawned on him that by avoiding the roads he had been warned not to take, he discovered that he was on his way to his destination. Similarly, the path to the truth is often littered with obstacles that we have to clear away first. Knowing what is not is a first step forward to knowing what it is. And the process is enormously helped when we ask questions and then subject received answers to careful scrutiny.[16]

The philosophical pursuit is a yearning for wisdom, a thirst for and a commitment to the truth. It is a declaration of an intention to cast aside superficiality or mere appearances insofar as one wants to penetrate to the essence of things, to reflect on it and to structure it. It wants to give the lie to frivolity or haste because it affirms that genuine satisfaction comes only after a search—sometimes a long one. It expects us not merely to react but also—and even more so—to lay foundations. It implies a way of thinking and even a way of life. Philosophy enables us to evaluate the details in the light of an encompassing vision. And for this reason, philosophy rejects what is merely fashionable because it champions lasting values. And for what? We should like to think that these lines from Ben Jonson's poem could very well apply: "Minds that are great and free/Should not on fortune pause;/'Tis crown enough to virtue still, her own applause."

And where does all this take place, this search for true wisdom? For the ancient Greeks, it was the *agora*, the marketplace, not unlike the social and political arena of Confucius' searchings. Contrary to certain perceptions, it is in the concreteness of life, the "raw stuff of life" that philosophical thinking takes shape, not in ivory towers. In philosophy, these concrete experiences are transformed into ideas. Philosophical questioning and thinking is the process of nurturing, testing, propagating and communicating these ideas. But it does not end there. These ideas have to be hammered on the anvil of life, tested in the furnace of concrete living. A.N. Whitehead again provides us with an insight when he remarked that

---

[16] Whitehead warns us of what he calls "inert ideas" which he describes as "ideas that are merely received into the mind without being utilised, or tested, or thrown into fresh combinations". He maintains that "education with inert ideas is not only useless: it is, above all things, harmful—*Corruptio optima, pessima.*", *Aims of Education*, p. 1.

speculative philosophy is like the flight of an airplane: it starts on the ground, takes off into the rarefied atmosphere of abstraction but lands back on the ground. It is useful to keep that comparison in mind as we consider the philosophical task.

Theories of Education

Let us now develop further this response to the challenge to education by turning to certain interpretations of education. These are particularly relevant to the present situation. Down through the years various theories of education have resulted in different aims and objectives which have been adopted by educators. These theories do not necessarily contradict one another. Often they are complementary although one may tend to emphasise one feature of the educative process while another may prefer to put the stress on another aspect. This variation is perhaps understandable in view of the fact that conceptions of education depend upon the needs of the time, the existing state of knowledge and the current attitudes towards life. Our contemporary situation is no exception.

One school of thought, for instance, regards education as a preparation for life or an apprenticeship to life. The educative process is merely the threshold; "real life" starts after school! What educators should aim at, therefore, is to equip the learner properly so that he or she can "face life" after school. Another view of education, on the other hand, looks at the training period as part of life itself. Life, if it is sacred, is sacred at all ages and not merely when one completes one's education. Hence, the learner should enter into meaningful learning situations suited to one's age though oriented towards experiences that one will likely undergo later in adult life. Schooling is a definite phase in one's life. Still another theory would maintain that the business of education is the transmission of accomplishments of past generations—the literature and values of the community. According to this conception of education the educand makes use of the knowledge and experience of one's ancestors. One adds one's own experience and knowledge to this heritage. In turn it is handed down to successive generations.

These theories and objectives—the list is by no means exhaustive—have had and still have advocates. This can be interpreted to mean that such theories and objectives embody much of what a number of people believe regarding education. For this reason, they have been quite influential. They also underpin the present discussion. As had already been indicated, it is for this reason that we need to critically examine these underpinnings and ask whether there is not a consequent neglect of the whole person—which we are arguing should be the focus of education. One could raise the question as to whether educators should be more concerned with the *educated* person (educated, that is, insofar as he or she has achieved the aim of a particular school of thought) rather than with the educated *person.* This may appear like a play on words, but the change in emphasis could lead to important goals for those responsible for the up-bringing of youth.

An Existentialist View on Education

It is this turn-about in perspective that existentialist thinkers are de-manding. Existentialism maintains that some theories of education make the mistake of believing that the young are things to be worked over in some fashion to bring them into alignment with a prior notion of what they *should* be. They argue that education ought instead to situate its aim and interest, not outside the learner, but within the learner himself or herself. The learner is the subject of education, not the object. The learner's activ-ity of learning should be aroused and promoted within one's own self-determination and self-realisation. This person-oriented outlook is consis-tent with the existentialists' general principle: the meaningfulness of hu-man living derives from within oneself. Reality is *lived* reality. To de-scribe the real, one must not describe what is beyond but what is in the human condition.

It is to the learner then that the educator must turn. Existentialism un-derlines one important moment in the learner's life. In the life of every individual there occurs what these thinkers call "the existential moment": when the individual discovers himself or herself as *existing.* The term it-self may not sound significant, but for existentialists "to exist" assumes a highly meaningful connotation. It means to "ex-sist", to stand out, to be aware of one's uniqueness.[17] This existential moment is the abrupt onset, the charged beginning of the awareness of the phenomenon of one's pres-ence in the world as a person.[18] Before this moment, there had been no such awareness.

The keyword then in the process of education, according to existential-ist thinking, is *awareness.* Education must somehow awaken awareness in the learner, existential awareness as a single subjectivity present in the

---

[17] See the poem in Chapter One.

[18] This could be compared to James Joyce's epiphany in *A Portrait of the Artist as a Young Man* (Oxford University Press, 2000) or the experience expressed by Elizabeth Bishop in her poem "In the Waiting Room," "But I felt: you are an I,/ You are an *Elizabeth,*/ You are one of *them.*" (lines 60-63).

world. Education must bring about the realisation that though one may not have had the choice of being brought into this world, nevertheless, one is the author of one's lifetime. For what a man or woman becomes is his or her choice and responsibility. He or she has the option of living an authentic or inauthentic existence no matter what the circumstances are. Education must set itself the task of awakening this awareness in the learner. As someone picturesquely said, existentialist education "grips a child by his moral collars and lifts him up to see over the crowd to the task of taking *personal responsibility* for being human". If this is what education should be, then an educated person is one who:

> becomes fully aware of himself as the shaper of his own life, aware of the fact that he must take charge of that life and make it his own statement of what a human *ought* to be—this is the individual who has been brought beyond mere intellectual discipline, beyond mere subject matter, beyond mere enculturation, beyond mere "fundamental dispositions" to the exotic but supremely human zone, the zone of value creation where selves create their own selves beyond the reach of teacher and textbook [19]

The challenge confronting educators is to provide the occasion and circumstances for the awakening and intensification of this awareness. Learning must become an act of discovery, discovery of responsibility.

Martin Buber, a thinker known for his philosophy of dialogue (and who provokes Richard's musings) illustrates this existentialist thinking on education in two essays: "Education" and "The Education of Character".[20] The child who is the subject of education is seen by Buber to be endowed with the "originative instinct". It is an autonomous instinct, not derived from others. This instinct causes the child to want to make things, to be the subject of something that is produced. Thus, a child is not content with merely accepting passively whatever is handed to it. It wants to put its stamp on it: it desires its own share in this becoming of things. This particular instinct is significant in education if it has to be guided. The child has also another instinct: the instinct for communion. Education would err if it were to base itself only on the training of the first instinct. To do so would be to prepare the child—no matter how skilled it will become or how developed his or her originative instinct will be—for a new human

---

[19] Van Cleve Morris, *Existentialism in Education* (N.Y.: Harper and Row, 196), p. 111.

[20] Martin Buber, *Between Man and Man* (Collins, 1971). Buber's philosophy is discussed further in Chapter Four. While Buber's context is the education of the child, what he says is applicable—appropriately contextualised—to various stages of the whole process of education of the learner.

solitariness. An originator, according to Buber, is a solitary man or woman. The originative instinct has therefore to be guided towards sharing in an undertaking and as a result of this guidance the child learns "to enter into mutuality". Entering into mutuality is what life is all about for Buber. It is being in dialogue, in an I-Thou relationship. It is only in such a relationship that the child can learn how to be fully a person.[21]

Consequently, education has an important role to play. Buber says that educators should not think that, once these instincts are given an outlet, they will take on a natural course benefiting the child. They are not to be suppressed, but at the same time they are not to be left on their own either. A certain selection of the various forces which influence the child has to be made by the educator. "Education, conscious and willed, means a selection by man of the effective world, it means to give decisive effective power to a selection of the world which is concentrated and manifested in the educator".[22] It has a definite purpose. To clarify what he means, Buber points to the master as the model for the teacher. The master in times past not only imparted his skill but also "the mystery of personal life". There has to be the element of the personal in education. The educator guides the child since as an educator he is capable of recognising values. What the child needs is not a moral or skilled genius but one who is wholly alive and able to communicate *himself* directly to the child. His aliveness—like the water in the Fonske—streams out to the child, affecting it yet without interfering with it.

But is this not putting the emphasis on the educator rather than on the child? And is it not possible that the educator would be influencing the child rather than awakening the child's sense of responsibility? Buber replies that the educator must realise that though he is a distinct element in the education of the child, he remains only one of the elements and that the aim of education is to enable the child to live the life of dialogue, a life of responsibility (responsibility in the sense of responding to the call of becoming fully human). This is what Buber means by "all education is education of character". Having been made aware of his or her responsibility, Buber's educated person will have the courage to shoulder life, to deny no answer to life and the world and to accept responsibility for everything that he or she meets. This person will also recognise that discipline and order are starting points on the way towards self-responsibility and that even great characters are not born perfect.

---

[21] It would be interesting to compare Buber and Whitehead on this point.
[22] Buber, *Between Man and Man,*. p. 116.

Concluding Comments

One could easily brush aside the existentialist approach to education as being too idealistic and too vague. Perhaps it is so. But it would be a pity, and indeed would be detrimental, if we did not take up this challenge and allow it to enable us to re-think our educational aims and methods. For after all there seems to be some truth in the accusation that schools today are not more than "educational factories where our children are processed and fashioned alike regardless of their personal uniqueness where teachers are forced, or think they are forced, into teaching along lines laid down for them."[23] For if education becomes distasteful to a large number of people or if all that our pupils want of education is "to get through", then it is probably time for us to re-examine our views on education and reshape the system which supports them. For somehow one has that feeling that in general an educated person should not be one who became an educated person in spite of the system.

How relevant is this to college and university education? How does this deal with the quest for wisdom? We believe that this fundamental point regarding the process and aim of education applies just as much at that level—particularly in the light of academic developments brought about by the Bologna process—since it is about educating human beings. Academia (and that, by the way, includes our subject disciplines) indeed needs to adapt but should continue to transform society and not just serve it. We need to acknowledge the climate of change, but we would also want in some respects to change the climate. We have transitioned from the information-society to the knowledge-society. Let us hope that we will soon move to the wisdom-society because of the work that we do in academia. Society will then, perhaps *only then*, be a community—*with* learning.[24]

---

[23] George F. Kneller, *Foundations of Education* (N.Y.: John Wiley, 1971), p. 263.
[24] John Henry Newman's phrase, to which the last sentence is a response, is "a community of learning".

CHAPTER THREE

WHAT OUGHT I TO DO?: THE QUEST FOR THE GOOD

Ethical Concerns

Ethics has become a particularly relevant topic for discussion and a subject for serious study. It has a very long tradition, of course; but nowadays one hears frequently of the need, because of abuses or concerns, to formulate and adopt ethical codes in various areas or professions.[1] Advances in science and technology resulting in new developments in various fields, including medicine, have presented fresh ethical problems, some of which could hardly have been anticipated. The perception of a loss of moral values in society has sparked off a persistent demand for more ethical training at home, in schools, and in society in general. There has also been a call to upgrade the moral status of a country.[2] For various reasons, not all of which are altruistic or disinterested, "ethical," "responsibility" and "accountability" have truly become buzz words in present-day society.[3] Ethics and ethical issues do indeed continue to challenge us.

---

[1] In her message to the Society for Ethics Across the Curriculum, which held its 9th International Conference in Dublin, President Mary McAleese of Ireland, writes: "Since the Conference was held in November 2007, our world has been turned upside down by the global financial and economic crisis. One of the dimensions of the crisis that has engendered considerable public anger and resentment has been the growing evidence of low ethical standards and values which have had devastating consequences." *Teaching Ethics*, IX, 1 (Fall 2008), p. 3.

[2] This was particularly evident in the 2008 American elections.

[3] Ethics has literally become fashionable! In the *Irish Times Magazine* (March 14, 2009), the article with the comment "Ethical fashion is big business." states: "At the recent London Fashion Week, the most extensive area in the Exhibition Hall was Esthetica, which was showcasing ethical designer fashion and which grows bigger each season.... It is all part of a growing awareness of how, where and in what conditions our clothes are made." p. 22. Moreover, *Fashion Theory* (December 2008) contains reflections on topics like slow fashion, ethical branding and the

Scholars, educators and practitioners have responded to this need and call by contributing the rich resources of their respective disciplines to the on-going discussion. Consequently, in addition to traditional courses and publications in ethics or moral theology, several more have appeared in specific areas, like bioethics, journalistic ethics, engineering ethics, business ethics, and the like. Ethics committees have been set up. Various consultancies, conferences and symposia have been organised. Programmes like "Ethics Across the Curriculum" have been offered. All these, and many others, seem to attest to the urgency and relevance of the topic.

The felt need for ethics, however, is translated into different expectations or conceptions of ethics and its challenges. There has always been a tendency to regard ethics as concerned with rules and regulations. Today that view equates ethics with codes of conduct. As a result, the ethical challenge is identified with the formulation, adoption and implementation of a set of clear guidelines that will regulate and evaluate behaviour or practice. This is particularly true in several professional bodies such as in medicine, science or business.[4] Increasingly, however, this understanding of ethics also seems to underlie the call for ethics among politicians as can be seen in the kind of ethics committees formed for that purpose. Politicians are even hauled before such committees to establish whether their behaviour can be deemed ethically appropriate. Another common conception of ethics is that it is a matter of taking a position or even having an opinion on specific situations. Many times the debates on euthanasia, abortion, or evolving family structures, come down to this. Behind such a view of ethics is the assumption that ethics is ultimately a subjective judgment or decision that one makes. In some cases, it is even equated with simply expressing what one believes about or even what one feels about the matter. It is an assumption that is at times expressed as "in ethics there are no right or wrong answers", a statement that results from realising the complexity of arriving at an acceptable ethical point of view; or "in ethical matters, I want to be able to assert my freedom or to have a choice.", a claim that emphasises the subjective nature of the decision. Still another conception of ethics, which has long roots in society, is that it is the general consensus of the individuals composing that society. That view is sometimes referred to as "conventional or the majority view". One's behaviour is expected to be in line with what is agreed upon by that society.

---

consumer, eco tech fashion and celebrity chick and the "green commodity fetish" (www.ingentaconnect.com).

[4] This is even true in tourism. The *Irish Times Travel Supplement* (every Saturday) also regularly carries a column titled "Ethical Tourism" which provides information to those who wish to take ethical considerations into account in their travels.

Sometimes this is equated with the culture of a particular people. Such an understanding of ethics especially comes to the fore as we become more aware of the diversity in the ways of life throughout the world.

But ethics and its challenges are much more than that—when we take into account the nature and status of the moral agents and the factors which make up ethical decision-making itself. In ethics, one is simply not talking about asking for directions or guidelines. Nor is the agent merely an implementer of a pre-established rule or guideline. Although in judging what is ethical or not and in deciding which course of action to take, there is greater involvement on the part of the agent, this does not mean that an ethical decision is merely a matter of preference or choice. It is not necessarily the majority view of society or the culture of that society either. Because of our make-up as human beings, endowed with intellect and free will, such decisions and actions should be characterised with a certain amount of reflection and freedom on our part. It is for this reason that one must distinguish mere instinctive behaviour from human conduct in various contexts and the cultural from the social. Furthermore, exercising one's freedom is not the same as exercising one's freedom responsibly.

An Ethical Dilemma

Before continuing with this discussion, however, let us first follow Rodrigo's reflections on the course of action that many in his country have to pursue given the situation that they find themselves in:

> But Rodrigo remembered very well that when Juan and Pepe graduated from elementary school, while Juan went to Manila to the minor seminary, Pepe himself reluctantly had to leave Guiuan, too. Pepe was not interested in going to high school. He needed to work to help support a rather large family—ten brothers and sisters, a mother and a father. Being the eldest he was expected to do that. But what probably turned the tide for Pepe was seeing his father spend so much time drinking *tuba* with his friends every single night. There was nothing else to do in Guiuan, his father regarding this as somehow justifying his behaviour. Pepe didn't agree, but he had to acknowledge the lack of opportunities in the town that he loved. He couldn't find a good-paying job. He had heard that in Tacloban he could earn a living selling newspapers, sweepstakes tickets or cigarettes. It was with a heavy heart that he temporarily abandoned his dream of doing something for Guiuan. He had to do something for his family first.
>
> Rodrigo wondered about the pressures put on many of the youngsters in the Philippines. Pepe was a good example. The West would never understand. How he wished they could indeed have the privilege of enjoying their childhood. But when one's family needs to survive, then one has to

accept appalling working conditions. The only other alternative is to let one's family starve.

As he thought of the many Pepes in the Philippines, Rodrigo recalled an entry he had made in his journal on the experience of poverty. Reflecting on the misery and degradation experienced by the poor, he had written: *"We may try to impart a theological, biblical or spiritual meaning to their plight, yet we cannot escape the economics of it. Nor can we ignore its psychological consequences. Poverty is extreme need or destitution. It means the way of life of the slum-dwellers or the homeless of Latin America or of the Philippines, of over-populated India, of the ghettos of America and elsewhere, of famine-stricken Ethiopia, Sudan and Somalia. Poverty hurts and oppresses people because it deprives them of the necessities of life. It creates the gap between the rich, over-fed landlord and the hungry, grief-stricken tenant. It makes a parent worry over the next crumb for the family. It forces a man or woman to stand in line at employment agencies in spite of the very slim chance of getting a job. Poverty is what causes grim-faced children to peer into restaurants to watch the more fortunate ones partake of life's bounties—as if the mere sight of food is enough to ease the hunger they feel. Poverty is certainly not a welcome word, and its effects are to be dreaded and avoided."* Those were not empty words. Rodrigo himself had first-hand knowledge of poverty.

So he cried to himself as these flashbacks haunted him. Do those who are fighting to rectify the plight of children by forcing these factories in developing countries to close or to put pressure on governments not to allow child employment—commendable though their efforts are in the long run—neglect to take into account that the short-term is sometimes more crucial? How are these families to live in the meantime? Are they forgetting that the culture of these people regards children as part of the workforce of the family? What right do these foreigners have in wanting to impose their understanding of what is right on other cultures?

Yet Rodrigo found himself angry at his own thoughts. Should he not know any better? Was he justifying the atrocities of landlords, factory-owners, multi-national corporations, some of whose working conditions were contributing to the ongoing poverty and degradation of the poor? Can culture be responsible for imprisoning the minds and the bodies of people? Did he not learn something from his stay in the West?[5]

Ethical Thinking

What does Rodrigo's situation bring to our attention in this enquiry? One point worth emphasing here is the importance of thinking in ethical matters. While it would be rather naïve and even mistaken to claim that in the various expectations and conceptions of ethics sketched earlier and the

---

[5] M.S. Sia, *Those Distant Shores* (forthcoming).

ethical task mentioned there is no thinking involved, it is nevertheless true that in some cases the injunction to simply "follow your heart", "trust your feelings", or "go with the flow" would convey that impression. The same point could be made with the insistence on "abiding by the code" or "following the laws of society." We need to *think through* the judgments we make and the decisions we take on ethical situations. We should *investigate more critically* the basis of such judgments and decisions—which Rodrigo was beginning to realise. Furthermore, in ethics, as well as in other areas of life, it is important to have an *overall vision* that should ground, inform and support any judgment or decision we make. Obviously, these claims belie a certain conception on our part: namely, that ethics is a rational activity that is undertaken by rational agents.

Philosophy, as an academic discipline, and not just in ethics, has always been associated with this line of enquiry. In fact, philosophy as the love of wisdom is indeed interested not merely in raising questions to advance our knowledge but also, and even more importantly so, in pursuing any answers received in the hope of arriving at a more consistent and defensible point of view. Regrettably, often philosophical thinking—in the view of many, including some philosophers themselves—is seen to be such an intellectual exercise that it is perceived to be divorced from the concrete concerns of ordinary life. Rationality is often interpreted—unfortunately, some philosophical squabbles illustrate this—to mean disembodied thinking! As we engage in more serious and protracted thinking, as is done in philosophy and in other disciplines, it could appear more and more abstract. This is inevitable. But hopefully this consequence of the pursuit of wisdom and of the good does not lessen the valuable advantage of philosophy to our daily lives or restrict our ability to conduct what is really a human exercise.

Ethical Theories

The contribution of philosophy to ethical concerns includes the formulation of ethical theories and teaching them. This poses a number of challenges. In addition to having to address the complexities of communicating philosophical ideas to people from different backgrounds, the teacher of ethical theories has to take account of the fact that a number of these people need to be convinced first of the importance and relevance of ethical theories. Those who have their professional or practical interests already clearly set out before them understandably wonder why they still have to engage in what they consider rather abstract thinking about practical matters To them one could reply that while certain ethical considerations do arise in specific professional contexts in a practical way, e.g. engineering, medical, business, the primary context is our human nature.[6] That is to say, ethical questions arise because we are first and foremost human beings in search of answers as to how we ought to behave as engineers, as medics or as business people. Ethical inquiry, no matter in what field, must be rooted in an examination of what it means to be a human being in a concrete world.[7] If this observation is correct, then all ethical debates by its nature is grounded in certain theoretical foundations. The exploration of specific ethical questions such as is done in engineering ethics, medical ethics and business ethics and of more philosophical questions stand on common ground. The ethical issues "emerge" or "arise" when we examine particular situations in life.

A Practical Question

"What ought I to do?" is a central question in ethics. It is for this reason that, despite certain assumptions on the part of many regarding any philosophical study, the study of ethics within philosophy is after all a practical discipline. It leads to action. It is more than that of course because the question is intended to lead to a specific kind of action; namely, one that can be characterised as good, moral or ethical. Despite varying answers as to which actions can be so characterised, given the competing ethical criteria put forward by philosophers, the question in the context of an ethical inquiry is a search for a definite *kind* of action. "What ought I to do?" translates into "What course of action should I pursue such that I can be said to be acting responsibly?"

The practicality of this question inevitably leads to the expectation of a solution. This is definitely the case when we examine specific situations, like keeping a promise when other lives are at stake, or supporting research into cloning, or reflecting on child labour as Rodrigo was doing. Given the particular circumstances and the clash of moral principles in such a situation, should one keep one's promise of confidentiality or not, or should one actively promote experimentation in cloning, or should one condone child labour? Ultimately, one can rightly expect that the end result of such an enquiry is a definite yes or no. Thus, this ethical question has led to the understanding that ethics is in the final analysis a matter of choice, a specific decision-making that hopefully is the right one. What all

---

[6] The notion of human nature is itself problematic. It is used here merely to mean our humanity.
[7] This, we believe, is the context of the ethical enquiry.

this amounts to is that the practicality of ethics and the urgency of certain situations lead some to equate ethics with a process of fact-finding, information-gathering, and the provision of definite guidelines that will enable those who find themselves in a moral dilemma not only to *know* the facts of the situation but also, and more importantly, to *respond* to it in an ethical way. It seems that the concentration of the ethical enquiry in fields such as medicine, business, engineering and others, stems from this need to address the specificity and practicality of the question "what ought I to do?" The expected answer has to be a definite one, a solution.[8]

The nature of this question thus makes some question the study of ethical theories, especially when they discover not only that there are a number of them but also that they even contradict one another. As far as they are concerned, if ethics is meant to answer the question "what ought I to do?" would it not be much easier if they were given the "right solutions" in the first place? At least, they would know whether they are acting correctly or not as medical or business people or as engineers. Furthermore, the word "theory" itself seems incompatible with the practicality and specificity of this ethical question. Instead it gives support to those who have misgivings about the relevance of ethical theories in what they consider to be "the real world".

From the Question to a Quest

In addressing these concerns, a helpful way of going forward in teaching ethical theories is actually to retrace one's steps! In this case it means revisiting our starting point by examining the basis and the nature of this question. "What ought I to do?" asked in the context of the discussion of a moral dilemma[9]—carried out at the very beginning—can be very effective in showing that the question and the expected answer are not as straightforward as they are in another context. In probing into the initial views of the students on what one should do in that particular situation, the teacher of ethical theories can show that several factors have to be taken into account, e.g. intention, circumstances, values, and so on. More importantly,

---

[8] This is not to say that the answer is a definitive or a clear one. It simply means that it leads to a specific course of action.

[9] A most productive discussion comes with the Heinz dilemma from Laurence Kohlberg. As explained in Chapter Two, note 7, this enables the teacher to *evoke* students' interest because of the problematic nature of the situation, and then *provoke* them by asking various questions on what they would do and by changing the characters in the situation.

however, it can lead to a more prolonged discussion on the very nature of moral decision-making.[10]

This question, associated with the process of making an ethical decision, is one that resonates well with the students' own experiences although not always in such a dramatic manner. Students readily appreciate that everyday we find ourselves in various situations where we need to pursue a particular course of action. But as the class explores this question, it inevitably leads to further questions: "What is the basis of one's judgment, and why does the question arise in the first place?" As they grapple with these further questions, they can be invited to investigate with the teacher the thoughts of various philosophers who had dealt with these questions far more extensively and at greater depth than the class can possibly do.[11] At this point it is beneficial to show to the class that by asking and pursuing this ethical question what they are engaged in is an "act of philosophising"—which every human being does at different levels—and "learning from the philosophers"—which they do in a philosophy class.[12] It is the stage where one can illustrate the correlation between an ethical enquiry and the philosophical act. Both acts arise and are developed because one wants to "think through" the question itself and any answer that may be given.

The phrase "ethical theories" will obviously feature. At this stage students need to be shown that such theories can be understood to have arisen and to have been developed in an attempt to provide a more consistent and more systematic answer.[13] In some cases the answer to the question "what ought I to do?" has to be a quick and even instinctive one. But in the ethical context, one's answer should be much more thoughtful. This does not mean that every time we find ourselves in an ethical situation, we cannot and should not act until we have undergone a prolonged and thorough process of thinking about the matter. Many cases, particularly medical ones, do not allow us that luxury for every problem. This is where ethical theories—and the study of these—can be of paramount importance as they can serve as a "theoretical framework" that enables us to work out an ethi-

---

[10] A particularly helpful resource that combines literature and ethics is Nina Rosenstand, *The Moral of the Story: An Introduction to Ethics*, 4th ed. (McGraw Hill, 2003).

[11] This would be to *invoke* the resources provided by the philosophers. See note 9.

[12] A question which one could ask students to consider is: if we are already engaged in ethical thinking in daily life, what value is there in turning to an ethical theory such as Aristotle's or Confucius'?

[13] This is not of course true with every ethical theory, e.g. Aquinas' natural law theory, insofar as his ethical theory starts with a more metaphysical vision.

cal solution to the problem. The basis for one's judgment, even those done in a hurry, can be more firmly grounded. In any ethical decision, there are underlying theoretical assumptions. What the study of ethical theories does is to expose those and subject them to a critical evaluation, thus giving us an "early lead" as it were in urgent cases.

In a way this is what is involved in the study of philosophy generally.[14] The sense of wonder that stirred in Socrates, Confucius, the Buddha and the other philosophers down through the ages also prodded them—and continues to do so in our times—to form and develop more reflective answers to the questions which interested them. Philosophical thinking can be described as, among other definitions, bringing to the fore, with a view to scrutinizing more critically, not just the questions we are asking but also and more importantly disclosing the underlying assumptions behind those questions. Furthermore, just as an ethical theory sets before us a framework in our investigation of moral matters, philosophy generally—or at least as understood in certain quarters—aims to provide us with a vision that enables us to view and appreciate reality more profoundly and more extensively. While an ethical inquiry is more focused and philosophical thinking is more extensive, the two complement and enrich one another since both are based on the same quest for "a more substantial answer".

A Human Question

Pursuing the question "what ought I to do?" in the ethical context also leads to a consideration of the nature of the questioner not just in terms of the nature of the "I" but also in regard to why the question arises in the first place. As the class follows through with an ethical discussion based on a moral dilemma, they also take a closer look at why the discussion is taking place at all. These lines from T.S. Eliot capture this quest beautifully: "…we arrive where we started/ And know the place for the first time."[15] The ethical issues are issues for us human beings and because we are human beings. "What ought I to do?" is a human question, and it arises because we are the kind of beings that that can distinguish between what is

---

[14] This is an occasion to discuss the nature and value of philosophical thinking while acknowledging the variety of answers that can be given as to what philosophy is.

[15] T.S. Eliot "Little Gidding," in *T.S. Eliot: the Complete Poems and Plays, 1909-1950* (Orlando, Fla.: Harcourt Brace, 1958), p. 145. A useful sourcebook that focuses on this issue—combining literature and philosophy—is Nina Rosenstrand, *The Human Condition: an Introduction to Philosophy of Human Nature* (McGraw Hill, 2002).

and what ought to be. Although we do not always know what ought to be, nevertheless we are aware that it differs from doing just anything. There is something about our make-up that leads us to make such a crucial distinction. It is a more fundamental sense than the desire to arrive at a definite answer in cases when we are looking for the right choice to be made as medical or business people or as engineers. In short, it is a human feature.

The practicality of the question "what ought I to do" should not mislead us into concluding that the ethical choice is essentially about ready solutions—a point already made earlier. Here one can draw the students' attention to the distinction between a superficial and a profound answer to that question. Inevitably, they put forward the importance of having all the relevant facts before one makes a decision. But as the discussion progresses and more questions are considered, they begin to realise that the gathering of facts itself presupposes an implied evaluation of those facts (even just the matter of "what counts" and "what does not").[16] Although it does not always emerge as readily as one would wish, the description of what is a profound answer to the question "what ought I to do?" changes to "where much thought has been given to it".[17] This of course leads to further questions: Why does it matter that we put much thought into our answer? When can one say that one has given it sufficient thought? Who judges ultimately that enough thought has been given to the answer that one has arrived at? What these and other questions disclose is that in our attempt to answer the ethical question "what ought I to do?" we do fall back, although not always consciously, not just on our desire to arrive at answers but also on our ability to give a *more considered* kind of answer.[18] We are the sort of beings to whom this situation applies. We are, as Aristotle had pointed out, rational animals.

As the class examines who we are in the light of the question "what ought I to do?" one can try to show the students that the significance of the question, in the context of an ethical choice, does not lie in its functionality (as it would be the case if one were merely faced with having to decide on alternative routes to a specified destination). Rather, it consists in its being grounded in our very rationality. Thus, not only does it arise be-

---

[16] The distinction between facts and values, between a scientific enquiry and an ethical one, is relevant here. However, there is no such a thing as a value-free fact; even in the selection and presentation of facts, there are always certain value-laden assumptions behind that individual's choice.

[17] In other words, it is not and should not be merely like the ad of a well-known sporting company: "Just do it!"

[18] This would be the stage of *convoking,* that is, arriving at some kind of an answer. See note 9.

cause, as rational beings, we are inclined to ask questions but the kind of answer that one can expect from us reflects our very nature. This can be a useful lead to a discussion of what is involved in characterising us as rational animals.

In pursuing the question "what ought I to do?" back to the questioner himself/herself, it will be clear that exploring the ethical question itself is an act of philosophising. It is an activity that we are engaged in precisely because we are human beings. If that is so, ethics has its place in the education of the human person, no matter what specialisation one is interested in.[19]

Developing Moral Sense

So far, we have highlighted the importance of ethical thinking and the contribution that philosophy can make. It should be noted, however, that such an activity is not intended, given the nature of the ethical enquiry and the ethical task itself, to lead to clear, detailed and conclusive answers to ethical dilemmas and situations. Admittedly, this can be frustrating. But one can and should expect ethical thinking to challenge our presuppositions and even our initial conclusions precisely in the hope that we can reject, modify and substantiate them. Unreflected viewpoints or perspectives have a way of leading us astray even if we also have to admit that any protracted and extensive enquiry can and does lead to more questions. This is true in any field, and compounded in a philosophical study.

Despite inherent difficulties with ethical thinking, however, it does highlight an important area in human life and helps to focus on an essential human concern and challenge: how are we to live? This is where the development of our moral sense is crucial. Ultimately, since we have to, and indeed do, make moral judgments, it is essential that we are guided by a moral sense that is being deepened and strengthened by continuous ethical reflections.

Moral sense is much more than moral sentiment or feeling.[20] It is not an intellectual ability that enables one to distinguish between right and wrong either. Nor is it simply a direction one takes when one exercises one's free will. And yet all of these come into play since moral sense is ultimately based on our very humanity. As human beings, we possess

---

[19] See Chapter Two.

[20] Moral sense as used in this book is different from, although comparable to, the way it has been used by philosophers like Frances Hutcheson and David Hume. Cf. Maria Elton, "Moral Sense and Natural Reason," *Review of Metaphysics,* LXII, 1, issue 245 (Sept. 2008), pp. 79-110.

feelings, imagination, intellect and free will, and when we ask what is ethical and what is not and draw a conclusion, we make use of all these gifts.

The word "sense" carries different meanings, each of which we can avail of to shed light on "moral sense" as used in the present context. "Sense", of course, means our five senses that enable us to be in contact with the outside world. The word is also used to refer to someone having "sense"; and we mean that that person does not just know but has the right knowledge. It can also mean simply "in a particular instance" as when we qualify a statement or claim made when we say "it is true in this sense". But "sense" can also have a stronger meaning as a more or less coherent overall view as when we talk of "life making (or not making) sense". The phrase "moral sense" draws on these meanings. It is through our senses that we accumulate experience, including moral experience, of the world around us. We require the right knowledge, and not just any knowledge, to enable us to act ethically. We need to be aware of the particularity of a situation to enable us to judge the appropriateness of our judgement or decision. More importantly, we ought to be informed by an overall per-spective that helps us not just to situate the particular moral situation or context but also to judge it more consistently. [21]

The various uses of "sense" and their applicability to the phrase "moral sense" means that ethical thinking should not be interpreted as solely a cerebral activity. It is a rational activity that involves all the abili-ties that human beings possess, including the use of our intellect. And since it takes place in concrete situations and particular individuals, it is an activity that draws on various sources, including gender, culture and relig-ion, whenever we resort to it. It is, to use Charles Hartshorne's phrase, "context-dependent". Ethical thinking enables us to appreciate our own status as agents and recipients: beings with "moral sense" that needs to be developed so that we can indeed give a responsible response to the chal-lenges of life.

In this respect other academic subjects can help further. Psychology probes into and helps us understand our feelings. Education and religion can facilitate the nurture of moral sense. Literature—since this chapter is a literary-philosophical enquiry, it deserves closer attention—is a strong ally for it can awaken our ethical sensitivities. Martha Nussbaum reminds us that ancient philosophers, like Aristotle, appreciated the educational value of drama since it provides us with valuable lessons about having proper feelings at the proper time, which in turn help with appreciating life and

---

[21] See Chapter One for the importance of context.

virtue in general. Aristotle was of the view that drama allows people to act out their emotions vicariously, and thus also has a cathartic effect. Nussbaum notes that our moral values are closely linked to our emotions, and it would be wrong to simply dismiss these as non-rational or even irrational. She claims that there is much cognitive value in emotions: providing access to values, to human relationships and to our self-understanding. The rational element in these emotions enables us to distinguish between emotional reactions which are morally relevant and those which are not; for example, "just anger". Emotional responses do involve decision-making and rational choices. Since narratives, the telling of stories, come naturally to us—Alasdair MacIntyre describes us as "storytelling animals"—reading them enables us to share basic experiences of values. The actual reading of these, rather than just an analysis of the content, can facilitate our understanding of the emotions. One could add that the sympathetic feelings aroused by the reading of such sources can help develop our moral sense.[22]

Taking a Moral Stance

An ethical enquiry should lead not just to knowing what is right and wrong—in the broad sense indicated above—but ultimately to doing that which is right and avoiding that which is wrong. For this reason, there is a justified expectation that ethical thinking, in our quest for the good, should facilitate our becoming more responsible, more civic-minded, and better behaved. Such an expectation is exemplified by the call for codes of conduct or the listing of virtues/vices. Ethical thinking should motivate us, at least we hope so, to work towards the betterment of ourselves, of society and of the world we live in. In short, the further question is: how does ethical thinking lead to our taking a moral stance?

Philosophers, like Aristotle and Aquinas, have always been aware of the distinction between knowing and willing, not just conceptually but also in reality. That translates to saying that knowledge of the good does not necessarily lead to wanting to do the good. Others, however, like Plato and Augustine, have insisted that the attraction of the good is such that it will make us pursue it. Thus, the more we get to know it, the more we would

---

[22] Martha Nussbaum, *Love's Knowledge* (N.Y.: Oxford University Press, 1990); *Uphheavals of Thought: the Intelligence of Emotions* (Cambridge University Press, 2001). It is interesting to compare Nussbaum's observations regarding the value of narratives with those of Carol Gilligan in *In a Different Voice* (Cambridge, Mass.: Harvard University Press, 1982). Gilligan turns to "women's stories" which she does not regard as fiction but as moral stories, i.e. women (and men) make sense of life by telling stories about themselves.

want it. For this reason, what bars us from ethical conduct is the veil of ignorance on our part. Common experience, however, would seem to favour the first point of view. We do need other incentives aside from knowledge, like law for Aquinas, to make us tread the ethical path. A more cynical observation would be that ethicists or moral philosophers and theologians, who spend their professional time studying and teaching ethics are not necessarily the most ethical human beings![23]

On the other hand, ethical thinking, while it may not necessarily lead to ethical conduct of the individual agent, nevertheless promotes and sustains it, at least indirectly. While knowledge of what is right needs other factors to make us want and pursue the good, ignorance of relevant information, including what is involved in making the ethical judgement or decision can easily lead to irresponsible or unethical conduct. The will to act, spurred by our passions, is not sufficient to ensure that we are indeed acting ethically. Too many misdeeds—also in the ethical sense—have been performed in the name of righteousness or God's will. Since acting ethically is dependent on our knowledge of the situation, the more we know the relevant factors, including our moral norms, the less we are in danger of acting unethically.

Even if we cannot provide an indubitable connection, at least in the ethical sphere, between thinking and willing in Plato's and Augustine's sense, it remains nevertheless true that one's moral sense, developed through ethical thinking, does lead to what could be described as exemplary conduct. Martin Luther King and Mahatma Gandhi easily come to mind since both individuals as moral agents were inspired and sustained in their way of life and their moral stance by the principles, arrived at through constant and protracted reflection, that they subscribed to. While one may have difficulties with Laurence Kohlberg's methodology and conclusions, one can still accept that moral reasoning does promote moral growth (not necessarily in the hierarchical order described by him) insofar as one has harnessed one's thinking powers to broaden one's perspective and increasing the likelihood of being guided by this. And that means that we are indeed developing our true nature and progressing towards our calling as responsible human beings.

In taking a moral stance—which leads to moral action—it is important once again to note that it is not simply a matter of deciding and then

---

[23] Shakespeare expresses this point quite well: "If to do were as easy to know what were good to do, chapels had been churches, and poor men's cottages princes' palaces. It is a good divine that follows his own instruction; I can easier teach twenty what were good to be done, than be one of the twenty to follow mine own teaching." *The Merchant of Venice*, Act 1, Sc. 2.

acting but of situating it against a wider background.[24] Situation ethics, which focuses almost exclusively on the particular situation or circumstance as dictating the morality of an action, ignores the need not only to be consistent in our ethical judgments—a lesson that can be learned from Kant—but also to be right about our judgment. In ethics, what is appropriate is not always the right ethical decision. We have to guard ourselves against making simply ad hoc decisions. In this respect developing a moral sense—a sense of responsibility that is spurred on by what we can do but is constantly guided by what we ought to do or not do—is particularly crucial. This underlies the need for the larger picture.[25]

Summing Up

While certain ethical considerations do arise in specific professional contexts in a practical way, e.g. engineering, medical, business, all ethical debates by its nature is grounded in certain theoretical foundations. "What ought I to do?" (and the expected answer) in the ethical context is not as straightforward as they are in another context. Probing more fully into it, we will see that even in that particular situation, several factors have to be taken into account, e.g. intention, circumstances, values, consequences and so on. It inevitably leads to further questions: "What is the basis for one's judgment, and why does the question arise in the first place?" We need to "think through" the question itself and any answer that may be given. We do need to go from the question(s) to a quest.

---

[24] Chapter One describes this as "context".

[25] This is where ethical theories—and the study of them—can have a role to play, *pace* Caputo. Cf. his, *Against Ethics: Contributions to a Poetics of Obligation with Constant Reference to Deconstruction* (Indiana University Press, 1993).

CHAPTER FOUR

THE NEED FOR ANOTHER—WHY?: THE QUEST FOR COMMUNITY

An Imaginary Conversation[1]

Let us first listen in to a conversation between Juan and his Novice Master. Juan is full of questions regarding his calling in life:

"Father, can I talk to you about something that has been going on in my mind," Juan decided to broach the topic with his Novice Master.

Juan was having his monthly interview with the Novice Master. To help the young novices on their individual journey into religious life, it was the rule of the novitiate that they hold regular *colloquia* with their Novice Master. They were fortunate in having as their guide a kind and understanding priest. Despite his large physique, he had a soft heart. He had served in the missions for a long time, and his talks were always laced with anecdotes from the mission lands where he had served. His perspective was shaped by the down-to-earth problems that faced missionaries as they struggled to bring the faith to distant lands. He was also known to be a holy man, who spent hours on his knees praying in front of the Blessed Sacrament.

"Certainly, Juan. You know you can always discuss any matter of concern to you during these *colloquia,*" Fr. Magister, as he was officially known, was reassuring. "Come, and sit down." He motioned to the chair in front of him.

"I. . .I don't really know where to begin. But . . .," Juan was clearly fumbling for the right way to bring up the topic.

"Don't tell me that you're finding Latin troublesome!"

With that both Juan and Fr. Magister had a good laugh since it was known that Juan was the top Latinist in his class. In fact, he had been asked by the Novice Master to do some translation of important ecclesiastical documents written in that "dead language". But it was a good opener that put Juan more at ease.

---

[1] M.S. Sia, *Those Distant Shores* (forthcoming).

"I suppose it is troublesome!" countered Juan. "But it's more the reality behind the Latin word *chastitas* that has become a problem to me. I'm not sure now whether I'm really called to a life of celibacy, Father Magister." Juan shifted in the chair. "I find the opposite sex attractive, and lately I've been wondering about a particular girl with whom I grew up."

"Well, that's very natural, Juan. That's human nature. Religious life won't take that away. In fact, it shouldn't."

Juan looked up at him in surprise.

"No, you see, Juan, one doesn't take the vow of celibacy because one hates or is not attracted to the opposite sex. That would be the wrong idea of this vow."

Juan needed some clarification. "But wouldn't that make it easier?"

"And what would be the point in that? To me it would seem as if the vow is then merely legitimising or covering up something. It would be making the vow for the wrong reason."

"But it becomes more difficult when one really desires to be with a woman." It must have been the Novice Master's fatherly concern that made Juan admit that.

"I know, Juan. And believe you me, out in the mission fields, it becomes even more difficult because of the loneliness. It can truly be a struggle. In a religious community, at least we have the company of our brethren. It can help, but as you are experiencing now, it doesn't go away."

"You mean, it will even get harder than what I'm feeling right now?" Clearly, Juan wasn't getting the reassurance that he had hoped for.

"That's right, and there's no point in denying that either. But one can tolerate it, one can cope with it. Or one can sublimate it."

"That's what I'm afraid of, Father. That perhaps I can't do any of those."

"Isn't that why we spend years preparing for this kind of life? The novitiate, and even the Scholasticate later on, is really a preparation time. That's why after the novitiate, we take temporary vows year after year until final vows."

"But some religious still leave after final vows—and sometimes for that reason." As if Father Magister needed to be reminded. There had been a couple of departures from the vowed community lately.

"That's true. And unfortunately, I do know of very fine confreres who left the religious life for that very reason, as you put it." Juan detected a certain sadness in the Novice Master's voice.

"If I do go ahead, Father Magister, I don't want to have to 'call it quits' later on. I would rather leave before that time."

"Do you think it's the life of celibacy or is it the fear of quitting later on that's bothering you, Juan?" The elderly priest adjusted his spectacles to have a better look at Juan.

"I suppose it's both. I can't really be sure," Juan instinctively shook his head. "One thing is sure, that I miss the companionship of a woman. And I hate to give up what I've never experienced, Father. You know, sexual intercourse," Juan stopped himself from adding, I have been wondering what it's like.

"You're right, it's difficult giving up what one has no knowledge of. How can one be sure that one's doing the right thing? Is that close to what's on your mind?" Fr. Magister smiled faintly.

"Sort of. It must be a beautiful experience." Juan hoped his face didn't betray what he was imagining.

"It is, Juan, it is. . . . Again, what's the point in giving up something that's not beautiful, or something that one doesn't appreciate. Augustine refers to the pleasure of sex as *remedium concupiscientiae*, that it is like an attraction so that human beings would be willing to take on the burden of parenthood. Calling it a 'remedy' is a rather one-sided view of this important aspect of our humanity. No, sex is good and beautiful not just because it leads to procreation but also because it bonds people. When people are really in love, sometimes there comes a point when they express that love also physically. In the married state, of course. At least, for Catholics. No, Juan, we don't give up that part of ourselves because there's anything disgusting about it. It's precisely because we value it that we are giving it up."

"I can see the point, Father, but is that sufficient? I mean, to realise that it's beautiful? Will that help me now and later on?" Juan glanced at the Novice Master, hoping for some reassurance. He caught a glimpse of the blue skies outside. Somehow, the sunlight, which illumined the room, actually darkened Fr. Magister's face.

"No, Juan, it won't. That's why we need God's grace. The life of celibacy, and indeed the life of a religious, is a vocation. It is truly a calling. If God calls us, then God will provide us with the grace. God doesn't expect something from us while leaving us out in the cold, as it were. Remember what I said about the testing time that we are given by our religious order? It's really the opportunity to find out whether we have a vocation to this way of life or not. And it is a way of life, not a profession." Father Magister stressed practically every word of the last sentence.

"I think that's what scares me, Father Magister. That it's a way of life. I suppose if it were a profession, one can always change one's mind. And that wouldn't be as bad."

"As bad as what, Juan?"

"As bad as quitting later on."

"I see your point now that for you it's probably the question of celibacy as well as the fear of quitting."

"It is, Father, and that makes me very confused as well. And doubly scared."

"We can't always know the future. In fact, we don't know the future. If we did, we would probably regret knowing it. Facing the future can be very daunting, you know. But we can prepare for it. Somewhat."

"How?" Once again, Juan was expectant of a more comforting answer.

"By being honest with ourselves, to start with. That's why in the novitiate we spend a lot of time in silence. Actually, it's not really silence. We need to converse with ourselves. We need to get to know ourselves. And we need to be at home with ourselves. That's when we also get to know whether we can be comfortable with ourselves."

"To prepare for the solitary life. Is that it, Father?" Did he sound sarcastic? Juan wondered, checking Father Magister's face. But the Novice Master must be used to all this as he remained unfazed.

"No, definitely not in the way you put it, Juan. It would be wrong to think that in the married state, one doesn't have to know oneself and be comfortable with oneself. The married state is not a cure for loneliness. It would be a pity if that were so, because then what you have are two lonely people, instead of one."

"Isn't it better than being lonely on one's own as it were, as at least you'll have company."

"And share in each other's misery? Again that's doing the right thing for the wrong reason.[2] Getting married is good, but to regard it as an escape from one's loneliness is not the best of reasons."

"I'm not sure I understand you, Father. I thought you said that our silences are meant to help us become comfortable with ourselves. But if I am so, then I don't have to be looking for anyone else." Juan moved back in his chair to be at ease.

"Do you really think so? The silences are meant to help us discover whether we want to embrace the religious life, with its vow of celibacy, or the married life. Whatever choice we make in life, we do need to learn to be at home with our individual selves. You see, Juan, strange as this may seem, it is such an individual that will make a good religious as well as a good married partner."

"That sounds contradictory. Doesn't it mean that one should be one and not the other?" Juan knitted his eyebrows quizzically.

"You're right, of course. It's a matter of one or the other. But to some extent what one brings into either way of life is the same. I mean in terms of being comfortable with oneself, of having learned to appreciate one's own company, of being, as I've already said, at home with oneself. Neither the religious life nor the married state should be a running away from oneself."

"But how will I know which one is for me?"

"God will let you know. That's what we mean when we say, God calls us to the religious life." Father Magister stressed the word, "calls".

"And to the married life?"

"The same way. The married life is also a vocation, not a profession."

"And how would I know to which one I'm being called?" Juan was clearly desirous of a more direct answer.

---

[2] T.S. Eliot puts this point across quite strongly: "The last temptation is the greatest treason: To do the right deed for the wrong reason." *Murder in the Cathedral* (London: Faber & Faber, 1965), lines 666-667.

"Perhaps we should take things one at a time. The main thing for you now is to converse with yourself. And ask God for guidance. And, you know, the different exercises of the novitiate life are intended to help us discover what way of life we are being called to."

Juan had several such conversations with the Novice Master. Somehow his doubts remained, but he continued to pray as had been suggested to him. And he was beginning to see that the life of celibacy was not the absence of love but its fullness. It might mean the giving up of a particular kind of love and its special way of expressing it. He was to realise too that celibacy was not meant to be the withdrawal of all contacts with the opposite sex but the openness for everyone. Not having one's own family was intended to be an appreciation of all families.

The problem, however, was that Juan was not sure whether that was meant to be his calling in life. How he wished he could be sure.

He was amused at some of the practical strategies they had been taught, like making sure that there was a physical object, such as table between them and the opposite sex. There was no point in risking it—his fellow novices and he used to remind one another!

But the way he was feeling, he needed more than just a barrier. Just as well Zenaida was several miles away.

A Reflection on a Human Need[3]

Let us now share in the recollections and reflections of other fictitious characters:

Enrique's questions kept nudging him on—to reflect on these matters. Perhaps, he reasoned it out, when one cannot see anything, one's mind wants to take over. As if it wants to provide one with another kind of vision. His experience in the countryside of Connemara and of the tranquility of Glendalough had made such an impact on him.

Away from all the activity and frenzy of fellow passengers, he didn't mind being in this situation. The more he reflected, the more he realised that there are times when we need to get away from other people, not necessarily to avoid them (even if at times this is the case) but more so to find the best atmosphere to think about the serious side of life—Enrique smiled, as he thought of his father's passion for walking alone. And some people prefer to be on their own, because they think that this gives them a chance to grow up, to learn to cope with life's challenges independently of others. Perhaps that was why Papa strongly encouraged him to travel on his own. According to his father, we become mature only when we have learned to carry the responsibilities of life on our own shoulders. Enrique was beginning to appreciate that.

---

[3] *Ibid.*

Enrique recalled an observation that his father had made, but at that time it meant very little to him. His father had commented that there is something in-built in every person that makes him or her sense a certain unity or closeness with others. When this link is cut, that person gets terrified. And also begins to feel lonely. Was that why in the past he had dreaded being on his own, of being cut off from others? It made him feel incomplete, as it were. When he discussed this with his father, Papa had replied that we are like that, we feel alienated because we need to be complemented by others.

"Other people," Papa explained—as he puffed on his pipe and crossed his legs when Enrique initiated this father-son conversation, "are really part of ourselves and we are part of them. That's why we can never be fully satisfied with just ourselves. We sense 'something' to be lacking in us. Thus we reach out, we go beyond ourselves, in the hope of finding satisfaction in someone or something outside of us."

But why, Enrique asked, and what is that someone or something? He sat up in the chair where he had seated himself opposite his father. His father's mahogany desk that stood between them matched the bookshelves that were stacked with impressive-looking books.

"Well, *hijo*." his father answered, "there are various explanations as to what this outside source of happiness is. Some claim it's God. That our hearts are restless until they rest in him. Augustine's famous words, you know. Others insist that it's other people. Our happiness will be complete only if we are united with them. That's why we miss an absent loved one. Still others would maintain that it's power, money or any other material good that we are seeking." Papa always tried to give different views. Then he continued, sounding like the *catedrático* that he was, "Whatever interpretation we may give to it, it points to the same incompleteness and consequent restlessness of human beings and the same longing for someone or something outside of ourselves. To be alienated from him or her or it is to be lonely." Lofty thoughts from a philosopher.

More to Enrique's liking, and sensing that he had gone above his son's head, Papa had climbed down the academic ladder, as it were, and explained, "When we create a gap, or if we build a wall between ourselves and others we become uneasy and lonely. Do you know why? Because it goes against our nature as human beings. Perhaps we could say that loneliness and uneasiness in ourselves remind us that we were never meant to be alone. That's what I meant by saying that we become alienated."

Why then did he like going for long walks on his own? Enrique couldn't reconcile his Papa's words with his practice.

"Aha, to get away from you, of course, *mi hijo*! What else?" Papa liked teasing him as well. "Seriously, I welcome the chance of being alone. Doesn't everyone? But it's temporary and brief. We're glad of these opportunities only because—whether we think of this or not—we can return to the company of other people. Like seeing you again." Enrique had smiled when his father had uttered those words. "We don't mind going for a solitary walk but it's a different matter altogether to be held in solitary confinement for a long time."

But Enrique persisted. He still wasn't clear as to how we can withdraw from the company of others for a while and yet not be lonely. So far anyway, that had not been his experience. What was it really about us, this thing that Papa called our human nature?

So Papa tried to address patiently his persistent questioning. This time he got up and sat sideways on top of his study desk, his right leg dangling. Enrique also remembered a shaft of light penetrating the room and casting a shadow on the chair that his father had vacated.

"The uniqueness of the individual. It means that each man, woman or child is important in themselves and is therefore irreplaceable. We're not like a cog in a wheel, you know. Its sole importance is being part of the machinery. The human being has in fact been described as a world to itself." Enrique had nodded. He liked the image of a cog in a wheel. His young mind could relate to that.

"In talking about this uniqueness of every human being, thinkers have stressed different ideas." The *catedrático* had returned—unfortunately, for Enrique's mind preferred a more down-to-earth explanation. "Some maintain that each of us, no matter how lowly by birth or by circumstance, is created 'in the image of God.' What they're referring to in this case is the dignity of the human individual. Each of us has the individual and personal attention of God. Aquinas, for instance, would say that. Other thinkers, I'm thinking now of the existentialists, like Sartre, for instance, emphasise the freedom of every human individual. Our will is free—no one can really force us to do what we don't want to do. We can still say 'yes' or 'no', even if pressure is placed on us. Our inner attitude remains free. We don't have to be swayed by the opinions of others. If we choose, we can say 'no'. So, *mi hijo*, the responsibility of living a happy or miserable life rests ultimately with every one of us."

Papa had suddenly broken off into laughter, to Enrique's amusement. "There's a film where Woody Allen, quotes—seemingly from the existentialists. . ."—this time, Enrique was more attentive—"He turns to his girlfriend and bursts out, 'I didn't ask to be born, did you? I had no choice. But I have it now. I can do what I choose to do!' I don't think those were his exact words, but that's the gist. Woody Allen's words sounded very much like Heidegger's.

"So you see, Enrique, these are two ways of looking at the uniqueness of the individual. And in saying that everyone's unique, we're implying that each one is a whole, and not just a part."

As if coming to the end of his lecture in a classroom, his father summed it up for disciple-like Enrique. "These are the two basic aspects of our lives: one, that we need others, two, that in spite of this need for others, we're also individuals. To describe ourselves as a 'part' is to try to give the reason for this felt need for others, and to call ourselves 'whole' is to help us understand the second point, that we are also independent of everything and everyone. We become lonely when we're alone because we are, as it were, a part. At the same time, since each of us is a whole or an individual, we can be alone without necessarily becoming lonely. That's why we don't always have to depend on others. We can detach ourselves, at least for a while. We can be on our own without having to feel lonely, without feeling alienated. That's why we can and do say, a person who enjoys his own company is very much at home with himself."

He asked his father to explain it again differently the next time. Too much philosophy was baffling for him. To which his father smiled, and this time the sun's rays seemed to fill the room, "It would be better for you to discover all that by yourself."

Conversing with Martin Buber

We have heard the questions of these fictitious characters—with some answers from their conversation partners. We will now turn to a well-known philosopher, Martin Buber.[4] Since Buber offers genuine insights into the questions and reflections of the fictional characters above, we can enlist his help with our enquiry into the quest for community.

Buber claims that he has no teaching: he merely points to reality, to "carry on a conversation with us", as it were. As he puts it, "I have no proof for this belief. No belief can be proved; otherwise, it would not be what it is, a great venture. Instead of offering proof, I appeal to that potential belief of each of my hearers which enables him to believe."[5]

Buber's important book, *I and Thou*, starts with a discussion of relationships. According to Buber, as human beings we do not engage only in activities which have a thing for an object. That is to say, we do not just do something, think of something, or feel something; we also have activities which establish relations. Thus, for instance, we can feel a certain kinship

---

[4] During his lifetime, Martin Buber, a Jewish thinker, had been praised by Herman Hesse and Reinhold Neibuhr as "one of the few wise men living on earth today". Ronald Gregor Smith, translator of *I and Thou* wrote that Buber might even be called "a world figure because of the remarkable influence his ideas made in many different spheres of thought and action." Buber combined thought with concrete existence. He made the realm of the personal and the "hallowing of the everyday" his chief concern. His ideas were not developed in academic seclusion. In all his works there is that seriousness to relate the intensity of his thought to the problems of our days. One finds this integral unity in Buber's very personality, a characteristic pointed out by the German educator, Karl Wilker.

[5] Martin Buber, "Politics, Community, and Peace," *Pointing the Way: Collected Reflections*, ed. and trans. by M. Friedman (N.Y.: Harper and Row Publishers, 1963), p. 238.

with another person so that he or she becomes "part of ourselves and enters into our very lives." In this particular activity, something takes place not only in us, but *between* us and the other.

This twofold existential experience of ours serves as the starting point for Buber for formulating the categories of "I-Thou" and "I-It" on which his philosophy of dialogue is based. For him, this state of relatedness is an existential reality such that the human person is said not to exist, except as related. For this reason Buber describes relation as a *primary* word. The categories of I-Thou and I-It always exist as combined words and are meant to differentiate the two kinds of relatedness. Moreover, the I of the I-Thou relation is different from the I of the I-It. Hence, the human person has a two-fold attitude: the attitude of the I-Thou and that of the I-It. Correspondingly, the world is also two-fold in that we can approach the same world in two diverse ways: as a Thou or simply as an It. If one approaches it as an It, one is doing so from a vantage point. This means that only part of one's being is involved in the meeting, something is kept outside of the relation. One does not completely reach out to the world which remains a detached object. On the other hand, if one says Thou to the world, one's whole being is involved, and one does not withhold oneself in the relationship. The world is addressed with one's whole being, without any defenses set up to block the I from the world.

This world to which we can be related in two different ways consists of things, people and spiritual beings.[6] Since it is manifold, our relationship—although we can have the same I-Thou relation with any of them—takes place in three spheres. In our life with nature, there is not much of a relation yet. Even when it is addressed as Thou, there seems to be no mutuality since nature does not seem to respond. But in our relationships with other humans, there can be full relationship for there can be mutuality in the sense that we can give and accept the Thou. In this relationship speech or the spoken word plays a dominant part. The same is not the case in our relation with spiritual beings since we perceive no Thou although we can sense that we are addressed and we answer—forming, thinking, acting—not with the use of verbal speech but with our being.

Focusing on the relationships with fellow humans, Buber maintains that we can be interested in a man or woman because they are aggressive or domestic, because they are social or reserved, because they are handsome or unassuming. Our interest in them is based on qualities which appeal to us as if they were a package of attractive and desirable qualities.

---

[6] In the original German edition of the *I and Thou*, the phrase is *geistige Wesenheiten* which R.G. Smith has translated as "spiritual beings". Buber, *I and Thou,* p. xi.

But we also find ourselves open to accept the other person in his or her wholeness, seeking the other's self, that which makes the other this particular individual person. We accept them for what they are. Because we long for the other to become present to us as "person", going out as we to the other, choosing and recognising us as we do them, we can be related to them in an I-Thou relationship. We may speak to them vocally or we may not, but we instinctively want to meet that other with our whole selves. We yearn to be more total in our response, to be able to bring everything that we are and are capable of in this encounter. There is evidently a basic difference in this second kind of relationship. The other "is not *He* or *She*, bounded from every other *He* or She, a specific point in space and time within the net of the world; nor is he a nature able to be experienced and described, a loose bundle of named qualities. But with no neighbour, and whole in himself, he is *Thou* and fills the heavens. This does not mean that nothing exists except himself. But all else lives in *his* light."[7] This person who has become a Thou for us is not relegated to a mere content or object of our knowledge. This Thou is no longer just one among other things in the universe; instead, the whole universe is seen in the light of the Thou and not the Thou in the light of the universe. The other's qualities count but not necessarily for as Thou it is his or her wholeness, the fact that he or she is, which confronts us. A definite kind of relationship exists between them and us, fundamentally different from the first kind—the I-It—that binds us to our Thou. It is the I-Thou, says Buber.

The I-Thou relationship, being a direct one, exists in the present[8] and is continuous and enduring. The I does not regard the Thou as something to be experienced and used (and therefore using the other as an object), and hence, should be laid aside after the encounter. One's knowledge of the other is not determined by his or her past, by what they have been, rather by what they are. One does not, as it were, set up a screen of prejudgments to filter their presence so as to be able to accept them. Because no past event or past knowledge guides us in this relationship, the I-Thou breaks away from the past, living instead in the present moment. This effect of directness and presentness in an I-Thou relation with fellow humans is, however, usually understood wrongly as one of feeling. Feelings may accompany the relation, but they do not constitute it. They may exist, but they do not cause the existence of the I-Thou relation. For when one

---

[7] *Ibid.* p. 8.

[8] The present for Buber is meant "not the point which indicates from time to time in our thought merely the conclusion of 'finished time' but the real, filled present, exists only in so far as actual presentness, meeting and relation exist." *Ibid*, p. 12.

says Thou to another, one accepts the wholeness of the other's being unconditionally, that is, regardless of what one feels for him or her.[9]

In contrast, for someone who has come to terms with the world of It, the world about changes. One's attitude of experiencing and using others develops as one becomes less inclined to enter into an I-Thou relation with them. Yet this changed attitude—which is the I-It—is the cause of progress: economic, scientific, cultural and others. Both the history of individuals and of humankind bears witness to the progressive development of the world of It which has in turn benefited humankind. Through the ability to experience and use, the primary connection of humans with the world of It, the world is enlarged. Nations grow, and cultures flourish. This I-It relation can also be beneficial even between human beings for many times we have "to look on men with whom we have to deal not as bearers of the Thou that cannot be experienced but as centres of work and effort, whose particular capabilities it is our concern to estimate and utilize".[10] A Thou will not bring in profit, but a He (or She) will. This is especially true in the economic sphere. If we do not think in terms of assets and work accomplished, on what men or women and workers can do to profit, then there is no sense in focusing our attention on the economy whose very purpose is to usher in material benefits for us.

Thus, one can see that for Buber the world of It is not evil in itself and is even necessary if we are to achieve prosperity. Our progressive life cannot dispense with it. It is of fundamental importance for the proper ordering of nature and of ourselves. Buber explains that although silence before the Thou leaves it free and unmanifest, human greatness lies in the strong response humans give, and which binds them, to the world of It. It is through this response that science, culture, economies and other related fields are developed. Though the return of the Thou into an It is described by Buber as a melancholy; nevertheless, he regards it as "exalted". According to him, what makes the I-It evil is to allow it to dominate.[11] When one is ruled more by the desire to profit and to progress to the neglect of establishing an I-Thou relation with others, there is an imbalance in one's

---

[9] The I-Thou relationship does not have to be mutual; however, for it to be full, it must be mutual. "Even if the man to whom I say Thou is not aware of it in the midst of his experience, yet relation may exist. For Thou is more than It relation realizes. No deception penetrates here: here is the cradle of the Real Life." *Ibid.* p. 9. The I-Thou relation, no matter how present and direct it is, will fade away into an I-It. In fact, a strong response to the Thou reduces it to an It (p. 39-43). But even if it does, it has the nature and disposition to be changed back into a Thou (p. 17).
[10] *Ibid.* p. 47.
[11] See Chapter Two.

life. When one cannot feel free to leave the world of It in order to set one-self in an I-Thou relationship, then the I-It has indeed become evil.[12]

As had already been mentioned, the I of the I-It is different from the I of the I-Thou. The difference does not lie in the recipient of the primary word that the I speaks but in the attitude towards the other. It is not the same I that relates itself sometimes to an It and sometimes to a Thou. Buber explains that the I of the I-It is a subject of experiencing and us-ing.[13] It is an individuality differentiated from other individualities.[14] It is set and detached; and it aims to fulfil its physical life, which is a "dying that lasts the span of man's life". This I, in Buber's rather picturesque lan-guage, thrills at looking at the world as if it were only a shop window where it can buy all that it can afford to buy. Other beings are just other goods in the market, as it were, goods that it can purchase if they are at-tractive enough. It seeks them just as it seeks prized commodities.

The I of the I-Thou, in contrast, is a person which finds fulfilment by entering into genuine relationship with other persons. It aims at contact with the Thou. It exists through a genuine intercourse with it, without any intention of appropriating the Thou for itself as if it were a commodity. This is the I that lives fully, and in Buber's view, the "real self [that] ap-pears only when it enters into relation with the Other".[15] As the I says Thou, that I becomes a particular kind of I. When it says Thou, it becomes more of a person, a subject. It achieves fuller existence since it becomes more of what it should be—a person. To be a person, from Buber's per-spective, is to achieve wholeness of being. And since the I says Thou with

---

[12] Buber, *I and Thou*, pp. 48-49.

[13] Buber, *Eclipse of God: Studies in the Relation between Religion and Philosophy* (N.Y.: Harper and Row Publishers, 1957), p. 128.

[14] To clarify for us his concept of individuality, Buber contrasts it with his concept of person: "An individual is just a certain uniqueness of a human being. And it can develop just by developing with uniqueness. This is what Jung calls individuation. He may become more and more an individual without becoming more and more human. I know many examples of man having become very, very individual, very distinct from others, very developed in their such-and-suchness without being at all what I would like to call a man. The individual is just this uniqueness; being able to be developed thus and thus. But a person, I would say, is an individual living really with the world. And *with* the world, I don't mean *in* the world—just in *real contact*, in real reciprocity with the world in all the points in which the world can meet the man. I don't say only with man, because sometimes we meet the world in other shapes than in that of man. But this is what I would call a person and if I may say expressly Yes and No to certain phenomena, I'm *against* individuals and *for* persons." Buber, *The Knowledge of Man*, p. 184.

[15] Buber, *I and Thou*, p. 63.

its whole being, it becomes more a person through its relationship with the Thou. To quote Buber, "The more direct the contact with the Thou the fuller the sharing. The I is real in virtue of its sharing in reality. The fuller its sharing the more real it becomes."[16] Thus, though this I may step out of the I-Thou relation, the reality of this I is never lost. Something of it remains, no matter how small. It will grow and mature again when it steps back into an I-Thou relation. Thus, this personal I recognises its existence as actually a co-existence. It is other-centred, even if it takes cognisance of the fact that it is a different being, an individual. It is aware that other beings exist beside and besides itself and that there is a reality and power existing between them and itself. This reality and power make it an authentic personality. Thus, since it is aware that it co-exists, the loneliness of the personal I, Buber claims, is never a forsakenness.

The Dialogical Principle

Buber develops the categories of I-Thou and I-It further in his discussion of the dialogical principle. According to him, dialogue comes about when one opens up one's whole being towards another without waiting for a response. It too is possible even if not mutual. It can occur even without words, gestures or any outward manifestations.[17] What is essential for dialogue to exist is the very openness of one's being. This is the basic presupposition.

No doubt, external manifestations such as word and gesture are characteristic of human dialogue. When humans, for instance, wish to communicate with one another, they design signs to convey their message. They make use of language to be able to do so meaningfully. They must rely on these if they want to be understood .But communication in the dialogue that Buber speaks of can exist even without these outward manifestations, although admittedly not in an objectively comprehensible form.[18] While communication in the usual sense calls for an interchange of content, at its highest moment, this interchange is surpassed by what Buber means by dialogue. For dialogue, according to him, is "completed outside contents, even the most personal which are or can be communicated."[19] Thus, in this context, it is more than just communication as we commonly understand that term. It is actually "communion"—the encounter of beings in their

---

[16] Buber, *Eclipse of God*, p. 97.
[17] Buber, "Dialogue," *Between Man and Man*, p. 3.
[18] Buber provides an example, *Ibid.* pp. 4-5.
[19] *Ibid.* p. 4.

openness. It occurs "where each of the participants really has in mind the other or others in their present and particular being and turns to them with the intention of establishing a living mutual relation between himself and them."[20] What is important, Buber explains further, is "that for each of the two men the other happens as the particular other, that each becomes aware of the other and is thus related to him in such a way that he does not regard and use him as his object, but as his partner in a living event."[21]

In dialogue—to return to the language of I-Thou—the I encounters the other in his or her very openness, and the I addresses them as much. The I does not ask what impression one's speech and being will make on the others for it is to their very being that I turn. I do not forfeit the other's person. He or she remains themselves. Neither do I leave my ground in order to meet him or her. I do not, so to say, trade in my uniqueness when I turn to them. Both of us therefore remain distinct from each other; yet, between us is a definite relationship.[22]

Because genuine dialogue is communion, it takes place in spite of conflicting opinions for it is independent of them. Neither of the participants needs to give up his or her point of view. In fact, essential views demand that whoever holds them maintains his or her stand. Accepting one's partiality as well as the limitation imposed by the other participant, one may still cling to one's own viewpoint. This difference of opinion should not, however, clam down the openness of each to the other. This point must be understood well, Buber warns, for otherwise dialogue may be interpreted as hemming in those who engage in it so that they find themselves not bound to say everything which in all righteousness they should say.[23] As he puts it, "If genuine dialogue is to arise, everyone who

---

[20] *Ibid.* p.19. To be distinguished from this kind of dialogue are technical dialogue and monologue disguised as dialogue, both of which are not intent on establishing a living mutual relationship: "There is technical dialogue which is prompted solely by the need of objective understanding. And there is monologue disguised as dialogue, in which two or more men, meeting in space speak each with himself in strangely tortuous and circuitous ways and yet imagine they escaped the torment of being thrown back on their resources." This latter kind of dialogue is what we *commonly*—to be distinguished from Buber's sense—refer to as a "dialogue" where the participants are simply waiting for a chance to speak without listening at all to the other.

[21] Buber, "Elements of the Interhuman," *Knowledge of Man,* p. 74

[22] Erich Fromm makes a similar point when he says that love is not the making of two people into one but making them one yet remaining two. Cf. his *The Art of Loving* (London: Unwin Books, 1972).

[23] To say everything which they should say does not mean simply anything they want to say. As Buber says, open dialogue should not be equated with unreserved

takes part in it must bring himself into it. And that also means that he must be willing on each occasion to say what is really in his mind about the subject of the conversation. And that means further that on each occasion he makes the contribution of his spirit without reduction and without shifting his ground."[24] One's basically different view about the subject of the conversation may even urge one to aim at convincing the other of the righteousness of one's way of looking at the matter. This desire to influence the other, however, does not mean the effort to change the other, to inject one's own "righteousness" (as Buber would say) into him. For as we have seen, genuine dialogue cannot come about unless one affirms the very otherness of the other and accepts it: "Everything depends so far as human life is concerned on whether each thinks of the other as the one he is, whether each, that is, with all his desire to influence the other, nevertheless unreservedly accepts and confirms in his being this man and his being made in this particular way."[25] For Buber, this strictness and depth of human individuation, what he calls "the elemental otherness of the other", is not merely a startingpoint to be discarded at a later stage, but is recognised and confirmed at all times. When one desires to influence the other, it means making an effort to "let that which is recognized as right, as just, as true (and for that very reason must also be established there, in the sub-

---

speech: "But in the great faithfulness which is the climate of genuine dialogue, which I have to say at any one time already has in me the character of something that wishes to be uttered, and I must not keep it back, keep it in myself. It bears for me the unmistakable sign which indicates that it belongs to the common life of the word. Where the dialogical world genuinely exists, it must be given its right by keeping nothing back. To keep nothing back is the exact opposite of unreserved speech. Everything depends on the legitimacy of 'what I have to say.' And of course I must also be intent to raise into an inner word and then into a spoken word what I have to say at this moment but do not yet possess as speech. To speak is both nature and work, something that grows and something that is made, and where it appears dialogically, in the climate of great faithfulness, it has to fulfil ever anew the unity of the two." Buber, *Between Man and Man*, p. 86.

[24] *Ibid.* p. 86. To explain what he means, Buber cites a personal experience that occurred during a conference at Easter 1914. Buber had raised a protest against a man's opinion concerning the Jews. He vehemently opposed this opinion, and he stood his ground with regard to his opposition. But in spite of their conflicting views, Buber and that man established a dialogical relation between themselves manifested by the exchanging of the kiss of the brotherhood. Buber, "Dialogue," *Between Man and M*, pp. 5-6.

[25] Buber, "Distance and Relation," *Knowledge of Man*, p. 69.

stance of the other) through one's influence take seed and grow in the form suited to individuation."[26]

This is why when one enters into dialogue, one enters a realm where the law of the point of view no longer holds. Buber explains that one suffers the limitations of human nature: the limitations by others, by one's own finitude, partialness, need of completion. Moreover, one's own relation to truth is heightened by the other's different relation to the same truth by being another individual.[27] Recognising and honouring these limitations, one allows oneself to be free and meets the other and really speaks to and towards that other.[28]

For Buber, therefore, dialogue is "not limited to men's traffic with another; it is, it has shown itself to be, a relation of one another that is only represented in their traffic."[29] He adds that where speech and communication are absent, dialogue essentially and minimally is the mutuality of the inner action: "The men thus bound together in dialogue must obviously be turned to one another, they must therefore—no matter with what measure of activity or indeed of consciousness of activity—have turned to one another."[30]

Given the topic of this enquiry into our quest for community, it is important to note that for Buber genuine dialogue is not a social or psychological phenomenon even if it is usually ascribed to the social realm. When Buber talks of dialogue, he is referring to an ontological reality. He goes further than a sociologist would, therefore. This occurrence *between* persons, the "interhuman", is a sphere in which one is actually confronted by the other: and in this confrontation or meeting, characterised by spontaneity, directness, presentness and the personal element, there is a definite reality—that of dialogue. Dialogue, thus, is not just the coming together of individuals, not even if in living together they become close to one another and share experiences and reactions with one another. To be thus bound up together—as a social phenomenon—means only that each individual existence is enclosed and contained in a group existence. It does not yet mean that they are tied together in any kind of personal relationships. True, they

---

[26] Compare this attitude with those connected with "propaganda" and "suggestion": "Opposed to this effort is the lust to make use of man by which the manipulators of 'propaganda' and 'suggestion' is possessed, in his relation to men remaining as in a relation to things, moreover, with which he will never enter into relation, which he is indeed eager to rob of their distance and independence." *Ibid.*
[27] *Ibid.*
[28] Buber, "Elements of the Interhuman" *Knowledge of Man*, pp. 79-80.
[29] Buber, "Dialogue" *Between Man and Man*, p. 8
[30] *Ibid.*

sense more belongingness which an outsider would not experience. They stick together, carried by the sense of collectivity which keeps them away from the feeling of estrangement. Their membership in the group consoles them in their loneliness and secures for them a definite place to turn to.[31] Frequently, too, especially in the case of smaller circles, the situation would favour the birth of individual relations. (Buber explains that the contrary would also be possible, that is to say, individual relationship could hardly be formed because collectivity aims at holding in check the inclination to an individual life by making the members concerned in the main with the activities of the whole group. Whatever takes place between individuals is held secondary). Such a grouping, however, does not necessarily involve an existential relation among the members. They are not necessarily living in the life of dialogue.

Dialogue is not just a psychological event either. Accordingly, to try to understand dialogue in this way is to miss the Buber's point. Likewise, to eliminate completely the psychological element is also to misunderstand dialogue. When two individuals are engaged in a conversation, the psychological is certainly an important part of the situation as each of them listens and each prepares to speak. But this merely accompanies that sphere which Buber terms dialogue and which is found neither in one of the two partners nor even in both of them together. It is in-between them. To bring this dialogue about, what is needed is an open attitude. As has already been noted, Buber speaks of the I as opening up itself, as giving its whole being, when it confronts its Thou. Their confrontation is direct and personal. The sphere of the interhuman or of dialogue assumes existence when this attitude is present.

The Life of Dialogue

The life of dialogue, Buber claims, is a situation of the everyday, formed by people, events, and things of day-to-day existence. There is nothing extraordinary about it in the sense that we do not go out of daily existence. As he puts it, our task is not to escape from everyday life but "to hallow it". Dialogue makes this possible as it affects our very lives. An attitude of bringing our whole selves to every encounter we make revitalises our lives. Yet life in dialogue is not ordinary or humdrum either, for it always offers fresh encounters for us. Something new awaits us; a new message seeks to be heard by us. We sense new freshness that renews all our contacts with reality so that every appearance and event is for us a

---

[31] Note the Novice Master's reply to Juan in the passage above.

vessel of meaning. We seem to unearth hidden dimensions of the world around us. Dialogue makes us aware that we are being addressed. The signs of daily happening speak to us—in the very air that we breathe, in the environment that surrounds us, in the very people that we deal with.[32] But many times instead of opening ourselves up to receive their message, we keep evading. We prefer to close ourselves in until we become convinced that there is no significance in what life has to offer, that everything is ordinary. Buber counters a possible criticism that in seeing meaning in daily life, we are presuming to put significance where there is none. He maintains that in the life of dialogue we become aware of and receive signs. Every sign is new; in fact, every message is unique and every address has an original significance.[33] Buber explains: "It can never be interpreted nor translated. I can have it neither explained nor displayed; it is not a what at all, it is said into my very being; it is not experience that can be remembered independently of the situation, it remains the address of that moment and cannot be isolated."[34]

Becoming aware is, however, not yet our decided attitude in the life of dialogue, not even if we become aware of the signs of the everyday as vessels of meaning. It is only the first step, Buber tells us. We can become aware and still shut ourselves in or step aside into our accustomed way. We can turn away still though "with an unhealable wound", a wound because we have become aware but unhealable because we have turned away instead of responding to it.[35] But we could venture to respond, to enter "upon the situation, into the situation, which as at this moment stepped up to us, whose appearance we did not and could not know, for its like has not yet been."[36] We could face creation as it happens. In that case it would

---

[32] Cf. Chapter One on the importance of such moments in life.

[33] Buber, "Dialogue," *Between Man and Man*, p. 12.

[34] *Ibid.* p. 16. To be contrasted with this response of becoming aware are those of observing and of onlooking: "We approach a man in another way. We can be interested in details, eyeing them intently. Our main concern then are the externals in this regard. The face of the man whom we approach is for us mere physiognomy, his movements mere gestures of expression. We are, so to say, observing this man. But we can also respond to this man's presence in another way. We can simply remain passive, letting his activities happen as they come without any intent on our part. In this approach we are onlookers. Divergent though these two responses may be, they converge on one point. In both the object of our response remained apart from us. There was noticeable detachment on our part. We did not claim any participation in the man. He was just an object cut off from us. He was an It." *Ibid.* p. 16.

[35] Hence, the importance of education as discussed in Chapter Two.

[36] *Ibid,* p.17.

be speech directed at us, rather than above us, affording us with the opportunity to appropriate it into our lived lives that would be more than just a sum of moments of responding. It will be a continuous responding and thus one of meaning. With no advance thought or routine, we face reality continually, accepting with our whole being presences that meet us. In this way we assume responsibility, the kind that exists only in lived life for "genuine responsibility exists only where there is real responding".[37] Then we shall not just exist, we shall exist meaningfully. We shall not just live, we shall live responsibly.

Communal Life of Dialogue

How does the life of dialogue affect our relations towards other beings? Buber replies that the I that says Thou relates itself to others but also wants that others say Thou to it, to confirm it in its existence, to acknowledge that it is good that this I exists. According to Buber, there is us that craving that our I-ness be accepted too so that whosoever accepts it could live a life of a living relationship. In a word, we long for mutuality, a longing expressed by the fictional characters in the passages above. "For every man wants to be confirmed in his being and in his existence. This is his avowed secret."[38] One, however, does not turn to the other and establishes an I-Thou relationship with them because one believes there are advantages in doing so. Nor does one do so only because one feels happy and free to be with them. Though these other considerations may be present, what Buber calls "this avowed secret" is really the principle of wanting to stand in relation to others, with others, in a relationship which one knows will vivify because it is mutual.

This, in Buber's view, is the basis on which genuine friendship, true marriage and real community life stand. With this in mind, Buber reminds us that a genuine friend is one who accepts you for what you are. Despite being conscious of your faults, such a friend does not let them block the genuineness of his or her acceptance of you. With no desire to dominate or possess you, a friend is concerned that you grow and unfold for your own

---

[37] *Ibid.* p. 16.
[38] Buber, "Community and Environment," *A Believing Humanism: 1902-1965,* trans. M. Friedman (NY: Simon and Shuster, 1967), p. 95. See also Buber "Distance and Relation," *Knowledge of Man,* pp. 67-68: "The basis of man's life is twofold, and is one—the wish of every man to be confirmed as what he is, even as what he can become by man, and the innate capacity in man to confirm his fellow man in this way."

sake and not for the purpose of serving him or her. However, Buber adds, a real friend will correct you if you go astray in your ways, but will still accept you even if you did. A true friend feels one with you but with you as you are, not as he or she needs you to be an object for their use. You yourself feel the same way for him or her. Between the friend and you is a deep, personal, dialogical relationship that passes as the test of being full because it is mutual.

Buber describes marriage as being built on the same principle: two people reveal the Thou to each other. This is what gives new life to the married couple, not their feelings for one another, no matter how strong these may be:

> Institutions of the so-called personal life cannot be given new life by free feeling (though indeed not without it). Marriage, for instance, will never be given new life except by that out of which true life always arises, the re-vealing of the Thou by two people to one another. Out of this a marriage is built by the *Thou* that is neither of the *I's*. This is the metaphysical and metapsychical factor of love to which feelings of love are mere accompa-niments. He who wishes to give new life to marriage from another source is not essentially different from him who wishes to abolish it. Both clearly show that they no longer know the vital factor. And indeed, if in all the much discussed erotic philosophy of the age we were to leave out of ac-count everything that involves experience in relation to the *I,* that is, every situation in which the one is not present to the other, given present status by it, but merely enjoys itself in the other—what then would be left?[39]

Each of the two partners accepts and confirms the otherness of the partner.[40] This person is other, essentially other than oneself. It is this otherness that the I means and confirms, wishing its otherness to exist, because it wishes this particular being to exist.[41] Buber explains further: "He who 'has entered on marriage,' who has entered into marriage, has been in earnest, in the intention of the sacrament, with the fact that the other is, with the fact that I cannot legitimately share in the present being without sharing in the being of the other, with the fact that I cannot an-swer the lifelong address of God to me without answering at the same time for the other; with the fact that I cannot be answerable for the other as one who is entrusted to me."[42]

---

[39] Buber, *I and Thou*, p. 46.
[40] Compare this with what the Novice Master said to Juan in the passage in the text.
[41] Buber, "The Question to the Single One," *Between Man and Man*, p. 61.
[42] *Ibid.* pp. 60-61.

From this same basis, Buber continues, one is led to the insight of what the vital factor of a real community consists in.[43] True community is based on this interpersonal relationship between the members, the genuine dialogue in which each allows the other to exist in his or her otherness and accepts that otherness in its wholeness and uniqueness:

> The true community does not arise through people having feelings for one another (though indeed not without it) but through, first their taking their stand in living mutual relation with a living Center and second, their being in living mutual relation with one another. The second has its source in the first, but is not given when the first alone is given. Living mutual relation includes feelings, but does not originate with them. The community is built up out of living mutual relation, but the builder is the living effective Center.[44]

Unless this togetherness is recognised and acknowledged, the coming together of human beings will merely form a crowd where the members subsume their personal and individual identity blindly to any of its movements. Buber compares the individual members of such crowd to a "stick in a bundle moving through the water, abandoned to the current or being used by a people from the bank in that or this direction. Even if it seems to the stick at times that it is moving by its own motion it has in fact none of its own, and the bundle too, in which it drifts has only an illusion of self-propulsion."[45] It is only in a genuine community that people live not alongside one another but *with* one another. There is a dynamic flowing from I to Thou, that basic mutual trust in each member because, being in mutual relation, they become communally minded. Where this is present, then a real community exists for a "people is community to the extent that it is communally disposed."[46] This does not mean that members of a community have an I-Thou relationship always, but their togetherness must include the possibility of such direct, mutual dialogue. Otherwise, their togetherness becomes a bundling together of individuals, as we have already noted, or a collectivity whose existence is acceptable insofar as its effects are. The group then loses its identity as a reality on its own, a consequence lamented by Buber..[47]

---

[43] Compare this with the conversation between Enrique and his Papa in the passage in the text.

[44] Buber, *I and Thou,* p. 45.

[45] Buber, "The Question to the Single One," *Between Man and Man,* p. 64.

[46] Buber, "Dialogue," *Between Man and Man,* p. 31.

[47] *Ibid.* pp. 30-31. See also Buber, "Comments on the Idea of Community," and "Community and Environment," *A Believing Humanism,* pp. 87-95.

A Concluding Note

The questions which Juan and Enrique raised, at the start of this enquiry, stem from their own particular concerns. Yet as we embarked on our quest for community and enquired further, it has become clear, as we probed into Buber's philosophical thoughts, that these particular questions—and others like them—arise because of our nature as human beings.

As we enlarge our horizons in this quest it is indeed worth our while carrying on the conversation with Martin Buber.

CHAPTER FIVE

HOW SHOULD WE INTERACT WITH ONE ANOTHER?: THE QUEST FOR POWER

Introduction

A particular conception of power has dominated much of the discussion regarding our dealings with one another; namely, unilateral control by one over another. Whether one is talking of the state (or a similar group) or of an individual, it is assumed that its power over the other or others means that it has the dominance or authority such that the other loses its freedom. Accepting its power means obedience, or compliance. Rejecting or resisting it can take various forms, such as revolution, revolt, civil disobedience and similar ones. Underlying both reactions is the same conception of power.

This enquiry, which focuses on a specific aspect of our interaction with one another, puts forward an alternative conception of power. Here power is understood as respecting the autonomy of the other; and the exercise of power takes the form of influencing, appealing or attracting the other rather than controlling it. Whether such a conception of power is credible and workable will need to be critically examined of course.

The Concept of Power

Power is generally equated with authority. Thus, when one possesses power, one is deemed to have some authority. An individual can have power, and so can a body of individuals, like the government or the state. In connection with this general understanding one could ask about the kind of power one has, its basis, its legitimacy, and even the extent to which it applies and so on.

But to some extent, power is really a relational concept. It does not simply connote possession but it also implies its exercise over another, the recipient of the action. Having power, despite the description, is thus more than just acquiring an entity or enjoying a particular status. There is the general expectation that whoever is regarded as powerful stands in a particular relationship with another, but the relationship is unequal since the powerful has authority *over* the other, and not vice versa.

The nature of that relationship, as exercised by the powerful, is the focus here. As was pointed out already, the usual understanding of power is that one has unilateral control over the other. Thus, an important corollary to it is the concept of freedom since the other can become restricted in its exercise of whatever freedom it has by accepting the authority of the powerful. Consequently, it is said that the more powerful one party is, the less free the other party becomes. On the other hand, assuming some freedom on the part of the other party, it can assert itself by opposing it. Hence, there is talk of the various forms of opposition noted above. Such talk will necessarily involve other issues, but it seems that it rests on "what one does with the control over one" by the powerful.

If this is true, then perhaps a case could be made for re-examining that very basis. The claim that is being made here is that a different conception of power will have significant implications for the way we interact with one another.[1]

A Walk—and a Tutorial

But let us pause and join Richard and Aisling as they walk around one of the inviting parks of the university town of Leuven[2]:

> Richard could see Aisling's point. Somehow their conversation was going back to what they had talked about regarding people's attitudes, perspective and perception.
> 'Were you always as idealistic as this?'
> 'Yes and no.'
> 'That sounds like a real philosophical answer,' teased Richard. 'We philosophers are always making distinctions. That's why we keep answering yes and no to most questions.'
> 'Or because you philosophers can't make up your mind,' Aisling teased back.
> 'Touché.'

---

[1] This point is well illustrated in the different understandings—with implications—of America's role in international politics in the context of the current crisis as articulated by Obama and by Bush.
[2] M.S. Sia, *The Fountain Arethuse,* pp. 273-279.

'Yes. Sean and I were always talking about our dreams and how we would live life to the full. Not materially. We could never do that with a teacher's salary. But we both thought life was a gift, that we were so lucky, that it would be ungrateful not to appreciate what God had given us.'

Aisling looked at the trees forming an honour guard, as it were.

'It was easy to be idealistic when things appeared rosy. But Sean was also realistic. Like the wayfarer in Pádraic Pearse's poem, he also was aware that the beauty of the world can make us sad because this beauty will pass. He was fully conscious too of the evil and the suffering around. He used to say that living life to the full didn't mean living it up. He meant not letting the disappointments, the difficulties and the dark side of life cloud the goodness that was everywhere in nature. And he used to quote the Latin saying, *Dum spiro spero*. He also maintained that living life to the full meant doing our share to bring out that beauty by working to correct the injustice, to lessen the suffering. That's why above all else he wanted to teach. He firmly believed in the power of education to change people's attitudes. And his enthusiasm was catching.'

Aisling looked up at the blue sky above, dotted with a few cotton-like clouds.

'No, I wasn't always idealistic. When Sean died, I couldn't understand how his philosophy of life could be the right one. After all, he was a victim of the cruelty of life.' She was fighting hard to hold back the tears.

'I'm sorry. I didn't mean our conversation to lead to this.' Richard put a comforting arm around Aisling's shoulder.

'It's all right,' smiled Aisling.

It was a smile amidst the tears. It was a strength that was breaking out of the grief. And Richard remembered what Aisling had earlier said about the admiration she had for a child who managed to smile while tears flowed down its cheeks. . . .

. . . Indeed, Aisling had been through a testing time. Her idealism was not coming from lofty speculation. It was rooted in the experience of life; it was a response to the challenges of life. And there is a big difference between someone who proclaims the ideals culled from books and someone who has undergone the ups and downs of life, who has gone through the crucible of life. Aisling had been through that. Sean's death had really torn her apart. She wanted to give up, she felt abandoned. Worse, she felt led on by life only to be dropped. What goodness had her Sean been talking about? She even lost her faith in God, the God that her Catholic upbringing had instilled in her. She could not continue to believe in a God who was described as a caring father, a concerned shepherd, the way the Irish nuns used to tell them at school. Her reality showed a God, if there was one, who was a tyrant, who delighted in punishing people, in laughing at them. She identified with Santiago in Ernest Hemingway's *The Old Man and the Sea* and with Kino in John Steinbeck's *The Pearl*. The experience of both characters was of a God who initially gave them hope, only to dash them down, who seemed to make fun of the human individual's valiant efforts. What she was going through reminded her of Thomas Hardy's 'Vast Imbecility' who 'framed us in jest, and left us now to hazardry'; of the capricious gods Gloucester was describing, for whom humans were like flies to wanton boys, killing them for sport; of the vengeful god depicted in Thomas Hardy's poem *Hap,* who mockingly calls to the 'suffering thing': 'Know that thy sorrow is my ecstasy! That thy love's loss is my hate's profiting!'

She was embittered, and she had a good reason to be so. She found it difficult being on her own. The nights were lonely, the evenings were long and dark, and the days were fraught with hardships. Many times she was mistaken for an unmarried mother, and she experienced the prejudice, the hatred and the narrowness of people's minds directed against such women even though she was not one herself. Many tried to take advantage of her the way they take advantage of widows, and helpless individuals. She was seen as easy prey by some men who thought that she was a lonely widow in need of protection and consolation, *their* protection and consolation, since they believed that they were God's gift to such women. She was the victim of those who judged her unaccompanied status before they asked what her true situation was.

She fought back, but she realised that she needed to fight herself. She knew that simply fighting back in rage and bitterness was not going to end the misery and frustration that she was experiencing. She was being hurt by others, and she was helping them hurt her even more by being bitter and angry. She was ignoring what she and Sean had talked about so many times. She was doing Sean's memory an injustice, thwarting whatever he had been living for. She was contributing to the seeming absurdity of life.

But Sean had made sure she would not forget. The young life that had been the result of his and her love kept reminding her of Sean's ideals, talked about in good times but now being tested in bad ones. She could hear Sean's words over and over again. And the infant whom she was cradling and who depended entirely on her wanted her to sail on. He seemed to be saying, 'Think of me and not just of you.'

. . .'No, I wasn't always idealistic. And I don't think I'm always idealistic. But it seems to me that we have to make an effort to be idealistic. For if we don't, we lose so much of what life and nature have to offer us.'

'You said, you lost your faith.'

'Yes, I stopped going to Mass. And in Ireland, that's a big sin. And I don't mean from a Catholic religious point of view. It's a social sin. Missing Mass is socially unacceptable. You might call it the result of years of conservative Catholicism, but that simply is the reality. It's changing now, of course. I didn't see any point. It was not just the ritual that had become meaningless to me. It was the very idea of paying homage to a God who couldn't care less about me. Why should I care about that God?'

'And what brought about the change? Was there a sudden conversion, like being knocked down from a horse?' Richard was trying to introduce a lighter note.

'Philip.'

'Philip? You mean he suddenly spoke and told you to shape up?'

'Yes!' Aisling could not resist returning the tease, particularly when she knew that Richard was not expecting that answer. 'He got up and spoke in a loud voice. No, seriously, it was not as spectacular as that. But have you ever thought of the power of the helplessness of a baby?'

Richard shook his head.

So Aisling continued. 'In your books that's probably a contradiction. But have you ever seen how the helplessness of a baby will get the undivided attention of everybody? I always tell the students at one of my lectures that I would bet that no matter how interesting somebody's lecture may be, if somebody brought a helpless baby into the lecture hall, everyone's attention would be directed to that cooing baby. There's power in that. It's a different kind of power. It doesn't dominate, it attracts. It doesn't threaten, it influences.'

'You must forgive me, but I don't see the connection between that and God.'

'I don't blame you. That was why I said that it wasn't a spectacular realisation. It took a long time. Perhaps it was just as well. When things move more slowly, they've more time to sink in, to get imbedded. The whole thing made me wonder what made me blame God. Well, I had been taught that God could do everything. So God could have prevented the accident. But the accident still happened. But what if God were like the helpless infant, like Philip a few years ago?'

'God, a helpless infant? And to think that I've been defending God's almighty power in my research!'

'But it doesn't make God any less powerful. Only that it's a different kind of power.'

'You mean, God like a helpless baby attracts, influences, doesn't dominate or threaten.'

'I think so—you're the philosopher. Let me say it in my unphilosophical way. We tend to make God a scapegoat for many of the ills around us. That was what I was doing, blaming God for taking Sean away from me. But it wasn't God who did that, it was the drunken driver.'

'In philosophy, we could still say that ultimately the responsibility could be traced back to God since from God, who is omnipotent, flows all power, couldn't we?'

'In your philosophy perhaps. And in your understanding of power. Let me try to explain it. I'm not sure whether this would make much philosophical sense to you. But as a mother responding to my baby's needs, I realised that often it is up to me to fulfil that need. I have that responsibility. And it's a responsibility that I've come to cherish. It seems to me that God allots the responsibility to make this world more liveable for you and me and for everyone else. God doesn't monopolise that responsibility. Whenever I saw the helpless Philip in front of me ...don't misunderstand me, don't think I would be thinking of this when he needed a quick nappy change or when he was shivering from a high temperature, but I would think of it as he slept soundly in my arms... I was grateful for having had that responsibility. But I could just have ignored my responsibility. In fact, I could have even thumped him or psychologically abused him. Sadly, there is much of that around. So it works both ways. When we don't live up to our responsibility, we can't blame God for the results. We should blame our irresponsibility.'

'And how does that tie in with the way you described power?'

'That God, because God has chosen to share the responsibility, appeals to us to exercise that responsibility. God doesn't force us. Just as a helpless baby does not and cannot. But when a baby looks up to you, you know through those teary eyes or smiling face, the baby is exerting an influence on you. The baby wants you to do something.'

'Doesn't that make God weak?'

'Is someone weak who enables you to do something? Is a teacher less powerful for inspiring others to accomplish more? Is a poet or an artist any less effective than a tyrant? Is a Muse irrelevant?'

'Answered like a good teacher. Answer a question with another question.'

'Don't we help our students think better that way?'

'I should really answer that with another question... but yes, you're right. Where does that leave us?'

'That God works through us. And God is as effective or as powerful, in the sense that I have described it, as we allow God to be. It really took me a while to realise this. It was only when I started to appreciate the love that surrounded me, my family's, my friends' and most of all, Philip's.'

'And Sean's.' There was a tinge of envy in Richard's voice. Sean had indeed been very lucky to have had Aisling.

Aisling smiled. This time it was she who reached out to pat Richard's face.

'God was showing me goodness and care in the people I love. It was through them that I could feel God's compassion, as they wept with me over the loss of Sean, rejoiced with me when Philip took his first step, felt hurt when I was victimised. God is in people, God is in nature.'

'Sometimes that's hard to believe.'

'It is, that's why we need to look. That's why I am still struggling to live by that—how did you put it?—idealism. And that's why, as teachers, we need to unveil the beauty that surrounds us and show it to our charges.... And speaking of charges, we'd better pick Philip up. Otherwise, he'll be like that forgotten child in the ad.'

Aisling was referring to the ad for a particular brand of floor cleaner which showed the mother who was using the rival brand unable to finish her work in time to pick up her child after school.

Creative Synthesis

Aisling's answers to Richard's questions, specifically regarding the concept of power, need further elaboration. Can it be supported philosophically? To find out we shall enlist the ideas of Charles Hartshorne whose metaphysical description of the workings of reality with the category of "creative synthesis" provides such a foundation.

Given the hostility in some quarters to anything that smacks of metaphysics, it is essential to add that the term "metaphysical" as used by him is quite different from the usage of that term that has led to the criticisms of those who have opposed any reference to metaphysics in any philosophical discussion. Moreover, such a conception—far from being a merely theoretical construct—is actually based on some scientific interpretation of the nature of reality.[3]

In Hartshorne's philosophy, "metaphysical" means that the description can be said to be applicable to the whole of reality.[4] Creative synthesis as a metaphysical category is thus a description that covers all of reality and is necessarily true of every reality. According to Hartshorne, in every happening or event there is an old as well as a new (or creative) element. The old consists of previous happenings or experiences which give rise to and which persist in the new. There is permanence since in the synthesis the prior data are preserved, the synthesis being the holding together of data. The many become one which in turn produces a new many, and so on. It is an accumulation of these prior acts or a "putting together" of factors into a whole. But the resulting synthesis is a new actuality or experience because a different kind of experience has emerged from the coming together of past experiences. Previously there was the separate existence of the included realities, but now there is a unity. Furthermore, the synthesis is spontaneous or free because none of these experiences—individually or collectively—dictated the exact unity that would arise.[5] A synthesis emerges rather than is determined. Hence, an experience or happening cannot be fully described in its total unitary quality merely by specifying

---

[3] Hartshorne and other process philosophers have been very much influenced by contemporary (as distinct from modern) physics.

[4] For further discussion of Hartshorne's understanding of metaphysics, see his *Creative Synthesis and Philosophical Method.* (London: SCM, 1970), chs. II and III.

[5] Cf. Hartshorne, "Religion and Creative Experience," *Unitarian Register and Universalist Leader,* 141 (1962), pp. 9-11; "Process and the Nature of God," in G. McLean, (ed.), *Traces of God in a Secular Culture* (Staton House: Alba House, 1973), pp. 117-141.

what its constituents are. Each experience enriches the totality of reality by being an additional member.

The concept of "creative synthesis" (or simply, creativity) is really Hartshorne's interpretation of causality. Every act is viewed by him as creative. However, each creative act is influenced by its past acts and does require them even if it cannot be determined precisely or fully by these antecedent acts, which are simply earlier cases of freedom. These acts, those of ourselves or of others, restrict the freedom of the new act, establishing and limiting the possibilities for an otherwise free and creative activity. On the other hand, they never determine them fully. Thus, Hartshorne defines causality as the way in which any given act of creativity is influenced or made possible, but yet not completely determined, by previous acts.[6] Because past free acts narrow down any creative act, there can be a certain measure of prediction. Hartshorne uses the analogy of the banks of the river which give the flowing water its direction but does not entirely determine its movement. As he puts it, "Causality is the boundary within which resolution of indeterminacies takes place. Causal regularities mean not the absence of open possibilities but their confinement within limits."[7]

Hartshorne thus repudiates the deterministic version of causality. In his view, absolute determinism regards a happening as already completely predefined in its antecedent causes, each state of the world described as containing in reality an absolute map, as it were, of all subsequent and all previous states. Absolute determinism does admit that humans will never be able to read the maps except in radically incomplete and inaccurate ways. But Hartshorne regards this doctrine as an incorrect reading of the universality of causation because it is too strict an interpretation. Causes, as far as he is concerned, never determine the effect in all its details. A cause is necessary in the sense that without it, there can be no effect. But when all necessary conditions for an event have been fulfilled, it does not follow that the event will take place in precisely the way it is predicted, merely that it may take place. A cause is necessary, but not the effect. There will be an effect but not a specific or a fully determinate effect. The creative aspect of a particular effect, therefore, lies in that it is never literally anticipated. According to Hartshorne, "To ask 'why may not the antecedent cases completely determine the given?' is to show that one has not

---

[6] Hartshorne, "Philosophy after Fifty Years" in P. Bertow (ed.), *Mid-Twentieth Century American Philosophy: Personal Statements* (Atlantic Highlands: Humanities Press, 1974), p. 143.
[7] Hartshorne, "Can Man Transcend His Animality?" *Monist.* 55 (1971), p. 216.

grasped the meaning and pervasiveness of creativity or spontaneity."[8] There is a certain originality or freshness in every effect. Inasmuch as it is creative, it is partly unpredictable, undetermined in advance.

Some Logical and Metaphysical Underpinnings

To understand more fully Hartshorne's concept of creative synthesis, we need to examine its logical and metaphysical underpinnings. It will be noted that the term "creative synthesis" indicates a certain amount of duality (as opposed to dualism) in the description as well as in reality itself. It is a concept that is grounded in the logic of what Hartshorne calls the law of polarity and supported by his general metaphysical scheme. To these we must now turn.

According to the law of polarity, which Hartshorne says he has taken over from Morris Cohen, "ultimate contraries are correlatives, mutually interdependent, so that nothing real can be described by the wholly one-sided assertion of [ultimate categories such as] simplicity, being, actuality and the like, each in a 'pure' form, devoid and independent of complexity, becoming, potentiality and related categories."[9] However, although polarities are ultimate, it does not follow that the two poles are in every sense on an equal status. As mere abstract concepts they are indeed correlatives, each requiring the other for its own meaning. But in their application to the reality itself, one pole or category includes its contrary.[10]

This law is said to pervade reality. If one reflects sufficiently, one can expect to find all of reality revealing certain abstract contrasts, such as complex-simple, relative-absolute and so forth, which are ultimate or metaphysical contraries. The two poles or contrasts of each set stand or fall together. Neither pole is to be denied or explained away or regarded as "unreal". If either pole is real, the contrast itself, i.e. the two poles together, is also real. Although only one expresses the total reality, its correlative also says something about that reality since it is included in the other pole. There is a basic asymmetry or one-sided dependence: what is concrete includes what is abstract, not vice-versa. As a result, metaphysical categories as exemplified by concrete realities are always to be found in pairs. No concrete individual is merely simple, it is also complex. There is no such thing as pure effect. The same entity is, in another aspect, also a

---

[8] Hartshorne, "Philosophy after Fifty Years," p. 143.
[9] Hartshorne (with William Reese), *Philosophers Speak of God* (University of Chicago Press, 1953), p. 2.
[10] Hartshorne, *Creative Synthesis and Philosophic Method*, p. 99.

cause. No concrete entity can be said to be solely necessary for in a different context it is also contingent. No happening is merely a synthesis, it is also creative.

The pairing of metaphysical categories runs through Hartshorne's metaphysical system. He does not see any contradiction in ascribing opposite metaphysical categories to the same reality provided they refer to different aspects of that reality. According to him the law of non-contradiction is incorrectly formulated as "no subject can have the same predicates p and not-p at the same time". What needs to be made explicit is that they cannot be applied *in the same respect*. Hartshorne explains that a person can change in some respects without changing in every way and the world may be finite spatially and infinite temporally. In all of these the predication of contrasting attributes is not on the same ontological level for one set refers to the concrete aspect while the other refers to the abstract.

Turning now to his metaphysical scheme, it should be clear at this stage that reality for Hartshorne consists of events or happenings, not substances. The concept of creative synthesis is in fact a description of activity or of action rather than of things. It is for this reason that the term "process" has also been used with reference to his philosophy inasmuch as process or becoming, rather than being, is the fundamental reality. Reality thus is a series of events or activities or processes, interconnected in creative synthesis.

Hartshorne introduces a metaphysical distinction which has a bearing on the concept of creative synthesis. Calling the concrete state of any reality its actuality, Hartshorne says that actuality is always *more* than bare existence. "All existence …is the 'somehow actualized' status of a nature in a suitable actuality, this actuality being always more determinate than the bare truth *that* the nature exists, i.e. in some actual state."[11] *That* the defined abstract nature is somehow concretely actualised is what Hartshorne understands by existence. *How* it is actualised, i.e. in what particular state or with what particular content, is what is meant by actuality. The abstract definition of something, its essence, exists if and only if it is actualised or concretised somehow or is in some concrete form. However, one cannot deduce actuality which is concrete from an essence which is the abstract definition of the thing. In other words, actuality *never* follows from essence. Thus, the essence "humanity" exists if there are men, no matter which men or what states are actualised. But from "humanity" one

---

[11] Hartshorne, "Tillich and the Other Great Tradition," *Anglican Theological Review,* 43, 3 (1961), p. 258.

cannot ascertain which men are actualised.[12] There is a manifest difference between existence (the truth *that* an abstraction is somehow concretely embodies) and actuality (*how* that embodiment occurs).

Since actuality is concrete, it is finite. This means that some possibilities are left out and thus prevented from being actualised. Actual reality in all cases is limited. Actualisation is determination which in turn implies partial negation. It is the acceptance of limitation. It means choosing this and therefore not that. Hartshorne maintains that concrete actuality must always be competitive; that is to say, it must at all times exclude something else which could be equally concrete. Thus, as events come together or are "synthesized", other events are being excluded. It would be more accurate in this metaphysics to say that the resulting synthesis comes into actuality (rather than into existence).

Creative Synthesis as a Conceptual Model for Power

Taking power in the first instance as implying a certain amount of autonomy—rather than exercising authority or control—creative synthesis means that there is truly a plurality of powers and that every reality is endowed with some power. In other words, to be **is** to have some power because it is the actualisation of some potentiality. This is because actualisation is to some extent self-creation. A plurality of beings therefore connotes a plurality of powers. For Hartshorne, every item of reality is creative and thus exercises varying degrees of power. It can to some degree decide what it wants to be. Every reality has its own appropriate form of creativity.

This variety means that every concrete effect has numerous real causes. But every cause is also an effect. Creativity means freedom and novelty, but it also signifies partial determination by previous creativities or creative acts. In being determined in this way, any creative act is at the same time, though not in the same respect, an effect. Activity and passivity are correlatives: what cannot act cannot be acted upon, and what cannot be acted upon cannot act. Power is thus acting upon other genuine powers. Every reality thus sets limits to the freedom of others but does not destroy it.

Recognising the genuineness of the freedom of others means, not taking away or preventing the freedom of others, but fostering and inspiring that freedom. The powerful—in this conceptuality—is like the creative

---

[12] Hartshorne, "How Some Speak and yet do not Speak of God," *Philosophy and Phenomenological Research,* 23, 2 (1962), p. 276.

orator, thinker and artist who inspire creative responses in others, as Aisling points out to Richard in the passage above.[13] The powerful is one who
encourages appropriate originality in others, rather than dictates specific
actions. The powerful ruler is one who places others in a position to make
fruitful decisions of their own. He or she awakens creativity in others, inspires them by providing them with opportunities and by fostering creativity in them. The powerful can impose limits on the disagreements, con-
flicts and confusions, but it cannot simply eliminate these confusions. For
that to be true, then there has to be monopoly of power—which is what is
rejected in this conceptuality. This is not to deny their existence since the
meaning of power is, contrary to its more frequent usage, not controlling
but eliciting responses which are partially self-determining or free. The
ideal form of power does not monopolise power, but allots to all their due
measure of creative opportunity.[14] It inspires freedom in others thus enabling them to act freely yet in such a way that a coherent and in general
harmonious world comes about. There is nothing ideal about possessing
total control and reducing others to powerlessness. Hartshorne maintains
that such idealisation is actually symptomatic of weakness. It is the inferior, weak beings who yearn to be able to manipulate everything. Concentration of decision-making in the one being is in principle undesirable because the values of life are essentially social, involving the interactions of
more or less free individuals.

Power over others—understood in this way—is comparable to the control of one mind over another. A mind is influenced by what it knows, its
object. A mind which knows A but not B would be different from one
which knows B but not A. A change is effected in the mind through a
change in the object. By altering the object of our awareness, the powerful
also influences us. When it changes, we as other knowers change in response to the altered state. The powerful thus influences us not by controlling every detail of our action but by determining its own action which is
the inclusive object of our thoughts. We can still disobey but not disregard
it. In reacting against its suggestion the disobedient is still influenced even
though negatively. A state of rebellion or resistance to a suggestion is not
the same as the state of unawareness of the suggestion.

---

[13] Aisling also attributes this conception of power to God. For a detailed philosophical development of this view, see Santiago Sia, *God in Process Thought: a
Study in Charles Hartshorne's Conception of God* (Martinus Nijhoff, 1985),
pp.77-85.
[14] Hartshorne, "Biology and Spiritual View of the World: a Comment on Dr.
Birch's Paper," *Christian* Scholar, 37, 3 (Sept., 1954), p. 409; also his, *Omnipotence and Other Theological Mistakes* (SUNY Press, 1984), pp. 10-26.

Hartshorne explains that governance in this scheme is taking each successive phase of development and making good use of that phase in one's own and furnishing others with such guidance or inspiration as will optimise the ratio of opportunities and risks for the next phase. According to him, the truly powerful sets the best or optimal limits to freedom. Optimal limits mean that they are such that, were more freedom allowed, the risks would increase more than the opportunities, and were less freedom permitted, the opportunities would decrease more than the risks. In Hartshorne's view, the powerful sets optimal limits for the free action of others by presenting oneself at each moment a partly new ideal which influences our entire activity. Thus, no guarantee of a perfection of detailed results for no power could ensure the detailed actions of others. There is no complete determination of any action by one will. Rather, all realities form themselves and form each other within limits. It is the setting of these limits, Hartshorne sums up, which constitutes the ordering of all activities.

Some Observations

Given such a conceptual model for power, what are the implications for our understanding of the way we should interact with one another? One important consideration is that such a description of the workings of reality—generalised to include human actions—means that the relationship of one cause to another does not result in the loss of freedom of the other causes—even when there is an attempt to do so. Rather, they become included or incorporated into the original cause, resulting in a new entity. In other words, there is no absolutising of the control that one exercises over the other. There is no robbing of anyone's autonomy. The other remains an entity in its own right, and there is no loss of its own power, so to speak Another consideration is that the attempt to exercise unilateral control—and it is merely an attempt in this way of thinking—actually has an effect on that party as well. It becomes an integral part of the actuality of that party, and therefore has a real consequence for it. Thus, one becomes a different reality because of what one does or tries to do.

It could be objected that such a conception of power is idealistic. If by this objection one means that it cannot be regarded as effective for bringing about change because it is dependent on its acceptance by those who have or are in power, that may well be true. It is for this reason that it is indeed legitimate to discuss various forms of resistance, even radical ones. It would, however, be regrettable if this is the only recourse we have. On the other hand, if by "idealistic" is meant that it is too theoretical, that would hardly be true if indeed we take into account, not how we perceive the workings of nature but how, at a deeper level, reality actually works. This conceptuality, as had been clarified earlier, is based on a certain scientific explanation of reality. If this is indeed correct, then it is in effect more realistic than idealistic.

Admittedly, this is not an easy task, and one would be naïve to think otherwise. Changing one's direction or adopting another perspective involves much more than just consenting to it. That difficulty becomes greater when one must also think of implementing it as would be the case if we are discussing not just a concept of power but also how the other would respond or react to it. It is for this reason that there is a real need to continue to reflect and evaluate various forms of resistance to power as traditionally understood. On the other hand, our difficulty at times is continuing with our entrenched conceptions in our discourse regarding human activity. We do need to engage in what Herder Camara called "a cultural revolution". Otherwise, an unfortunate consequence here is not just confusion but also questionable behaviour. And if we are to correct that, it is important that we do regularly and consistently uncover our assumptions and subject them to a critical appraisal. In the present context, the challenge of re-thinking our conception of power really means that there is a need to direct people towards a fundamental issue as it will have implications not just on how we are to think but also on how we are to live.

Such a philosophy of action would have an impact on, among others, ethics.[15] If ethical responsibility, for instance, is measured not just by one's intention but also by the amount of control that the agent has on one's action, then it seems that one must also take into consideration the nature of the action itself. In many cases our understanding of causality shapes our attribution of responsibility. In this interpretation of causality as creative synthesis, action is both given as well as free. If freedom is necessary for ethical responsibility, then every action has ethical significance since it has an element of freedom. Action is not merely the necessary or expected effect of circumstantial or societal factors. It means that every action carries a certain amount of ethical worth. It should be noted, however, that here it is the action itself (and not just the agent in the Aristotelian sense that is free). Because it is free it could have been otherwise; because it could have been otherwise, there is a need to account for the actuality of the action. In this sense no action can be regarded as "value-free". It is good to remind ourselves that since there is a hierarchy of freedoms, as explained above, it would be wrong to conclude that ethical re-

---

[15] For a fuller discussion of this topic, see Ferdinand Santos and Santiago Sia, *Personal Identity, the Self and Ethics* (Palgrave Macmillan, 2007).

sponsibility is being attributed to all forms of creative synthesis, merely that it has ethical worth.

At the same time, however, such a philosophy of action recognises that no action is totally free either; thus, the ethical dimension can never be regarded as exhaustive, i.e. complete. Because every action is a result of the interplay of various other actions, it is always influenced. Such an interpretation accepts, but only partially, the claim of those who insist on the role of external forces which leave every action determined. There is some truth in the claim that praise and blame—to use Aristotle's terms—must take into account that one's action is not completely one's own after all. Hartshorne's concept of creative synthesis, which is a metaphysical one, translated into a philosophy of action can provide a possible grounding of an ethical theory that is cognisant of both freedom and restriction.

In such a philosophy of action, which makes a distinction between the abstract and the concrete, one can also see in discussions of rights, e.g. freedom of speech, that one can indeed uphold the existence of such an abstract right but the concrete exercise of such a right may have to be more circumspect. This point has become particularly relevant in the debates regarding the alleged freedom of speech which was used to justify the publication of what was considered by many as insulting cartoons on a spiritual leader. The exercise of any right does not occur in a vacuum. The identification of the abstract with the concrete can lead not just to conceptual confusion but also to unfortunate tangible consequences.

The distinction between the "creative" and the "synthesis" aspects of our action can be helpful too in grounding the notion of responsibility towards the future, e.g. in environmental ethics, inasmuch as the givenness that we create by our actions now will shape the kind of situation that future generations will have. We owe it to those who come after us to ensure that their environment is suitable for their own development. Just as we are the recipients of what had happened in the past, we are contributors—in a real way—to what will be the future. It is our efforts, or lack of them, that certain possibilities are or are not actualised for others.

CHAPTER SIX

"SEEING GOD IN ALL THINGS"—
EVEN IN SUFFERING?:
THE QUEST FOR A RATIONALE

Questions

A question is revealing: it not only asks for information, but often also discloses what is going on in the mind of the questioner. From the questions that are being posed we are given some insight into the questioner's thoughts. This is even more true if we pay attention to the very way the questions are phrased.[1] A question, furthermore, sometimes shows up the questioner's prior knowledge of what he or she is asking about. Hence, there can really be no "stupid" question, only perhaps an idle one, for a question bears within it an implicit answer, no matter how vague it may be when the question is asked. For if the questioner had no knowledge at all of the answer, he or she would not have been able to raise the question in the first place. To ask "Why?" for instance, presupposes a knowledge of an observed fact, that something is, so that the question "why?" is really a progression, an explicitation.[2]

A question also points to an enquiring mind. To ask a question means to search for more; it shows that one has perceived something behind the apparent· and has gone beyond instinct. Perhaps this is why human beings are regarded as questioners; humans are always searching for answers. (Significantly, *question* and *quest* are related.) Because they are endowed with the capacity to wonder, they have reflected. This has caused them to look for deeper meaning, to be dissatisfied with what is transitory, and to seek what lasts.

Raising a question usually leads one to new and deeper knowledge or,

---

[1] Allowance must, of course, be made for fluency and a good grasp of the nuances of the language.

[2] Questions are asked against a "background" or "horizon" of implicit knowledge rather than of ignorance

at times, to a new awareness of what one had known previously. The latter is best exemplified in the often-heard expression, "Oh, of course, I knew that before!" It is a sudden recognition of what one already knew. Sometimes, however, a question is not meant to be answered, perhaps not directly. Sometimes we search even if we can expect no answers, at least no immediate answers. This is because there are some questions to which no answers are at hand, though only for a while, but the answers may emerge later if we chance to glance back.

There are times when in raising questions one is transformed. Then the questions, viewed in the light of one's transformed state, become irrelevant. Perhaps this is because one becomes aware of the wider context: Such an experience, for example, occurs when one is "plunged into the depths". Profound questions about the meaning of life are often asked in moments of distress, anxiety, and suffering. But strangely enough, when one is back in "good form" everything seems clear again and the questions that were so pressing before lose their urgency and even their importance. This is so because one has been transformed rather than because one has simply returned to one's usual self. One has not gone back but gone further. One's answer came in the form of a transformation.

Existential Questions

But what questions do we raise? Humans, it may be argued, have the distinction of being perhaps the only kind of creatures who can ask fundamental questions about existence. While requiring basic items such as food and drink in order to survive, humans nevertheless are often made aware that the fulfillment of human existence needs more than these. Shakespeare expresses this well when he makes Hamlet cry out: "What is a man,/ If his chief good and market of his time/ Be but to sleep and feed? A beast, no more."[3] It seems that humans ask for more. Unfortunately, the answer to these existential questions is rarely clear. What is less unclear is a certain uneasiness or even dissatisfaction with merely satisfying one's immediate needs.[4] Hence, questions like: What makes us truly human? Is life worth living? Is there a purpose to life? are asked.[5] Humans, unlike other living beings, can and sometimes do wonder about the significance of being alive.

It would be naïve to think that we humans always ask these questions

---

[3] *Hamlet,* Act IV, Scene 4, lines 33-35.
[4] Henry Vaughan's poem "Man" captures this sentiment.
[5] See Chapter One.

in such an explicit way. Nor do we address the issue of ultimate meaning with uniform concern and interest. Moreover, an examination of our list of priorities in life would hardly reveal such in-depth existential values. In fact, we generally seem to be contented with setting ourselves certain goals, striving after them and, when attained, with looking for others.[6] Nonetheless, the question as to how life can have any meaning at all is a human one not only because, as far as we know, humans alone are capable of reflecting on it but also because every human being—although at times implicitly rather than explicitly—is confronted by it.[7] As a matter of fact, we more or less presume the meaningfulness of life by carrying on with our daily routine. We assume that there is some sense to life by engaging in the various activities that we do. Otherwise, we would not do them. This is not to say that when queried we can always provide an adequate or enlightening reason. Yet the fact that we are actually carrying them out implies some confidence in the meaningfulness of our specific tasks and even of life in general.

Job's Question

Job is a very good example of someone who asks such existential questions when he finds himself in a situation where he is forced to speak out and hurl accusing questions at God.[8] He raises one of the most difficult

---

[6] Some, like Kai Nielsen, argue that there is no evidence that there is a purpose *of* life, but that we can fashion for ourselves purposes *in* life, e.g. freedom from pain and want, security and emotional peace, human love and companionship, creative employment and meaningful work. These can be sources of happiness and therefore provide some meaning to life. Cf. his *Ethics Without God* (Prometheus Books, 1973). This argument, however, fails to recognise that having only relative purposes in life is giving purpose to life. That is to say, there is a tacit acceptance of the ultimate significance of possessing a number of relative goals in life.

[7] Cf. James Fowler, *Stages of Faith* (Harper and Row, 1981).

[8] This discussion of Job is limited to a consideration of the message he has for us today in the light of the topic of this book. Therefore, no persistent attempt has been made to distinguish between the author of Job, the book itself or the character Job. Nor has there been an effort on our part to take note of the two portraits of Job presented in the book. Cf. Bernhard W. Anderson, *The Living World of the Old Testament,* 2nd ed. (London: Longman, 1971), pp. 507-508 or to avail of more detailed exegetical studies of this book. Our reflection on the Book of Job is indebted to the following: Peter Ellis, *The Men and Message of the Old Testament* (Minnesota: The Liturgical Press, 1963); Gerhard von Rad, *Wisdom in Israel* (London: SCM Press, 1972); John L. McKenzie, *The Two-Edged Sword* (London and Dublin: Geoffrey Chapman, 1965); Bernhard W. Anderson, *The Living World*

questions. Because of his unique experience, he is dissatisfied with the usual answers to the suffering of the innocent. He cries out for a more satisfactory one. In fact, he comes to the point of challenging the Almighty. Job's questioning illustrates the kind of questioning that results in a transformation. In his questioning, Job is changed radically. He is brought to a certain experience that reduces his previous questions to insignificance.

The question that is usually made to appear as the question with which Job is grappling is the suffering of the innocent: How can one reconcile the idea of a good God, without whose will and knowledge nothing can happen, with the idea of a person who has not committed a sin and yet is made to suffer severely and for a prolonged period? To maintain that this is the theme around which the Book of Job revolves is certainly true. The author takes pains to point out that not only does Job claim that he is innocent but also that Yahweh regards him so (1:8, 2:3; cf. 1:1). With this consciousness of his innocence, Job cries out for the reason of his affliction because it appears to him utterly nonsensical that he, an innocent man, should be made to suffer.

Job's question goes much deeper, however, as the very analysis of the question of suffering will indicate. It raises the associated question of the nature and character of God and how human beings stand in relation to God. Job's suffering, then, is more than just the physical agony he is experiencing. He is racked and torn mentally as well. He is in mental agony not just because he is searching for the meaning of his sufferings, but more because he cannot comprehend the nature of this God he is dealing with.

His friends propose some reasons for his sufferings. These are the traditional answers to the question of suffering. One reason given is that suffering or punishment is traceable to a guilty deed. Especially in the case of a monstrous human crime, it was believed that sooner or later disaster would return to the person who had committed it. For this reason Job's friends insist that he examine his conscience to find out what guilty deed he has done (4:7-9; 8:20; 11:6) and to renounce it (11:14). Only then would he find peace again.

The explanation of suffering as corrective is also brought up. Sometimes suffering comes to people for apparently no reason; that is to say, there seems to be no recognisable sin. Yahweh was believed in this case to be secretly but, in the end, clearly pursuing the task of correcting men and women. Job is reminded of this (5:17-27; 33:15-30) and urged to return to God, to prayer, and to cultic confession. What is presupposed here is that

---

of the Old Testament; and Gustavo Gutierrez, *On Job: God-Talk and the Suffering of the Innocent* (Maryknoll, N.Y.: Orbis Books, 1987).

Job's life was not in order. For suffering, according to this explanation, was being offered in order to "turn man aside from his deed and cut off pride from man" (33:17).

Job's friends also recall the doctrine of the sages, the doctrine of material rewards and punishments. They assert the correlation between the morality of people and their well-being: good people are prosperous and the prosperous are morally good. If the wicked appear to prosper, this is only for a while. Their prosperity cannot endure; hence, to them death is dreadful, for it means leaving behind their possessions. Disaster always lurks for the wicked (20:4-29). Job's friends maintain the connection between sin and suffering. In their view every person who suffers has sinned; there was no such thing as a good person whose situation is evil. Job, who claims to be innocent, was a contradiction because, according to the traditional understanding of which his friends are exponents, innocence and suffering together are impossible. The blame must be on Job, the friends argue, for it could not be on God. God is righteous, whereas human beings are not (5:6-7; 34:12). Hence, his friends ask him to submit to God's correction so as to win God's favour again.

Job insists otherwise. He protests his innocence (9:20-21; 27:5-6, chapters 29 and 31). He is not aware of any crime or misdeed. His friends are accusing him of an imagined, or cleverly deduced, wickedness. He believes he is in the right with regard to his relationship with God because he feels himself unable to admit in his own case the correspondence which is asserted by his friends between guilt and punishment. If indeed his suffering comes from God, then it must have some other reason or purpose, but not his guilt. He wants his claim of standing in a right relationship to God, however, not to be based on his own estimate of himself. He wants to find some reassurance in a declaration from God. It was a reassurance which had been available to him long before, enough to enable him to claim himself to be innocent. But Job is aware that it is the justificatory verdict of God that matters, not his own protestations of innocence.

A Deeper Question

If it is not Job who is at fault, then it must be God. Cost what it may, he must force God to speak since he cannot make sense of his afflictions. This distress leads him to an even deeper problem: What kind of God is he involved with? His experience seems to contradict his belief in a just God. For how could there be such a God when it is obvious that there is no justice in a world where the wicked prosper and the just suffer and suffer intensely? He could not reconcile this God of his experience with the God

of tradition who was very much involved in human history and had in fact
entered into a relationship with the people of Israel. The God of old was
always identified as being on the side of the poor and the sick. God was
their saviour. To those who had been deprived of justice, God was their
defending counsel. Yet this God whom Job is experiencing now seems to
be capricious, to be toying with him, an innocent person. (One could also
add that God was acting more like Thomas Hardy's "Vast Imbecility", a
mighty builder but impotent caretaker, who "Framed us in jest, and left us
now to hazardry,"[9] or Pietro's God who plays a cruel dice game with creatures in Morris West's novel, *Lazarus*.[10] Gloucester's description of the
gods also seems to be more applicable to this God he is experiencing: "As
flies to wanton boys, are we to th' gods;/They kill us for their sport."[11]) Is
God truly capricious?[12] Job comes to the point of accusing God of appearing as a sinister enemy. Instead of caring for a creature, God is like a capricious tyrant (9:18-19), a savage beast (16:7, 9), a treacherous assailant
(16: 12-14). In a display of wild imagination, Job likens himself to the
mythical sea-monster (Tiamat or Rahab), the arch-enemy of God, over
whom God has set a watch (7:11-12).

   Job's question, therefore, assumes larger proportions: How credible is
God? What does God mean to him, to Job? This is what has become prob-
lematical. Perhaps there is no essential difference between good and evil.
God seems to destroy both the blameless and the wicked; the same fate
seems to await both (9:22-23). And yet, being a believer, Job cannot accept this. He believes in the supreme moral will of the Lord. But why the
apparent ineffectiveness of this moral will in human life? If the will of the
Lord is for good, and if the divine power is supreme, then why does not
the good that God wills come into being and why does God not remove
evil?

   Job demands an answer. He cannot understand and with desperation
he complains: "I cry to thee and thou dost not answer me" (30:20), and
again: "Oh, that I had one to hear me! Here is my signature! Let the Almighty answer me!"(31:35). Yet God seems to turn a deaf ear.

   But God *does* answer. The answer given is not to the question why the
innocent Job is suffering, but to the more profound point which Job had
raised: God's nature and the human being's relationship to this God. The
response is at the same time a rebuke and a challenge to Job. Instead of a
clear-cut reason for his suffering, Job is brought to an existential aware-

---

[9] "Nature's Questioning" lines 13-16.
[10] Morris West, *Lazarus* (N.Y.: St. Martin's Press, 1990). p.164.
[11] *King Lear,* Act IV, Sc. 1, lines 36-37.
[12] Compare Job's lament about his God with Aisling's experience in Chapter Four.

ness of how he stands with God: the God who is wise enough and power-ful enough to be able to govern the universe in all its complexity must be great enough to direct the course of human events. Human beings cannot comprehend God's purpose; they cannot penetrate the secrets of God's providence. Human wisdom consists in serving God, not in being equal to God in the knowledge of divine providence. In the face of this experience, Job's response is one of faith and humility (42:1-6).

The answer which Job receives is not in the form of words but in the form of an experience; that is, a realisation of creaturely existence in the presence of the Creator.[13] It is not the time for questions but for faith and humility. Job comes to the stage where his original question of why he is suffering in spite of being innocent becomes irrelevant. He has been trans-formed and in the context of his changed state, that question slips into ob-scurity. He has learned that "the beginning of wisdom is the fear of the Lord". Thus he withdraws his question because he has grasped that he is a creature and his destiny is well protected by this mysterious God who de-mands complete surrender on Job's part.

"I have heard of Thee but now I see"

The Book of Job offers many points worth reflecting on. It is no won-der that it seems to have a lasting significance. Whoever wrote the book—and did it with such style that commentators refer to its literary merits[14]—had remarkably sensitive insights into human problems. The author deals with these as one who really appreciates the complexity of human nature.

In raising the problem of suffering, the author touched upon one of the most bothersome human questions. The problem is even more acute for somebody who, like Job, believes in an all-good and all-powerful God, because the reality of evil and suffering is a direct challenge to that belief. As Gustavo Gutierrez puts it, "The problem of speaking correctly about God amid unjust suffering is not limited to the case of Job, but is a chal-

---

[13] According to Gustavo Gutierrez, God's answer to Job is "'a forceful rejection of a purely anthropocentric conception of creation", *The God of Life* (Maryknoll, N.Y.: Orbis Books, 1991), p. 160.

[14] See, for instance what P. Ellis wrote: "His work has been called the greatest poem of ancient or modern times, the most wonderful poem of any age or lan-guage, one of the grandest things ever written with pen. The author himself has been ranked with Homer, Dante, and Shakespeare, and his language and theme have fascinated and stimulated readers down the centuries," *The Men and Message of the Old Testament,* p. 478.

lenge to every believer."[15] Theists, therefore, have turned to the Book of Job for an answer to this question. Their reactions have varied depending on how acceptable or unacceptable they have found the response that the author gives to the question of Job's suffering.

But, as we have noted, the author of Job seems to have been concerned with a much more fundamental question: What is one's relationship with God? Job's suffering had provoked that more basic question. Perhaps this is the reason why what is offered to Job is not an explanation of his miserable plight but an experience that enables him to cope with it. The series of questions that Job raises leads him to an existential awareness that the God who is able to govern the entire universe with much care and wisdom certainly provides for human beings as well as the rest of creation. This awareness does not really "solve" the problem although to some extent it "dissolves" it, as it were. In the greater insight into the kind of relationship that he has with God, Job's original question somehow fades into the background. Now he can truly claim that he is in touch with God, not just that he has heard of God. In his suffering Job experiences God differently. He wanted to know why he was suffering, but he ends up relating more to his God. He was dissatisfied with the answers provided by his friends because these were attempts to justify suffering, but what matters more is his relationship with this God.

Hopkins' Question

Gerard Manley Hopkins asks his God a question similar to Job's. In his sonnet "Thou art indeed just, Lord" Hopkins explains his wretched plight to God.[16] He seems much worse off than the wicked despite his ef-

---

[15] Gustavo Gutierrez, *On Job*, p. 11

[16] The speaker or *persona* in many of Hopkins' poems, especially those written during his stay in Ireland, can be said to be no other than the Jesuit Gerard Manley Hopkins himself. Support for this interpretation (which underlies the following explication) can be found in the letters which Hopkins wrote to his friend, Robert Bridges. In some of these letters he comments on the content of his poems and the frustration, doubts and difficulties which he was experiencing. In "Thou art indeed just, 0 Lord" there are references in his own prose which will throw light on this interpretation of his work. In a letter dated Sept. 1, 1885 Hopkins wrote: " ... So with me, if I could but get on, if I could but produce work I should not mind its being buried, silenced, and going no further; but it kills me to be time's eunuch and never to beget". In another letter on January 12, 1888, he again describes himself as a eunuch: " ... Nothing comes: I am a eunuch—but it is for the kingdom of heaven's sake." A third reference can be found in notes made at a New Year's Day retreat: "I was continuing this train of thought this evening when I began to enter

forts. Thus, he remonstrates with God who seems to permit the wicked to prosper and thrive while all his own efforts are thwarted. Hopkins finds himself unable to accept this situation; having devoted himself to God's service by becoming a priest, he expects more from God. Although he is complaining, his tone like Job's nevertheless expresses reverence rather than utter despair. Knowing God's goodness and trusting in God's ability to rectify things, he can pray that God would inspire him to achieve something of value.

The Latin quotation at the very beginning of the sonnet is taken from the Vulgate and comes from Jeremiah 12:1.[17] Jeremiah 12 in fact seems to be the basis of the entire sonnet:

> Thou indeed, 0 Lord, art just, if I plead with thee, but yet I will speak what is just to thee; why doth the way of the wicked prosper: why is it well with all them that transgress and do wickedly? Thou has planted them, and they have taken root: they prosper and bring forth fruit: Thou art near in their mouth and far from their reins. And thou, 0 Lord, has known me, thou has seen me, and proved my heart with thee (Jer.12:13).

---

on that course of loathing and hopelessness which I have of often felt before, which made me fear madness, and led me to give up the practice ... I am like a straining eunuch". Cf. Jeffrey B. Loomis, "Chatter With a Just Lord: Hopkins' Final Sonnets of Quiescent Terror," *The Hopkins Quarterly,* VII, 2 (Summer 1980). pp. 54-55. Hopkins' sonnet "To R.B." also lends itself to this interpretation: "Sweet fire the sire of Muse, my soul needs this;/ I want one rapture of an inspiration" (lines 9-10). The following explication is thus based on the understanding that the *persona* of the poem is Hopkins himself. The edition used here is taken from *Chief Modern Poets of Britain and America, Vol. I: Poets of Britain,* ed. Gerald DeWitt Sanders *et al,* 5th ed. (Macmillan, 1970).

This explication is indebted to: Kunio Shimane, "The Sonnet of 'Endeavour': "Thou art indeed just, Lord", *The Hopkins Quarterly,* VII, 2 (Summer, 1980), pp. 65-81; Peter Milward, *Landscape and Inscape: Vision and Inspiration in Hopkins' Poetry* (Grand Rapids, Michigan: William B. Eerdmans Publishing Co., 1975); Norman H. MacKenzie, *A Reader's Guide to Gerard Manley Hopkins* (Ithaca, N.Y.: Cornell University Press, 1981); W. H. Gardner, *Gerard Manley Hopkins* (1844-1889): *A Study of Poetic Idiosyncracy in Relation to Poetic Tradition,* Vol. II (London: Martin Lecker & Warburg, 1949). For a different reading of the poem, see Jeffrey B. Loomis, "Chatter with a Just Lord: Hopkins' Final Sonnets of Quiescent Terror," *The Hopkins Quarterly,* VII, 2 (Summer, 1980), pp. 47-64; Jeffrey B. Loomis, *Dayspring in Darkness: Sacrament in Hopkins* (Lewisburg: Bucknell University Press, 1988).

[17] This quotation gives us the title which is usually rendered in English. The first three lines of the poem are a paraphrasing of the Latin quotation: "*Justus quidem tu es, Domine, si disputem tecum: verumtamen justa loquar ad te: Quare via impiorum prosperatur?*"

Right from the beginning Hopkins asserts his belief in God's justice. He is convinced that if he should "contend" (line 1), to debate a matter with God, God would listen and be fair. Accordingly, he has the courage to make his plea which he believes to be "'just" (line 2). Paul Mariani describes Hopkins as "pleading in the role of a skillful *advocatus* before the *dominus.*"[18] Hopkins is seeking an answer to his question: "Why do sinners' ways prosper? and why must/Disappointment all I endeavor end?" (lines 3 and 4). In putting his case so directly to God, Hopkins shows his willingness to believe in a fair system.

His reverence for God is noticeable in his use of "sir" (line 2). This reverence remains in evidence when he addresses God: "O thou my friend" (line 5): there is love between the speaker and his Lord. If God were his enemy (judging by the way God treats him as friend), could God possibly mistreat Hopkins any more than God seems already to be doing? Behind these lines one can hear the echo of the familiar saying: "With friends like you, who needs enemies?" The extent of Hopkins' suffering is coming to the fore.[19] Since one justly expects better treatment from one's friends than from one's enemies, Hopkins becomes more hurt when he realises that those who do wrong prosper while he who has committed his whole life to God's service does not. At this point in the poem Hopkins' feelings are so intense that the structure of the poem reflects them. The lines cannot contain the feelings, and they run on with an enjambed line carrying the speaker's protest into the sestet: " ... Oh, the sots and thralls of lust/Do in spare hours more thrive than I that spend,/Sir, life upon thy cause .. ." (lines 7-9). Hopkins conveys his frustration and disgust that "the sots and thralls of lust," i.e. drunkards and slaves, prosper without even trying while he fails despite his best endeavours.[20]

---

[18] Paul L. Mariani, *A Commentary on the Complete Poems of Gerard Manley Hopkins* (Ithaca & London: Cornell University Press, 1970), p. 302. According to W. H. Gardner, "Hopkins complains to God of his crippling sterility in lines of taut and impressive poetry." Cf. his *Gerard Manley Hopkins,* p. 364.

[19] Lines 5-7 rely on antithesis (enemy-friend), strange syntax, and alliteration (wouldst, worse, wonder) for their effect.

[20] The word "lust" may be significant given Hopkins' priestly vocation and the demands of celibacy. He refers to himself as "Time's eunuch" (line 13) so that perhaps sexual frustration is added to his complaints. Certainly the debauched ways of the wicked are implied in lines 7-8. The positioning of "Sir" (line 9). stressed as it is, re-emphasises a formal appeal and recalls line 2. It also draws attention to the alliterative value of this word and the word "'See" which is also in a stressed position in this line. Cf. Kunio Shimane, "The Sonnet of "Endeavour," p. 73. Hopkins makes good use of alliteration ("s" sounds, "b" sounds and "th" sounds) in this poem, thus giving the impression that the poem is to be heard and

The poem was written in spring in Dublin (17 March 1889), a few months before Hopkins' death. The season of spring as well as the plant imagery in the Jeremiah passage may account in part for Hopkins' turning to nature in the sestet of the poem:

... See, banks and brakes
Now, leavèd how thick! lacèd they are again
With fretty chervil, look, and fresh wind shakes
Them; birds build—but not I build, no, but strain,
Time's eunuch, and not breed one work that wakes.
(lines 9-13)[21]

Here Hopkins is once more taken up with the beauty and bounty of nature, a sentiment which can be seen in many of his poems (for example, "God's Grandeur", "Pied Beauty", and "Spring"). This shift from religion to nature in this part of the sonnet enables Hopkins yet again to combine two of his great strengths in this one poem: the power of his religious poetry and the beauty of his nature poetry. The image of nature in this poem is one of lushness and great productivity and contrasts starkly with the poet's own unproductive stasis. As John Pick puts it, Hopkins "contrasts his own interior desert with the fecundity around him".[22] Hopkins points out that the

---

not just read. He also repeats words like "just", "Lord", "sir", and "thou" thereby helping us to focus on the object of his address and maintain the dramatic situation created in the opening line of the sonnet.
[21] According to W. H. Gardner, with these lines "[Hopkins] drops into a more subdued but richly figurative and allusive style." *Gerard Manley Hopkins,* p. 364. The style is less detached and more emotional than the octave. The fruitfulness and fertility of nature add to his misery since they uncover his own sterility. In his own harsh view of himself, he has produced nothing of real value or worth. The use of the word "See" (line 9), followed by the comma, is interesting as it reveals how much force Hopkins can get from a simple monosyllabic word. It is comparable to the force with which evidence, e.g. exhibit A, is shown in court. In addition, it draws attention to the "banks and brakes" (line 9) which have rich, luscious growth. Again alliteration is employed and lends forceful emphasis to the things of nature. Not only are the banks and thickets thickly "leavèd" (line 10) but they are also covered with intertwining herbs and cow-parsley, "fretty chervil'" (line 11). as if to add insult to his injury. The use of "fretty" (line 11) recalls Hopkins' predilection for coined words, one of the innovative techniques which he used as he broke away from the traditional 19th-century stanza forms and developed his system of Instress/Inscape and Sprung rhythm. In line 11 the arresting position of "look" recalls his earlier use of "See" (line 9).
[22] John Pick, *Gerard Manley Hopkins: Priest and Poet* (London: Oxford University Press, 1943), p. 152.

leaves are being shaken by the "fresh wind" (line 11). His use of the adjective "fresh" gives the picture of energy, movement and newness in nature unlike his own stale plight. We sense the essence, i.e. the "whatness"—inscape, of the wind and its power breathing new life into things. Nature is thus renewed.

But Hopkins returns to his frustration. While birds build, he himself does not.[23] The nesting image augments the fertility and creativity of nature and underscores Hopkins' frustration in not being able to achieve or accomplish such security for himself. He is trying hard, but all his efforts leave him straining as "Time's eunuch" unable to "breed one work that wakes" (line 13).[24] His enslavement, unlike that of "the sots and thralls of lust", does not produce any success.[25]

Hopkins makes a final plea: "Mine, 0 thou lord of life, send my roots rain." Calling the Lord "mine" and "lord of life", Hopkins indicates his close relationship with God and his belief and trust in God. Hopkins is like a plant without water.[26] This desire for "rain" is a desire for the life-giving force of water, so necessary to nature for spurting growth in spring. Spiritually, it is a desire for grace which can rejuvenate. Divine inspiration will help Hopkins' priestly and poetic life.

The last line is distinct from the rest of the sonnet. It encapsulates a plea from his heart to God to justly reward the just. It reinforces the theme of the poem—justice—and reaffirms the poet's belief in his opening asser-

---

[23] In W. H. Gardner's view, the abrupt pause after "Them;" (line 12) ushers in the climax of the poem. Cf. *Gerard Manley Hopkins,* p. 364. Line 12 continues the constructive energy referred to earlier and concretises it with the alliterative "birds build" in contrast to Hopkins' own state: "but not I build." The use of plosive labials adds force to the climax.

[24] Hopkins had referred to this in letters to his friend, Robert Bridges. He may have in mind the sexual restraints of celibacy (not being able to reproduce or give life to a child) or he may be using the image of slavery (since eunuchs were frequently used as servants or slaves) to show his own enslavement. Cf. John Robinson, *In Extremity: a Study of Gerard Manley Hopkins* (Cambridge University Press, 1978). pp. 156-158.

[25] Perhaps since he is a poet and priest the words "one work that wakes" means a good poem or some satisfying result of his ministry. Norman H. MacKenzie observes that ironically, this poem is one of his most enduring sonnets in a form for which he is renowned. Cf. *A Reader's Guide to Gerard Manley Hopkins,* p. 204. Be that as it may, he longs for a more tangible, visible reward from his life of dedication and hard work.

[26] The pause at the end of line 13 is dramatically effective. It prepares us for the final plea and request of line 14. The final line of the sonnet extends the nature-fertility metaphor and links it with religion.

tion: "Thou are indeed just, Lord, if I contend/With thee; but, sir, so what I plead is just" (lines 1-2).

A Question without an Answer?

It would be presumptuous to conclude that Job and Hopkins answer the question of suffering in its various forms.[27] Being assured of God's providence or justice will not silence our questioning. The question will continue to bother us again and again because suffering, especially that of the innocent, seems irrational and unjustifiable. Like Pietro we will still ask: "Why, why, why? We live in faith and hope, we are the givers of love. Why is this torment visited upon us and upon our children."[28] The reality of suffering is one of the facts about life that may escape a solution but not an investigation. Hence, one may rightly suspect any allegation that the existence of suffering is a pseudo-problem or the wrong question. It is a real problem. When one experiences excruciating pain or watches helplessly the agony and misery of others, then one realises how genuine the problem of suffering is. Anybody who tries to make light of someone else's miseries through well-intentioned interpretations should try exchanging places with the sufferer.

One of the greatest tragedies that humankind has ever experienced as a result of its own enormous cruelty and unbelievable ignorance is the Holocaust. While we can indeed point our finger to the perpetrators of this crime, it has nevertheless challenged the conception of an almighty and omnibenevolent God which somehow makes the stance taken by Job and Hopkins rather less certain. Much has been written on this topic, but let us share the questioning and thoughts that it has generated in a fictitious character, Professor Malachowski:

> His search for answers came from a personal experience of a bitter kind of existence. That was why the Majdanek camp was more than a symbol, it was reality. The ashes which he regularly saw were those of his parents and of thousands of others. It was not like the water in the Fons Sapientiae, which symbolised knowledge. Truth stared him in the face as he meditated on the events which led to the death of his parents. As he

---

[27] It is interesting to note what Aldous Huxley wrote: "Never, I think has the just man's complaint against the universe been put more forcibly, worded more tersely and fiercely than in Hopkins' sonnet. God's answer is found in that most moving, most magnificent and profoundest poem of antiquity, the Book of Job'" Quoted by John Pick, *Gerard Manley Hopkins,* p. 153.

[28] Morris West, *Lazarus,* p. 164.

wandered about the camp, a routine that he religiously followed, looking in distress at the piles of shoes of the former inmates, as he dodged the wire fence that had trapped his parents and several others in a pitiful existence, as he imagined the bitterness and the frustration that reduced humans to mere skeletons, he often asked why, why did such evil things happen? Why was suffering perpetuated by evil people?

Amidst all this, the professor had sensed an abiding faith even among those who suffered intensely. While others felt, and felt strongly, that God had abandoned them, there were many others who persisted in their religious faith. Perhaps they needed to cling to something. One had to have some hope; otherwise one was lost completely. In the sea of fear, of shadows, and misery, one had to have a plank. No matter what. For if not, one would sink to the bottom. Faith in God was one such plank. But what Dr. Malachowski could not understand was why they would cling to God. Were those who rejected God not right in abandoning God? After all, that was what this so-called all-good and almighty God had done. One with inferior qualities would not allow that to happen. So why were they turning to God? Why had his parents persisted in praying to God?

He toyed with a psychological answer. Maybe it could all be described and explained by psychology. He did not doubt that, since all human reactions can somehow be explained. But there was something more. He turned to religion, starting with the Book of Job. The character Job was wrestling with the same problem. Job dismissed many of the answers his tradition had to offer him. Dr. Malachowski found that book sharpening the question he was asking: who is this God that a suffering people are dealing with? Job supplied an answer: a mysterious God whose ways are not our ways. But Dr. Malachowski asked for more. Surely more could be said about this God. It did not make sense to be endowed with an intellect and to be left wandering about in murkiness when it came to this crucial question. That was when he turned to philosophy. Not because he was confident he would get an answer, but because philosophy, at least the philosophers he had come to know, challenged him to dig deeper.

But philosophy let him down. He read Augustine, Aquinas, von Hügel voraciously. In the professor's view they presented a God that was causing all the problems he was having. A God who should have been able to do something about the situation because this God had all the power. A God who should have cared about what was going on because this God was all-benevolent. It did not match. Such a God needed to be defended against the charge of atheists. But he did not believe such a God should be defended. So Dr. Malachowski abandoned the task of looking for a defence of God. A God who had to be defended in the face of suffering must not be a caring God. Why should he care about such a God? The answer presented by the

philosophers he read seemed irrelevant in the face of his experience of suffering—of his parents' and countless others' tragic lives.[29]

In addition to the questions raised by Professor Malachowski, the existence of such suffering presents a practical challenge; namely, that we
have the obligation to remove the causes of suffering whenever possible.
Especially where suffering is the consequence of injustice and selfishness,
then we must not only alleviate suffering but also actively seek to root out
its causes. Accepting the fruits of people's wicked deeds will only
strengthen their greed and perpetuate their crime. We should feel obliged
to make this world a happier place in which to live for everyone. Human
creative powers are meant to be used to reduce the gravity and extent of
suffering brought about by evil people or by natural causes. Although this
world may never be perfect, it can be less imperfect, thanks to what
women and men, individually and collectively, can do.

But there is another side to this quest for an answer to suffering. It
may account for the change of direction in the mind of the author of Job
when he dealt with that question and for Hopkins' firm belief in God's
justice. For it seems that the question of suffering is one of those questions
mentioned at the beginning of this enquiry to which we can expect no
ready answers, yet they can transform us. The change that comes about in
us makes us look back only to realise that the questions we have raised
now appear so superfluous.

When the "chips are down" (as they were for Job and Hopkins), when
our sufferings make us see only a very hazy future, then we tend to ask
whether life has meaning at all. At times like this the meaninglessness-of-
it-all makes its painful presence felt.[30] Then we are tempted to call it quits,
wondering whether the struggle is worthwhile. When port and home seem
distant and the boat we are in is rocked by angry waves and tossed about
by strong gales and rough seas, then we can get sick and feel tempted to
jump overboard. Only the stout-hearted will want to hang on and sail on.
And yet when everything is calm again, when the stormy weather breaks
up to give way to sunny spells, then life again becomes not only bearable
but exciting and the light that glows from life seems to dispel the gloom.

---

[29] M.S. Sia, *The Fountain Arethuse*, pp. 183-184. Prof Malachowski raises a question that needs more attention: In the light of suffering, what kind of God can we
continue to believe in? What can philosophical thinking contribute to the debate?
We have addressed and pursued these and other questions in our book, *From Suffering to God: Exploring our Images of God in the Light of Suffering* (Basingstoke:
Macmillan, 1994), Part II.
[30] Cf. Chapter One.

Everything stands out again so clearly that we begin to wonder why we had questioned whether there was any meaning in life itself. Everything is so buoyant once more, everything is so meaningful again.

Some would call this experience simply the "different moods" or the "ups and downs" of life. But it is more than that. Instead, it is a matter of coming to grips with the reality of life rather than being simply carried by life's currents, now into still and calm waters, now into churning waters. Neither the author of Job nor the poet Hopkins was giving us an analysis of "moody" human beings. They were debating the very existential question that is still being asked today: how do human beings stand in relation to their God? Job's suffering and Hopkins' plight are situations that really cause such a question to arise. Both of them underwent an experience that many of us at one time or another have undergone or are now undergoing. Like them, we are confronted by suffering, ours as well as that of others. But for many of us it stands in the way between God and ourselves or sours any personal relationship with God. In other words, the question of suffering leads us to call our relationship with God into question, sometimes angrily. Such a reaction is understandable given the baffling aspect of suffering.

Learning from Job and Hopkins

But the message that the author of Job and the poet Hopkins have for us even today is that it need not lead to that. But why not? Because the irrationality of suffering is not everything about it, even if the fact of suffering appears to militate against the belief in a just and powerful God. The writer of the Book of Job wants to show us that Job wrestled with the same problems, but instead of turning his back on God, he made the question his route to God. Hopkins wondered and even complained but still found God just. It may be that suffering, disappointments, the roughness of life are our opportunity of feeling closer to our Creator, just as they were for those two. They could turn out to be shady colours which balance the lighter ones so that the intricate pattern of life will come more fully into view and hence be more valued. They could become, as it were, punctuation marks at significant places of life so that we can properly read and understand God's message or the pauses in the musical score of life so that the music may be better appreciated.[31] Much depends on us. We may not understand why there is suffering (sometimes one is at a complete loss to

---

[31] This should not, however, be taken to mean that God deliberately causes suffering as if God were a sadist. See Chapter One.

explain it, never mind justify it), but we can transcend the situation by letting it lead us to a more authentic relationship with God. Job may have been a fictional character, but there have been too many concrete examples of people who have refused to allow suffering to become a barrier between God and themselves for us to ignore this point. Someone once said that in moments of distress and loss we experience God first as an enemy, then as a void, and finally as a friend. Our sufferings could be the very factor which will enable us to experience God's compassion, something which one finds only in a true friend. It could be that the rough side of life will be our means to say to God: "I had heard of thee by the hearing of the ear, but now my eye sees thee" *(Job* 41:5). It may even, despite appearances, still enable us to cry out with Hopkins: "Thou art indeed just, Lord."

CHAPTER SEVEN

"O, DEATH, WHERE IS THY STING?": THE QUEST FOR DELIVERANCE

In this chapter we shall probe into certain literary meditations on death. We shall do this by explicating specific poems, arguably an effective way of presenting the poets' insights while preserving the rich imagery and the concreteness of their language. Although these poems were written by different people, they form a certain unity of thought.

Attitudes to Death

What is troubling about the moment of death, thereby causing much distress and anxiety, is that we all know that one day each of us will die; yet there is much uncertainty about death. Consequently, the thought of it grips our whole being, leaving us bewildered. Or it could be the parting with loved ones or perhaps leaving behind an unfinished task which makes death a sad and unwelcome moment. John Keats's poem "Terror of Death" certainly expresses the tragedy of being separated from loved ones or being unable to complete a piece of work. Maybe it is the fact that there is no turning back after—to use Alfred Tennyson's words—one has "crossed the bar" that terrifies us. Dylan Thomas' advice, therefore, is:

> Do not go gentle into that good night,
> Old age should burn and rave at close of day;
> Rage, rage against the dying of the light.[1]

We are afraid that death may reveal our lives to have been a sham, and it would render us powerless to change them.

Nevertheless, there are some for whom death is welcome. Just as there are varied reasons for fearing it, there appear to be different reasons for welcoming it. To some, death will be the longed-for break from life's toils.

---

[1] "Do not go Gentle into that Good Night," lines 18-20.

As Shakespeare puts it:

> Fear no more the heat o' the sun
>   Nor the furious winter's rages;
> Thou thy worldly task hast done,
>   Home art gone, and ta'en thy wages:[2]

It will be like the respite that one looks forward to after a hard day's work. Then again there will be those for whom death marks the end of an absurd existence, enabling them to slip into oblivion. For these life has had no meaning; what better choice than to cut it short? Others will have a rather stoic attitude towards death. Caesar in Shakespeare's play wonders: "Of all the wonders that I have heard,/It seems to me most strange that men should fear;/Seeing that death, a necessary end,/Will come when it will come."[3] Humans are destined to die; hence, the best that one can do, it is claimed, is to put up with it. Still others, like John Donne in his poem "Death, be not Proud", challenge death and maintain that it does not in fact have power:

> One short sleepe past, wee wake eternally,
> And death shall be no more; death, thou shalt die[4]

The Symbol of Light and the Meaning of Death

The different literary passages cited above articulate what possibly various individuals feel about death. There is no doubt that the reality of death is a source of much questioning even if for some it is something not to be feared. But someone once claimed that death is a tragedy only when we know nothing about it. If this is true, then just how much do we know of death? If we had some idea of its significance, would there be less fear in us? Would we be less scared at the prospect of it since it would not be a plunge into the unknown or a leap into the dark?

A poet whose attitude toward death is worth looking into is Henry Vaughan. In his poem which has been given the title of "They are all gone

---

[2] This song is from Shakespeare's play *Cymbeline,* Act IV, Scene 2.
[3] *Julius Caesar,* Act II, Scene 2. In his book *Human Immortality and the Redemption of Death* (London: Darton Longman and Todd, 1990), Simon Tugwell discusses various ancient attitudes to death and mortality found in a number of literary and philosophical writings. He also traces the evolution of Christian eschatology from its beginnings up to the end of the Middle Ages.
[4] "Holy Sonnets" 10, Lines 13-14.

into the world of light!" he uses the symbol of light to reflect on the meaning of death for him.[5] In this poem he also voices his hope for deliverance.

Light has always been an illuminating symbol in religion and literature since it is capable of revealing many meanings, thus helping us gain an insight into what is otherwise difficult to comprehend. Henry Vaughan certainly finds the symbol of light useful. In the poem referred to above the proliferation of words and images associated with light underlines the importance of this symbol for him: *star, kindle, flames, burn, bright, fair, glows, glitters, jewel.* Furthermore, by contrasting these with terms connected with darkness, such as *dark, sad, gloomy, cloudy, dull, hoary, mists, blot,* the impact of the symbol becomes greater. For Vaughan, light represents God, heaven, immortality, happiness, knowledge, vision, freedom; whereas darkness stands for damnation, mortality, misery, absence or separation from God, ignorance, blindness, bondage.[6] Commenting on Vaughan's use of these two images or groups of images, Sandbank writes that they "serve to re-enforce a dramatic world-picture in which the opposition between heaven and earth, Grace and nature, is a very basic distinction."[7]

The imagistic contrast of darkness and light gives unity to Vaughan's poem.[8] One can clearly see this contrast in the very first stanza:

They are all gone into the world of light!
And I alone sit ling'ring here;
(lines 1-2)

The word "they" refers to those people who have died (including his younger brother William and his own wife, Catherine); they have passed from this world into the world of light (in another work of his, "The World", he also describes the next world in terms of light: "I saw Eternity

---

[5] The versions of Vaughan's, Donne's and Herbert's poems being used here are those which are included in *English Seventeenth-Century Verse,* Vol. I, ed. Louis L. Martz (New York: W. W. Norton & Co., 1969). In his book, *Language Recreated: Seventeenth-Century Metaphorists and the Act of Metaphor* (Athens: University of Georgia Press, 1992) Harold Skulsky shows how figurative language is used in that century, particularly in the poetry of John Donne, George Herbert and Henry Vaughan.

[6] Cf. S. Sandbank, "Henry Vaughan's Apology for Darkness,"*Essential Articles for the Study of Henry Vaughan.* Ed. Alan Rudrum (Archon Books, 1987), p. 129; James D. Simmonds, *Masques of God: Form and Theme in the Poetry of Henry Vaughan* (University of Pittsburgh Press, 1972), p. 54.

[7] S. Sandbank, "Henry Vaughan's Apology for Darkness," p. 129.

[8] Cf. James D. Simmonds, *Masques of God,* p. 54.

the other night/Like a great *Ring* of pure and endless light", lines 1-2). The radiance of that "world of light" makes this earthly world very dark, adding to the isolation of the poet (speaker), which we can sense in the phrase "I alone". From such a dejected state the poet would like to escape.

The next two lines reinforce the contrast by repeating the pattern of opposition:

> Their very memory is fair and bright,
> And my sad thoughts doth clear.
> (lines 3-4)

Their "fair and bright" memory is set off against his "sad thoughts". At the same time, however, the poet seems to want to introduce a less sombre note. While the word "sad" is not one to be associated with light but with darkness, the sad thoughts are "clearing". In addition, the opening of the second stanza describes his memory of them (and hence, by implication, his thoughts) in this way:

> It glows and glitters in my cloudy brest
> Like stars upon some gloomy grove,
> (lines 5-6)

The alliteration in "glows" and "glitters" highlights the dazzling power of the departed even in his "cloudy breast". The imagery of light and darkness—condensed in one line—has the effect on him of stars on a gloomy grove. The light of the stars, more obvious and appreciated, dispels the darkness and gloom. The poet continues his thoughts with references to "faint beams" which shroud the hill after "the Sun's remove" (lines 7-8).

The third stanza directs our attention to the gulf which exists between the quality of his mortal life and the immortal life of the departed. They walk "in an Air of glory,/ Whose light doth trample on [his] days" (lines 9-10). In contrast, he lives in an earthly life which is very imperfect: he feels his days are "dull and hoary" at best. James Simmonds notes that, "Implicit in this contrast between two kinds of life which the speaker 'sees' is a contrast between two kinds of knowledge, one that sees the surfaces of things and one that sees beyond them."[9] In this world, Vaughan appears to be saying, we do not have the fullness of knowledge nor sight.

Vaughan believes that it is through death that we can be raised "High as the Heavens above!" (line 14). Death is a necessary stage through

---

[9] *Ibid*, p. 55.

which we must pass to reach the higher plane (or as Donne puts it: "And soonest our best men with thee doe goe,/ Rest of their bones and soules deliverie.")[10] The imagery of light is seen once again in the word "kindle" (line 16). Death kindles in Vaughan's heart a passion: it is now "beauteous death" (line 17). It is "the Jewel of the Just,/ Shining no where, but in the dark;" (lines 17-18). Making use once more of the contrast between light and darkness, he describes death as leading us to the brightness of immortality. But we cannot see beyond this world because of our limited light (here the symbol of light has evolved to mean understanding and vision). Thus, post-mortem mysteries remain unsolved while we are in this world:

> What mysteries do lie beyond thy dust;
> Could man outlook that mark!
>
> (lines 19-20)

Vaughan is expressing a wish or desire for greater understanding and insight—to see things as they really are. His wish echoes verses 12-13 of 1 Corinthians: "For now we see in a mirror dimly, but then face to face. Now I know in part; then I shall understand fully, even as I have been fully understood."

In the next stanza Vaughan shows us what it is to see as mortals, emphasising once more the difference between that sight and true vision or understanding. He illustrates it by citing our limited knowledge and range of sight on seeing that the bird has flown the nest. We do not have enough "light" (that is, intelligence, understanding) to see "what fair Well, or Grove he sings in now," (line 23). We are in the dark about these things (incidentally, the reference to grove and well is, according to E. C. Pettet, to details of the Old Testament landscape). [11]

But even in such darkness, there is a glimmer of hope. The phrase "And yet" (line 25) introduces it. Just as Angels call to the soul in brighter dreams when we are asleep, so "strange thoughts"—flashes of light, divine inspiration—help us to "transcend our wonted theames" (line 27), giving us a peep into glory. At times with God's help we overcome our limitations and catch glimpses of "glory" (line 28). In another work, Vaughan makes a similar point:

> When on some *gilded Cloud,* or *flowre*
> My gazing soul would dwell an houre,

---

[10] John Donne, "Death be not proud", "Holy Sonnets" 10, lines 7-8.
[11] E. C. Pettet, *Of Paradise and Light: a Study of Vaughan's Silex Scintillans* (Cambridge University Press, 1960), p. 158.

And in those weaker glories spy
Some shadows of eternity;
. . . .
But felt through all this fleshly dresse
Bright *shootes* of everlastingnesse.[12]

Returning to the poem "They are all gone into the world of light!" one can see that the symbol of light is further evident in these lines:

If a star were confin'd into a Tomb
  Her captive flames must needs burn there;
                    (lines 29-30).

The burning flames encased in a tomb represent the soul enclosed in our mortal body. The longing of the soul for freedom is fulfilled by the death of the body (opening of the Tomb) since it releases the soul whereupon "She'l shine through all the sphaere" (line 32). As he puts it in another poem entitled "Ascension Hymn", souls "must be undrest" (line 6). The soul, once liberated from the captivity of the body, will join all those who are "gone into the world of light" (line 1). Each soul adds its own star, a light to the world of light.[13] E. C. Pettet observes that this reference to the Tomb confining a star (in line 29) has intimations of the Resurrection.[14] Immortality for us mortals was brought about by Christ's Resurrection, which has ensured Vaughan's "liberation from the tomb" and entrance into "the world of light".

The ninth stanza is an appeal to God to release the spirit from this world of slavery into true freedom. The stanza thus conveys more explicitly Vaughan's attitude to this life and to the next. He affirms his faith in God, recognising God as the Father of eternal Life and of all creation.

Believing that we will not be truly liberated until we understand fully and can see clearly, Vaughan presents in the final stanza two ways of being liberated:

Either disperse these mists, which blot and fill
  My perspective (still) as they pass,
Or else remove me hence unto that hill

---

[12] Henry Vaughan, "The Retreate," lines 11-14, 19-20.
[13] In his "[Joy of my life! while left me here]" (line 17) Vaughan regards "God's Saints" as "shining lights"). Included in Mario A. Di Cesare, ed. *George Herbert and the Seventeenth-Century Religious Poets* (N.Y.: W.W. Norton & Co., 1978).
[14] E. C. Pettet, *Of Paradise and Light,* p. 161.

Where I shall need no glass.
(lines 37-40)

In these lines Vaughan indicates the forms of liberty he desires. Again he pursues the light-and-darkness imagery: mists result in diminished sight which blot the clear or total picture. The true brightness is not seen by mortals because of the darkness and the cloudy nature of mists—ignorance, mortal understanding, mortal sight. Thus, he asks God to "disperse these mists". One is reminded here of Emily Dickinson's "Of all the Souls that stand create":

And this brief Tragedy of Flesh—
Is shifted—like a Sand—
When Figures show Their royal Front—
And Mists—are carved away
(lines 7-10)

Vaughan's second choice is to be removed from this world (dark vale) to that other world of heaven (bright hill) where all is revealed. Only then will he be enlightened and join those who are already stars in the world of light. This option of being taken out of this mist-obscured world into the illumination of heaven neatly ends the poem. Thus, for Vaughan "to lose this life is, in fact, a gain, the shedding of the dross which is the material world and the gaining of the pure light of God and eternity."[15] Or, as Vaughan himself puts it in "[Silence, and stealth of dayes!": "But those fled to their Maker's throne/ There shine and burn;" (lines 24-25).

One can easily see that in Vaughan's work the symbol of light with its rich connotations of heaven, immortality, happiness, knowledge, full vision, freedom (and often contrasted with the symbol of darkness) pervades the whole meditation on the meaning of death for him. It is a symbol capable of bearing simultaneously several kinds of interpretation.[16]

---

[15] George Parfitt, *English Poetry of the 17th Century* (London and New York: Longman, 1985), p. 104.

[16] It is worth quoting Pettet at length on this point: "There is no other short poem in the language more brightly and continuously luminous. From the dazzling impact of its opening lines, through images that interpenetrate, are modified, and are sometimes repeated, it evokes the earthly, visible light of sunset, stars, and jewels (produced, according to hermetic theory, by the action of the sun), the strange radiance of 'some brighter dreams', visited by shining Angels, the divine, ultimate light. kindling as well as illuminating, that links life and death, heaven, the departed spirits, and the human soul. And all this pervasive luminosity is emphasised by Vaughan's typical, Rembrantesque chiaroscuro of stars against 'some gloomy

The Death of Jesus[17]

In his meditation on death Vaughan mentions the liberating effect of Jesus' death. The fact that Jesus died on the cross seems to make a difference to the way Christians view death. They believe that Jesus' death enables them to see meaning in their own deaths and this gives them hope. For them part of the significance of that historical death some 2000 years ago lies in their being able to untangle some of the knots that surround death. Because of that event, death for the Christian is not a plunge into the unknown or a leap into the dark. The reality of death assumes a meaning which comes from Christ's meritorious death on the cross: the process of dying becomes a participation in Christ's saving act. And because death is made meaningful, then life itself is seen as an important challenge since it is the situation where the Christian is given all the opportunities of fulfillment at death. It is in this sense that contemporary Christian theology talks of life as "death in anticipation".[18]

To regard Christ's death as giving meaning to our own death is not, however, to ignore the deep-seated dread of death that Christians share with other people.[19] Death, more than anything else brings before us the

---

grove', of the heavenly 'world of light' over and against the dull glimmering of mortal life, and most striking of all, of light in darkness, light triumphant over darkness, at the moment of death." *Of Paradise and Light*, p. 162.

[17] In this reflection the death of Jesus is seen in its soteriological significance. For an account on what is discovered about God from the fact that Jesus was executed, see Jon Sobrino, "The Epiphany of the God of Life in Jesus of Nazareth" in his *The Idols of Death and the God of Life: a Theology* (Maryknoll, N.Y.: Orbis Books, 1983). pp. 88f. See also, Dermot Lane, "The Cross of Christ as the Revelation of God" in his *Christ at the Centre: Selected Issues in Christology* (Dublin: Veritas Publications, 1990), pp. 53-79. Also, William A. Beardslee *et al.*, "Preaching on the Death of Jesus" in their *Biblical Preaching on the Death of Jesus* (Nashville: Abingdon Press, 1989), pp. 75f.

[18] In pointing out that Christ's death gives meaning to our own since it gives us a focus and a participatory role, we are not implying that we should be obsessed with death the way that some people in the past were. Cf. Norman Pittenger, *After Death: Life in God* (SCM 1980), p. 2. Michael Wheeler writes about the literary and theological evidence of the Victorians' obsessive interest in death in his *Death and the Future Life in Victorian Literature and Theology* (Cambridge University Press, 1990), pp. 25-68.

[19] John Donne captures this sentiment well. In his "To Christ" (also known as "A hymne to God the Father") he expresses ultimate fear that he would not be saved:
"I have a sinn of feare, that when I have spunn
My last thred, I shall perish on the shore;
Sweare by thy self, that at my Death thy Sunn

radical finitude of our existence. It threatens to nullify everything. W.B. Yeats describes the situation graphically: "An aged man is but a paltry thing,/A tattered coat upon a stick, unless/ Soul clap its hands and sing, and louder sing/ For every tatter in its mortal dress,"[20] In the document "Church in the Modern World" Vatican II stated that "it is in the face of death that the riddle of human existence becomes most acute. Not only is man tormented by pain and by the advancing deterioration of his body, but even more so by a dread of perpetual extinction."[21] W.B.Yeats again expresses this feeling in rather poetic terms:

> Consume my heart away; sick with desire
> And fastened to a dying animal
> It knows not what it is; and gather me
> Into the artifice of eternity.[22]

There is an instinctive desire in every one of us to want to live forever.[23] Hence, we feel restless and anxious as we become painfully aware that like everything else, we too must pass away. Death is the most tangible expression of human finitude. It is a real threat. No wonder it has been described as life's sharpest contradiction, the absurd arch-contradiction of existence.

Good Friday and Easter

Two poets who meditate on the Christian understanding of the death and subsequent resurrection of Jesus are John Donne and George Herbert. In a poem entitled "Good Friday, 1613, Riding Westward" Donne reflects on the meaning of that event while Herbert brings out the significance of Christ's resurrection in his poem "Easter". Both of these works are replete with images of the God they believe in and of their relationship to that God.

The title of Donne's meditation "Goodfriday, 1613, Riding West-

---

> Shall shine as it shines now, and heretofore;
> And, having done that, Thou hast done.
>   I feare no more." (lines 13-18)

[20] W. B. Yeats, "Sailing to Byzantium," (lines 9-12), *The Works of W. B. Yeats* (Wordsworth Editions, 1994).

[21] W. Abbot (ed.), *The Documents of Vatican II.* "The Church in the Modern World," art.18.

[22] W.B. Yeats, "Sailing to Byzantium," (lines 21-24).

[23] Cf. Chapter Eight.

ward" arrests our attention for a number of reasons. The poem commemo-
rates the crucifixion and death of Jesus Christ, but the date "1613"—so
prominently positioned in the title—reminds us that Donne is concerned
with his own observance of the anniversary of that event and its implications for him rather than with the actual historical occurrence.[24] The phrase
"Riding Westward" implies a journey but one in the opposite direction
from that expected in relation to Good Friday and its Eastern connections.[25]

The first line of the poem sets up a hypothetical analogy: "Let man's
Soule be a Spheare" (line 1). As a sphere, the soul is subject to the principles which govern the other spheres—here we are introduced to Donne's
"conceit" which sees the movement of the soul in terms of the movement
of the spheres.[26] The human soul, like the other spheres, has a guiding Intelligence. Devotion should be its guiding principle. Its movement should
be towards devotion (especially on Good Friday); but, like the other
spheres, the soul is also subject to "forraigne motions" (line 4) which
cause it to lose its own direction.[27] The soul as sphere is buffeted everyday

---

[24] Cf. Murray Roston, *The Soul of Wit: A Study of John Donne* (Oxford: Clarendon
Press, 1974), p. 205.

[25] Commenting on the poem itself, Barbara Kiefer Lewalski writes that Louis
Martz in his *Poetry of Meditation* notes that "it is a classic Ignatian meditation: the
extended comparison in the opening lines presenting the preparatory stage; the
long central section constituting an intellectual analysis of the crucifixion in terms
of its manifold paradoxes; and the final lines containing a heartfelt colloquy or
prayer to Christ emerging from the meditative exercise." *Protestant Poetics and
the Seventeenth-Century Religious Lyric* (Princeton University Press, 1979), p.
278.

[26] According to A. C. Partridge, this conceit is based on the Ptolemaic cosmology
with the ultimate support of Plato's *Timaeus:* "In Plato's cosmology the Creator
imposed on his universe a certain order, the first being a division of heavens into
inner and outer spheres, namely, those of the planets, and those of the supposedly
fixed stars. The earth was regarded as the centre around which all moved, once in
twenty-four hours. The orbits of the fixed stars took a different direction from
those of the planets. The sphere of the fixed stars (called the Same) moved in a
circle from left to right; the seven planets (called the Other) had contrary motion
from right to left." *John Donne—Language and Style* (Andre Deutsch, 1978), p.
143.

[27]Helen Gardner explains the basis for the comparison: "The spheres had more
than one motion. Their own natural motion, each being guided by an Intelligence,
was from West to East; but the motion of the Primum Mobile hurled them against
this, from East to West, everyday. Other motions, such as the trepidation of the
ninth sphere, prevented the separate spheres from obeying their 'natural forme', or
directing Intelligence." *The Metaphysical Poets* (Penguin, 1970), p. 87.

and rarely obeys its "naturall forme" (line 6). The next lines state clearly what interferes with the progress of the soul towards devotion:

> Pleasure or businesse, so, our Soules admit
> For their first mover, and are whirld by it.
>   (lines 7 and 8).

Distracted from its true course, the human soul gets caught up in the attractions and demands of this world and is no longer moved by devotion to God. In thus likening the soul to a sphere, subject to the movement of other spheres, Donne has given us a striking comparison.

This comparison also explains the direction of his journey. Like a mathematical problem clearly demonstrated—if we have followed his argument so far—Donne's reason for taking this direction becomes explicit:

> Hence is't, that I am carryed towards the West
> This day, when my Soules forme bends toward the East.
>   (lines 9-10).

Today of all days (emphasising the significance to Donne of Good Friday, and his wish to observe it properly) his "Soules forme bends towards the East" in devotion and gratitude to his Saviour. Yet, he is moving towards the West. Temporal attractions exert a great force on him (he is going to Montgomery Castle in Wales) preventing the soul from obeying its "naturall forme". Donne knows what he should see at Calvary in the East:

> There I should see a Sunne, by rising set,
> And by that setting endlesse day beget;
> But that Christ on this Crosse, did rise and fall,
> Sinne had eternally benighted all.
>   (lines 11-14)

Through his use of paradoxes he shows his Christian belief that the salvation of human beings was brought about by the setting of a "Sun".[28] The imagery of the sun is effective in depicting what Jesus Christ accomplished by his death and resurrection: he begot "endless" day and immortality for mortal humans. The absence of the sun is conveyed by the words "eternally benighted" stressing that without Christ's death on the Cross (setting sun) and his resurrection (rising sun) we would not have been re-

---

[28] This pun on Sun/Son is also seen in "To Christ" (also known as "A Hymn to God the Father"): "Sweare by thy self, that at my Death, thy Sunn/ Shall shine as it shines nowe, and heretofore;' (lines 15-16).

deemed and sin would have permanently covered all in darkness. Here again Donne is contrasting East and West (rising and setting sun), thus connecting the second movement of the poem (lines 11-32) with the first.

Yet Donne is almost glad not to see the crucifixion. It is a "spectacle of too much weight" for him (line 16). He would not be able to face up to the horrifying spectacle of the tortured, crucified Jesus. To look at God's face is tantamount to death: "Who sees God's face, that is selfe life, must dye;" (line 17—a reference to Exodus 33:20). But how much worse to view God die: "What a death were it then to see God dye?" (line 18). It is not surprising that Donne finds "that spectacle of too much weight" (line 16) for him since it had such profound consequences on nature, as seen in this metaphor:

> It made his owne Lieutenant Nature, shrinke,
> It made his footstoole crack, and the Sunne winke.
>   (lines 19-20)

These lines are reminiscent of Isaiah 65:1 and Matthew 27:5155. The enormity of the event (crucifixion) is mirrored in disturbing phenomena—an earthquake and eclipse of the sun.

The difficulty he experiences in facing the crucifixion is further brought out in his rhetorical question: could Donne look on "those hands which span the Poles,/ And turne all spheares at once" (lines 21-22) and witness the marks of the nails in Jesus' hands stretched out on the Cross? Once again the idea of opposites and extremities (North-South poles and the right-left arm of the Cross) and the movement of the spheres are kept before us. God is given the role of turning all spheres. Thus, this section of the poem is linked with and reinforces the opening movement (lines 1-10). Donne wonders whether he could bear to look on Jesus Christ—humbled, suffering the ignominy of the crucifixion:

> Could I behold that endlesse height which is
> Zenith to us, and our Antipodes,
> Humbled below us? ...
>   (lines 23-25)

It is a terrifying contemplation which reminds one of another Christian paradox—the greatest shall be least.

Donne's next rhetorical question asks if he could behold that blood which is:

> The seat of all our Soules, if not of his,
> Make durt of dust, or that flesh which was worne

> By God, for his apparell, rag'd and torne?
> (lines 26-28)

He focuses on the shedding of Christ's blood and its mingling with the earth and on the tortured state of Christ as his flesh is injured and mutilated by human beings—paradoxically, for their salvation.

In his meditation Donne considers next the possibility of reflecting on the suffering of Mary "Who was God's partner here, and furnish'd thus/ Halfe of that Sacrifice, which ransom'd us?" (lines 31-32). Perhaps he can relate to Mary and appreciate her suffering (as parent) and the sacrifices demanded of her as Mother of God. Her sufferings also helped to win our salvation.

Throughout the second section of the poem (lines 11-32) we are kept aware of the religious implications of Good Friday and of the paradoxical notion that the West (setting sun-Christ's death) leads to East (rising sun-resurrection and immortality). All the ideas and images are thus held together.

Donne then informs us that since he is riding westward, he cannot actually see these sights (suffering, crucifixion, resurrection) before him; nevertheless, he is mindful of them. Thus, he can make an appropriate act of meditative devotion even as he rides westward. The sights which are "present yet unto [his] memory" (line 34)—traditionally located at the back of the head, according to A. C. Partridge[29]—enable him to contemplate his sinfulness and the ever-watchful presence of Christ. His "memory" is looking East even as he rides towards the West. Therefore, God (in the East) is looking towards him. It is at this stage in the poem that God becomes personal for Donne:

> ... thou look'st towards mee,
> O Saviour, as thou hang'st upon the tree;
> (lines 35-36)

He feels unworthy. Maintaining the metaphor of his movement to the West, Donne points out that his back is towards God, not because he is rejecting God but because he wishes to expose his back to receive God's punishment which will clear him of his unworthiness:

> I turne my backe to thee, but to receive
> Corrections, till thy mercies bid thee leave.
> (lines 37-38)

---

[29] A. C. Partridge, *John Donne—Language and Style*, p. 145.

Donne wishes to suffer his own scourging personally from God to atone for his wrongdoings.[30] He wants to be punished so that he can get closer to God:

> O thinke mee worth thine anger, punish mee;
> Burne off my rusts, and my deformity,
> Restore thine Image, so much, by thy grace,
> That thou may'st know mee, and I'll turne my face.
>   (lines 39-42)

Donne realises that he is tarnished by sin and that unless he is cleansed and purged he cannot be united with God.[31] Only when he is made free of sin through punishment will he be able to turn his face towards God. This turn at the end of the poem reiterates the conceit of the movement of the sphere (soul) obeying its "naturall forme" and turning to devotion—he will turn his face from the West to the East. The poem's thought has, as it were, gone full circle: just as West meets the East, the human individual who emanates from God returns to God.

George Herbert's poem "Easter", beautifully complements Donne's poem since in Christian thought Good Friday and Easter are not separated. Thus, Herbert's reflections can be said to develop further the significance of Jesus Christ's death.[32]

The structure of the poem is worth a mention. The poem consists of thirty lines, grouped in six stanzas. The first three stanzas, comprising six lines each, form the first movement of the poem while the remaining

---

[30] As Donne puts it in another work, "They killed once an inglorious man, but/ Crucifie him daily .. " ("Holy Sonnets" 11, lines 7-8).

[31] In another work of his, Donne makes the same point: "That I may rise, and stand, o'erthrow mee, and *bend* /Your force, to breake, blowe, burn, and make me new" ("Holy Sonnets" 14, lines 3-4). The same sentiment is expressed by Ben Jonson: "Use still Thy rod,/ That I may prove/ Therein, Thy Love" ("A Hymn to God the Father" lines 4-6). This poem illustrates the significance of Christ's death and resurrection, as Jonson sees it, for humankind but also raises the question of human sinfulness despite God's generosity. Our reference to Donne and Jonson on this point does not mean agreement with their image of a God who punishes. One of the reasons for exploring our images of God is precisely to bring out not only what is tenable but also what must be rejected. See, the Introduction of our *From Suffering to God: Exploring our Images of God in the Light of Suffering*, pp. 1-15. See also, S. Sia, *Religion, Reason and God: Essays in the Philosophies of Charles Hartshorne and A.N. Whitehead* (Peter Lang, 1994), pp. 4-7.

[32] In fact, in another poem "Love (III)" George Herbert shows the significance of the crucifixion and death of Jesus Christ. In the final stanza of that poem Herbert offers assurance that Christ's sacrifice redeems us.

twelve lines, divided into three 4-line stanzas, form the second movement of the poem. The line-length is irregular: long and short in the first movement, and the lines rhyme in couplets. In contrast, the line-length is much more regular in the second movement, and the lines rhyme alternately. It is no wonder that in some editions of this poem it is printed in two separate parts as "Easter I" and "Easter II"[33] A probable reason for this is that the two movements or parts of the poem look distinct, at least on first sight. But a closer examination of the poem reveals a certain unity: the second movement answers the first. That is to say, "Easter II" is the speaker's response to the call in "Easter I" for his lute to awake.[34] Furthermore, both appear to be hymns, making it more credible to refer to the underlying unity in this work.[35]

The first movement begins with a formal call to praise:

Rise heart; thy Lord is risen. Sing his praise
                    Without delayes,
          (lines 1-2)

Herbert bases this movement on Psalm 57, one of the Proper Psalms for Easter matins:

My heart is fixed, 0 God, my heart is fixed: I will
          sing and give praise.
Awake up my glory, *awake* Lute and Harpe: I my selfe
          will *awake* right earely.
I will give thanks unto thee, 0 Lord, among the people:
          and I will sing unto thee among the nations.
                    (lines 8-10, italics added)

According to Chana Bloch, in the first stanza of his poem, Herbert

---

[33] In John Wall's edition, the two parts are separated. However, he explains that in 1633 (Le. 1633 edition of Herbert's religious poetry) the two are printed as one poem. This editor favours the division found in MS Jones B., 62 (in Dr. Williams' library, London) since critics agree that the second part is the speaker's response to his call in the first part. Cf. John Wall, *George Herbert: The Country Parson and the Temple* (Paulist Press, 1981), p. 155. The argument for regarding the two as really one is precisely that the two parts (call-response) form a unity.

[34] *Ibid.* p. 63

[35] There is another sense in which one can see a connection between the two movements thus pointing to a much closer unity of the two parts than Wall is prepared to acknowledge. From the content of the first movement, one can imagine it to be the preparation and tuning up of the musical instruments for a performance and the second movement as the recital itself.

transforms the biblical sequence of verbs, "awake, awake, I will awake" into a new Christian *sequence—"Rise* heart, thy Lord is *risen,* thou mayst *rise".* Herbert's use of the word "rise" takes on three different senses: wake up, Christ has been resurrected from the dead, you may be reborn to a new life of the spirit.[36] The reason for singing and giving praise is that Christ's saving deeds in the Crucifixion and Resurrection guarantee immortality for us mortals. We are restored to eternal life and have just cause to celebrate and sing:

> Who takes thee by the hand, that thou likewise
>> With him mayst rise:
> That, as his death calcined thee to dust,
> His life may make thee gold, and much more just.
>> (lines 3-6)

Mere "dust'"has been transformed into "gold". Christ has justified us.

Now that the heart is ready to sing, Herbert calls—at the beginning of the second stanza—on the lute:

> Awake, my lute— and struggle for thy part
>> With all thy art.
>> (lines 7-8).

It is not an easy task. Because of the importance of the event, one needs to exert effort to celebrate this Easterday in an appropriate manner. Herbert continues:

> The crosse taught all wood to resound his name,
>> Who bore the same.
> His stretched sinews taught all strings, what key
> Is best to celebrate this most high day.
>> (lines 9-12)

Christ's sinews were stretched taut on the Cross. Likewise, the strings on Herbert's lute must also be stretched to the correct tension to achieve the proper key.[37] It was by his suffering—"stretched sinews on the

---

[36] Chana Bloch, *Spelling the Word: George Herbert and the Bible* (University of California Press, 1985), p. 249.

[37] This comparison is particularly striking since Herbert played the lute and used it to achieve the musical quality, so obvious in his poems. In fact, many of his poems are sung and have been set to music. For instance, the first 18 lines of "Easter" have been set to music by George Jeffreys in "Rise, heart, thy Lord is risen: Verse anthem for Easter day" for STB soli, SSATB chorus and organ. See, also, Vaugh

cross"—that Christ conquered death. However, Herbert focuses not so much on the pain but on the results of it: the liberation, resurrection, eternal life. Consequently, Easter is a time of joyous celebration. Herbert proclaims that the wood of the cross has shown how all wood, including the wooden bridge of his lute, should give praise to God. For his own part he will use his talent to praise God. As he expresses it in another work, "The Thanksgiving":

> My musick shall finde thee, and ev'ry string
>> Shall have his attribute to sing;
> That all together may accord in thee,
>> And prove one God, one harmonie.
>> (lines 39-42)

Indeed in still another poem "Providence" he considers praise of God to be our chief function.

In the opening line of the third stanza of this first movement of "Easter" Herbert joins the "heart" of stanza 1 and the "lute" of stanza 2 together:

> Consort, both heart and lute, and twist a song
>> Pleasant and long:
>> (lines 13-14)

He also announces the song, which seems to extend from line 19 to line 30.[38] Music is made up of three parts; if he is to produce such music, a third part must be supplied. This third part is the "blessed Spirit", often associated with inspiration:

> O let thy blessed Spirit bear a part,
> And make up our defects with his sweet art.
>> (lines 17-18)

Human efforts are not sufficient; hence, God's role remains essential. This third "component" takes our "dust" and once again turns it into "gold".

The three stanzas taken together thus form what Anthony Low calls a "paean celebrating the most joyful of the Church's feasts".[39] The first

---

Williams' musical settings for Easter.

[38] Structurally, this is an important development as it helps to summarise stanza 1 and stanza 2, thus preparing for the conclusion (in this stanza) of the first movement (it also introduces the second movement).

[39] Anthony Low, *Love's Architecture: Devotional Modes in Seventeenth-Century English Poetry* (New York University Press, 1978), p. 85.

movement of the poem, with its three stanzas, is somehow evocative of the
Trinity, especially due to the reference to the Spirit. Moreover, the movement resembles a musical arrangement. In the first stanza the heart rises
and sings while in the second the lute enters, playing counterpoint to the
singing heart. In the last stanza the Holy Spirit, like another musical in-
strument, plays his part, thus completing the three-part harmony to round
off the concert. As Low again observes: "The poem, constructed on this
musical metaphor, seems also to provide us with a program for its musical
setting."[40]

The second movement of the poem begins with line 19 and runs to the
end of the poem. This movement also consists of three stanzas, thus linking it to the structure of the first movement. But the regularity of the lines
by contrast is immediately noticeable. Low refers to this part of the poem
as "the simplest and most lyrical of Herbert's songs".[41] The measure, four
lines in tetrameter or Long Meter, could be sung to many established tunes
and was thus a favourite of hymn and psalm writers. Its simpler style,
compared to that of the first part of the poem, meant that music would
bring out the harmonious contrast.[42]

The fourth stanza, which initiates the second movement of the poem,
opens with the following lines:

> I got me flowers to straw thy way;
> I got me boughs off many a tree:
> > (lines 19-20)

It is clear that Herbert is anxious to do something, to do his part. But God
does not need the flowers nor the boughs:

> But thou wast up by break of day,
> > And brought'st thy sweets along with thee.
> > (lines 21-22)

These lines echo Mark 16:1-6: the women had brought sweet spices to

---

[40] *Ibid.* p. 86.

[41] *Ibid.*

[42] In describing this second movement, Low says that Herbert appeals to more than
one of the senses. The poet, he claims, employs a meditative technique by situating
his singer in the Palestinian landscape where he gathers flowers for his offering.
There is no conscious effort nor strain such as that which characterise a "Holy
Sonnet" or a formal Ignatian exercise. Instead, it is done with ease, allowing the
meditation to blend with harmony. The result is a small but perfect specimen of the
meditative hymn. *Ibid.* pp. 86-87.

anoint Christ's body in the tomb, only to find that he had risen from the dead. Richard Strier notes that in this same stanza one can see that the shift in pronoun emphasis—from I, to thou and thy—is significant because it puts the focus on Christ, his Resurrection, his independent nature.[43]

The fifth stanza contrasts the rising of the Sun with the Resurrection. The difference is immense: the Resurrection is unlike the rising of the sun and everything else in nature. Herbert expresses it thus:

> The Sunne arising in the East,
> Though he give light, & th'East perfume;
> If they should offer to contest
> With thy arising, they presume.
> (lines 23-26)

The Sun and the East mentioned in the first line of this stanza are united in the "they" of the third and fourth lines. The rising of the sun in the East ushers in the day; but the Resurrection, which brings about the first and last everlasting Day, is far superior to the sun's day. It would be presumptuous of them to think that they could outshine the Resurrection. The sixth and final stanza clarifies this point by asking:

> Can there be any day but this,
> Though many sunnes to shine endeavour?
> (lines 27-28)

The answer is, of course, *No*: "There is but one, and that one ever" (line 30). Our futile efforts and calculations are again referred to: "We count three hundred, but we misse:" (line 29). Herbert's "I" and "they" become joined in "we". He, like many sons (suns), endeavours to shine, only to realise that human attempts are finite and fallible.[44] Our notion of time, punctuated by sunrise, is not able to make us comprehend the essential magnificence of the Resurrection and the Infinite, Infallible One.

The chords of Herbert's hymn have, as it were, struck a chord as it dawns on him that "There is but one, and that one ever" (line 30). That one everlasting day is the Resurrection. Richard Strier maintains that "this ending is one of the most astounding moments in Herbert. A vista opens up in relation to which all our 'countings' like all our acts of 'natural piety' (getting flowers) fail, but we are here left contemplating the vista itself rather

---

[43] Cf. Richard Strier, *Love Known: Theology and Experience in George Herbert's Poetry* (Chicago & London: University of Chicago Press, 1983), p.59.

[44] Along the same lines he bemoans in his poem "Miserie" (lines 31-36) the fact that imperfect humans are not capable of praising the perfect God.

than our failures in relation to it."[45]

In this poem then, which consists of two movements, Herbert unites himself with God. The first stanza is devoted to the heart, the second to the lute. In the third, the heart and the lute unite with the Holy Spirit. Having completed the first movement with an expectation of a song on our part, Herbert introduces the second movement. This movement is also composed of three stanzas— "since all musick is but three parts vied/ And multiplied;" (lines 15-16). With God's help the song is complete. Herbert contemplates the Resurrection in stanza 4. In stanza 5 he considers how the Sun and the East cannot rival the glory of the Resurrection. Finally, he proclaims the mystery of the Resurrection.

Death, Sin and Christian Hope

So far we have been listening, as it were, to the poets, who despite their fears and anxieties continue to express their Christian hope.[46] The significance of their work for theological reflection is well brought out by David Jasper: "The poet speaks in metaphor. and analogy; theology itself cannot abandon the language of similitude and speak of the mystery of God in the language of science and analysis, for God is no analysable system. The poet is always there to remind theology of this, and of the reticence, obliquity and indirection of its Truth"[47] On the other hand, there is a sense in which poetry needs theology for "theology meanwhile works upon the language of religious faith, straining in its careful way beyond poetic analogy and poetic inspiration .... Poetry itself then finds in doctrine and the language of belief a precise means by which to apprehend the human mystery."[48]

Donne's and Herbert's poems reflect Christian theological tradition which regards death as the consequence of original sin affecting all people and leading to their fall from the gift of immortality. Death in Christian terms is punishment for sin. "Death spread to all men because all men sinned." (Rom 5:12). Edward Schillebeeckx describes death as "a sentence of doom that man because of his sinfulness called down upon himself and

---

[45] Richard Strier, *Love Known; Theology and Experience in George Herbert's Poetry*, p. 60.
[46] For a more philosophical treatment of the topic, cf. Emannuel Levinas, trans. Bettina Bergo, ed. and annotated by Jacques Rolland, *God, Death, and Time* (Stanford University Press, 2000).
[47] David Jasper, *The Study of Literature and Religion: an Introduction*. Studies in Literature and Religion (London: Macmillan, 1989). p. 35.
[48] *Ibid*. pp. 35-36.

all mankind."[49] Since it was sin that brought about death, we have a genuine reason to be afraid of dying. For death may unveil our lives to have been lived in falsehood, thus sealing us off in a monument of folly.

But there is another side to the reality of death and sin, one that is not clearly brought out in the Christian interpretation presented above but of particular relevance to our quest for deliverance. In many places one cannot but speak of a situation of death caused by what has been referred to as "sinful structures". Certain structures or policies have directly or indirectly contributed to the utter wretchedness of life so much so that people get no chance at all to participate in what life has to offer. Sometimes even the opportunity to hope is taken away from them. It is not surprising then that we hear of individuals, governments or societies being given the label of "perpetrators of death". In an ironic twist the explanation of death as the consequence of sin is certainly true since it is *their* sinful actions which result in the horrible and unnecessary deaths of many.

But, as we have noted in the poems by Vaughan, Donne and Herbert, Christians also believe that the tragic aspect of death is not everything about it because Christ's death has conquered sin. Indeed Christian theology clearly affirms that by overcoming sin, Christ has won over death which is the result of sin. What Christ has achieved was victory, not in the sense that humans will no longer die, i.e., not that we will no longer undergo physical death, but in the sense that our death has taken on a new meaning. The punishment attached to death because of sin becomes meritorious penance. Schillebeeckx explains: "So by the fact that Christ as a holy man who is God entered lovingly into it, death has obtained a redemptive worth. Death remains a punishment for and a consequence of sin as a result of which Christ died; but the punishment now becomes reparation, satisfaction and meritorious penance. The punishment is now a constructive, salutary punishment; it receives something that of its own self it could not possess and has got only through God's merciful intervention— a positive saving worth."[50] Thus, Christ's death has given us hope.

In the same tone Karl Rahner writes: "What was the manifestation of sin becomes, without its darkness lifted, the manifestation of an assent to the will of the Father which is the negation of sin. By Christ's death his spiritual reality which he possessed from the beginning and actuated in a

---

[49] E. Schillebeeckx, "The Death of a Christian," *Vatican II: The Struggle of Minds and Other Reflections* (Dublin: Gill and Son, 1963), p.68. In this chapter we explore the Christian meaning of death. For a discussion on how death is viewed by different religious traditions, see John Bowker, *The Meanings of Death* (Cambridge University Press, 1991).

[50] *Ibid.* p. 74.

life which was brought to consummation by his death becomes open to the whole world and is inserted into this whole world in its ground as a permanent determination of a real ontological kind."[51] In other words, Christ's death has radically altered our own. His acceptance of death has turned a natural phenomenon into a significant one. It has enabled the Christian to reject the claim made by people like Sartre that our death is the absurd last chapter of our absurd book of life. Christ's death gives meaning to our own in that our own deaths could be the culmination of our daily attempts to turn to God. Instead of being merely the end of our existence, it could be the very occasion of our meeting with God. Death, Christ has shown us, could be looked upon as our final encounter with God.

Christians regard Christ as the fulfillment of all the Father's promises to us. Salvation history sees in him the fullness of God's actions on God's people. All along it was Christ who had been foretold by the prophets of old as the Messiah, the One who would bring redemption to his people. He accomplished this through his death: by his death and subsequent resurrection we are saved. As St. Paul puts it: "But God shows his love for us in that while we were yet sinners Christ died for us. Since, therefore, we are now justified by his blood much more shall we be saved by him from the wrath of God" (Rom. 5:8-9). Paul saw the death and resurrection of Jesus as the work which freed us from slavery to sin and death and raised us to new life in the Spirit.

Thus, according to Christian thinking, Christ's death removes the meaninglessness of our deaths and of our lives. But in what sense is it liberating? Vaughan, Donne and Herbert have shared with us their interpretations. We have also looked at a theological answer. These have shown us that Christ's death gives us a purpose, a goal to work for. Those of us who have had the experience of grappling with the senselessness-of-it-all, of searching for answers to the existential questionings which inevitably are raised by thinking animals and of discovering some of those answers will know how liberating that last step is. It is more than a passing relief. There is nothing more pitiful than a serious questioner for whom an answer is fundamentally necessary but who is left with a question mark. He or she is like a clock which continues to tick but has lost its hands, or a person who extends a hand in anticipation of a handshake which never comes. To Christians, these situations do not arise because of Jesus' death. We are not, of . course, claiming that it is only the Christian who finds meaning in life or in death. Rather the death and resurrection of Christ provide mean-

---

[51] Karl Rahner, "Death," *Sacramentum Mundi,* p. 61

ing to the Christian, and this is liberating.[52] It is their form of deliverance.

Within the Christian context, the decisions one makes in life can participate in Christ's redemptive act because life has been thoroughly transformed by his death on the cross. Furthermore, it· is an invitation to us to also participate in the process of liberating others from a meaningless existence and death-causing situations. To the Christian, the world as a whole and as the scene of personal human actions has become different from what it would have been had Christ not died.[53] Genuine possibilities have been opened up for the personal action of humans, individually and collectively, which would not have existed without that most eventful death. Although that death happened at a given time in the past, it continues to save us at all times so long as the possibilities he has bestowed on us are genuinely appropriated by us. Christ's act is continually being made present so that it happens, not literally or factually but nonetheless truly, over and over again in the experiences of people throughout history.[54] We are saved by our actualising within us those possibilities provided to us by Christ when he died on the cross.

Thus, the Christian, despite experiencing the uneasiness of knowing that he or she must die or that loved ones will die, believes that dying is not really "a sailing into unknown horizons". Moreover, the Christian realises that dying may after all be the final affirmation of a life in which one has responded affirmatively to the many invitations Christ has offered us so as to save ourselves and others.

---

[52] Christian theological thinking on the significance of the death and resurrection of Jesus Christ is much more profound than what we can discuss here. Our focus in this chapter is dictated by the approach we have adopted in this work.

[53] Cf. "Religion as Context" in Chapter One.

[54] Donal Dorr, "Death," *The Furrow* (March, 1968), p. 146.

CHAPTER EIGHT

"YOU STILL SHALL LIVE"—FOREVERMORE?: THE QUEST FOR IMMORTALITY

The Mortality of Life

The sense of life's painful and poignant facets comes to and moves individuals in different ways. For Shakespeare this sense finds its expression in his obsession with time, death and mortality, which can be seen primarily in the sonnets addressed to the young man but also in the Dark Lady sonnets. It troubled him greatly that beauty is prey to and subject to temporality and mortality. In the sonnet sequence he explores the savage, destructive nature of Time, together with the sadness and pain caused by death. Temporal and mortal existence is profoundly upsetting since it is mutable. As Shakespeare himself expresses it in Sonnet 64: "Ruin hath taught me thus to ruminate,/That Time will come and take my love away."(lines 11-12). For Shakespeare the fear of losing a loved one is so painfully poignant that he says: "This thought is as a death, which cannot choose/But weep to have that which it fears to lose."(lines 13-14). With such an awareness of human mortality it is little wonder then that his poetry deals with different ways of overcoming the power of Time and Death In this enquiry we shall focus on three ways of so doing as explored by Shakespeare in his sonnets. These are: (1) by breeding or physical reproduction, (2) through the immortalising power of his poetry and (3) through the power of the soul to attain eternal life. We will then pursue the quest for immortality by turning to Charles Hartshorne's philosophy to see what we can learn from it.

Immortality through Reproduction

In the first seventeen sonnets Shakespeare advises the young man to immortalise his beauty by reproducing himself in a child. Sonnet 1 begins with these lines: "From fairest creatures we desire increase,/That thereby beauty's rose might never die,"(lines 1-2). This thought sets the keynote for the first group of sonnets although, as Joseph Pequigney points out, one appreciates this more fully only later on. He observes that "Shakespeare's Sonnets hardly look promising as a holistic work when Sonnet 1 is perused. It lacks the introductory features regularly found at the outset of other Renaissance love-sonnet cycles—Astrophel and Stella, for instance, or Amoretti."[1] The first sonnet does not contain the usual references to love, a lady, the muse or the poet, nor does it state an overall intent.

On the other hand, the sonnet bears some resemblance to those of the Petrarchan poets. It has the lavish praise of personal beauty although readers may be surprised that it is masculine beauty which is so extolled in contrast to the "red and white" paragons of female virtue and beauty normally praised. In line 5 there is some mention of "bright eyes", which normally exert tremendous power in sonnet sequences. The praise and blame usually found in sonnet sequences and attributed to the female for refusing sexual relations surfaces in Shakespeare, too. But here it is the male who is not being virtuous by refusing to have sexual relations and so produce a child—clearly he is at fault since it is his duty to procreate.

A little further on in the sonnet sequence, Shakespeare writes: "Look in Thy glass and tell the face thou viewest/Now is the time that face should form another," (Sonnet 3, lines 1-2). The young man is again reminded of his duty: he must not be selfish and refuse to procreate. His beauty must not die with him. If he has a child, he will pass on his traits to that child thereby living on in the child and in his children's children: "This were to be new made when thou art old,/And see thy blood warm when thou feel'st it cold."(Sonnet 2, lines 13-14).

This form of immortality will be a source of consolation to him in his old age. Shakespeare is keenly aware of the power of Time, which will destroy the young man's beauty:

> When forty winters shall besiege thy brow,
> And dig deep trenches in thy beauty's field,
> Thy youth's proud livery, so gazed on now,
> Will be a tottered weed of small worth held.
>   (Sonnet 2, lines 1-4).

David Kaula notes that the grammatical arrangement which the procreation group of sonnets uses is complex. The friend's present perfection "so gazed on now" (Sonnet 2, line 3) is sharply offset by the certainty of

---

[1] Joseph Pequigney, *Such is My Love: A Study of Shakespeare's Sonnets* (The University of Chicago Press, 1985), p. 7.

its eventual destruction "When forty winters shall besiege thy brow" (line 1). To counterbalance these two indicative tenses the poet introduces the subjunctive "should" of desire or duty and the conditional future expressed through the "if" construction: "If thou couldst answer... "(line 10).[2] Throughout the sonnets Shakespeare makes frequent allusions to Time. Presenting it in various allegorical disguises—a thief, a tyrant, a ravaging giant—he always shows its relentless, merciless, destructive side. His wish is to overcome Time and with it Mortality and Death. Hence, he advises the young man of the urgent need to procreate. If, on the other hand, the young man turns down this advice, he runs the risk of being forgotten: "But if thou live remembered not to be,/Die single and thine image dies with thee."(Sonnet 3, lines 13-14) But since Shakespeare does not believe his friend will want to be forgotten at death, Shakespeare continues to admonish him to have children. By so doing, his friend will cheat death:

> Then what could death do if thou shouldst depart,
> Leaving thee living in posterity?
> Be not self-willed, for thou art much too fair,
> To be death's conquest and make worms thine heir.
> (Sonnet 6, lines 11-14)

In Sonnet 11 Shakespeare further exhorts his friend to have children, arguing that if all of us decided not to beget children, the world would quickly end: "If all were minded so, the times should cease,/And three-score year would make the world away."(lines 7-8) In Hubler's view, "Nothing is more basic to Shakespeare's thought than the conviction that a man has an obligation to nature, that he is the steward and not the owner of the qualities."[3] The young man ought to play his part in perpetuating his qualities and in fighting against Time. This powerful arch-enemy must be vanquished. In Sonnet 12 Shakespeare tells his friend bluntly: "And nothing 'gainst Time's scythe can make defence,/Save breed, to brave him when he takes thee hence." (lines 13-14) Time's cruel scythe mows us down, and unless we have an offspring to replace us and keep us living, Time is the victor.

At this point in the sonnet sequence Shakespeare's fight with Time has reached war-like proportions; he intends to prevent Time from annihilating his friend: "And, all in war with Time for love of you,/As he takes

---

[2] David Kaula, "'In War with Time': Temporal Perspectives in Shakespeare's Sonnets," *Studies in English Literature,* 3 (1963), p. 49.
[3] Edward Hubler, *The Sense of Shakespeare's Sonnets* (Westport, Conn.: Greenwood Press, 1976), p. 69

from you, I engraft you new."(Sonnet 15, lines 13-14). Shakespeare will do his part to immortalise the beauty and memory of his friend: he will "engraft" him new. He is undertaking a task similar to that performed by Spenser:

> My verse your vertues rare shall eternize,
> And in the hevens wryte your glorious name.
> Where when as death shall all the world subdew,
> Our love shall live, and later life renew.
> *(Amoretti*, Sonnet 75, lines 11-14)

Both Spenser and Shakespeare have a sense of their power as poets.

There is a significant change in the sonnets because it proposes a new possibility for defeating Time. The full significance of de-emphasising biological engenderment as a means of cheating time, and death will be seen in the rest of the sonnet sequence as the power of his poetry to immortalise grows in strength. Although Shakespeare is proposing a second means of defying Time, he does so tentatively at first and without undermining the advice already given to his friend. This can be clearly seen in Sonnet 16 where he reiterates his initial position:

> But wherefore do not you a mightier way
> Make war upon this bloody tyrant Time?
> And fortify yourself in your decay
> With means more blessed than my barren rhyme?
> (lines 1-4)

and again in Sonnet 17: "But were some child of yours alive that time,/You should live twice, in it and in my rhyme." (lines 13-14).

Immortalising Power of Poetry

Sonnet 17 marks the end of the first group of sonnets addressed to the young man. Pequigney claims that in Sonnet 17 propagation and poetry together will ensure the perpetuation of the friend's beauty.[4] This union of the two means of conferring immortality on his friend neatly takes us into Shakespeare's true forte—the power of his poetry pitted against the power of Time. In Sonnet 18 he immediately sets a new tone in the third quatrain with the confident use of the emphatic "shall":

---

[4] Joseph Pequigney, *Such is My Love: A Study of Shakespeare's Sonnets* (The University of Chicago Press, 1985), p. 25.

> But thy eternal summer shall not fade,
> Nor lose possession of that fair thou ow'st
> Nor shall Death brag thou wand'rest in his shade,
> When in eternal lines to time thou grow'st.
> So long as men can breathe or eyes can see,
> So long lives this, and this gives life to thee.
>
> (lines 9-14)

Through the immortalising sonnets, Kaula says, "the pattern is essentially twofold: on the one hand, the comprehensive activity of time encompassing past, present and future indistinguishably; on the other, the permanent testimony of the poet's verse, usually expressed as an indicative certainty."[5] Shakespeare will bestow on his friend new and continued life through his poetry. This life will last as long as humankind lasts—to the end of time. This means is more powerful than the possibility of continuity offered by procreation, firstly, because through procreation only an "image" of the person is passed on to the child. Besides, that child would also have some characteristics of its mother. Shakespeare was not at all concerned with the woman who would bear the child of the beloved. His wife would be a mere requirement for keeping his own beauty alive. Secondly, the line could be broken by the son's failure to have a child. At any rate, the traits inherited would be changed by then. In contrast to the first flawed means of achieving immortality, Shakespeare offers then the promise of a more reliable kind of perpetuity to his friend to the end of life on this earth.

Shakespeare has grown in confidence; he no longer regards his rhyme as "barren" and is even willing to challenge Time in Sonnet 19: "Yet do thy worst, old Time; despite thy wrong,/My love shall in my verse ever live young."(lines 13-14). Shakespeare can more than match the power of Time. The theme of poetry overpowering Time re-surfaces very powerfully in Sonnet 55: "Not marble, nor the gilded monuments of princes, shall outlive this pow'rful rhyme," (lines 1-2). Shakespeare's poetry is mighty and can confer immortality on his friend. The art and energy of his poetry enables the poet to make his friend "shine" through all ages. Cleverly taking the artificial inanimate memorials of princes, he shows how "sluttish Time" will erode and destroy them. Unlike his poetry they do not and cannot stand up to Time. As a consequence, his poetry is much more desirable as a means of achieving immortality than the customary marble monument.

---

[5] David Kaula. "'In War with Time': Temporal Perspectives in Shakespeare's Sonnets," *Studies in English Literature*, 3 (1963), p. 49.

According to Booth, Sonnet 55 echoes two famous classical passages.[6] Their influence on Shakespeare is apparent, but the tone of Shakespeare's poem is quite different. The first classical passage is Ovid's *Metamorphoses*, XV (translated by Arthur Golding):

> Now have I brought a woork too end which neither Joves feerce wrath,
> Nor swoord, nor fyre, nor freating age with all the force it hath
> Are able too abolish quyght. Let comme that fatall howre
> Which (saving of this brittle flesh) hath over mee no powre,
> And at his pleasure make an end of myne uncertyne tyme.
> Yit shall the better part of mee asuured bee too clyme
> Aloft above the starry skye. And all the world shall never
> Be able for too quench my name. For looke how farre so ever
> The Romane Empyre by the ryght of conquest shall extend,
> So farre shall all folke reade this woork. And tyme without all end
> (If Poets as by prophesie about the truth may ame)
> My lyfe shall everlastingly bee lengthened still by fame.
>   (lines 871-879)

The second is Horace, Odes III, xxx, (Loeb translation): "I have finished a monument more lasting than bronze and loftier than the Pyramid's
royal pile, one that no wasting rain, no furious north wind can destroy, or
the countless chain of years and the ages' flight. I shall not altogether die,
but a mighty part of me shall escape the deathgoddess. On and on shall I
grow, ever fresh with glory of aftertime." (lines 1-8)

It can be seen from comparing these two passages with sonnet 55 that
Shakespeare is no mere slavish imitator. The reference to "Jove's fierce
wrath" in Ovid is discarded and replaced by the image of Mars, the god of
war. This image gives a concrete example of the destruction to which
tombs are subject. The battered, wasted, toppled, and corroded monuments
cannot equal the "living record" of Shakespeare's sonnet. Ovid has a reference to the "Romane Empyre" which Shakespeare assimilates and en-
dows with his poetic skill. Lever points out that in Shakespeare's sonnet
the "conquest of Time is also a conquest of space; and the Friend's praise
will still 'find room'—and Rome, which is all the world—until the last
judgement of the quick and dead, when he himself shall rise."[7] Time may
wear everything else away until the day of judgement but the poem will
not be affected.

---

[6] Stephen Booth. *A Reflection on Shakespeare's Sonnets* (New Haven and London:
Yale University Press, 1969), pp. 227-228.
[7] J. Lever, *The Elizabethan Love Sonnet* (London: Menthuen & Co. Ltd., 1978), p.
271.

The most important difference between Shakespeare's sonnet and the classical passages is that Shakespeare places the emphasis on his friend's fame and immortality:

'Gainst death and all oblivious enmity
Shall you pace forth; your praise shall still find room
Even in the eyes of all posterity
That wear this world out to the ending doom.
(lines 9-12)

whereas the classical poets are more self-centred. Shakespeare is not concerned with his own posthumous fame but with immortalising his friend. In developing this very point, Philip Martin says that "the Romans say 'Because of my poem I will never die' whereas Shakespeare says 'Because of my poem you will never die'"[8]

Shakespeare is aware of Christian belief in the after-life. In this way his friend will achieve immortality. Nonetheless, he affirms the role of his poetry in immortalising his friend: "So, till the judgement that yourself arise/You live in this, and dwell in lover's eyes."(lines 13-14). It seems that Sonnet 55 is the climax of his eternalising sonnets and shows Shakespeare's ability to write a "monumental" poem. Stronger in poetic terms than mere inanimate monuments, it must "outlive" and not just "outlast" other monuments. It outlives these by being the "living record" of his friend. Hubler believes "that this work is a deservedly famous poem but that it ends in a couplet of diminished force."[9] While Hubler's assessment of the poem is right, one can question his judgement on the couplet because of Shakespeare's statement of Christian after-life mentioned here and developed more fully in Sonnet 146, to be discussed later. Although Sonnet 55 is indeed the strongest expression of the power of Shakespeare's poetry to keep alive the memory of his friend, we do not reach the end of this theme in the sonnet sequence. We see it again in Sonnet 60, where the main body of the poem deals in detail with the destructive nature of Time, while the couplet drives home his defiance of Time and confirms the power of his poetry.

One might think that the concentration on the theme of the power of Time and of ways to overcome it might have become tedious by the time we have reached Sonnet 60. But this is not the case. The imagery of this

[8] Philip Martin, *Shakespeare's Sonnets: Self, Love and Art* (Cambridge University Press, 1972), p. 157.
[9] Edward Hubler, *The Sense of Shakespeare's Sonnets* (Westport, Conn.: Greenwood Press, 1976), p. 26.

sonnet concretises the power and destructive nature of Time and testifies to Shakespeare's facility with language to explore a theme fully without becoming boring. The first quatrain of Sonnet 60 opens with an explicit matter-of-fact statement that life goes on just like the waves which move towards the shore. Booth [10] maintains that these lines of Sonnet 60 recall Ovid's *Metamorphoses,* XV, lines 181-184 (translated by Golding) (552):

> For neyther brooke nor lyghtsomme tyme can tarrye still. But looke
> As every wave dryves other forth, and that that comes behynd
> Bothe thrusteth and is thrust itself: Even so the tymes be kynd
> Doo fly and follow bothe at once, and evermore renew.

Again the influence of Ovid is marked, but Shakespeare makes it his own as he uses the waves to convey the struggle of life within the power of Time. The words "toil" and "contend" bring out the idea of "struggling" which appears in the poem as a whole. The simile of waves and minutes effectively conveys the speed with which Time passes. A sense of loss exudes from these lines as one realises the transience of life.

The second quatrain opens with the abstract noun "nativity". The quatrain shows Shakespeare's ability to enrich his images:

> Nativity, once in the main of light,
> Crawls to maturity, wherewith being crowned,
> Crooked eclipses 'gainst his glory fight,
> And Time that gave doth now his gift confound.
> (Sonnet 60, lines 5-8)

The word "nativity" suggests the birth of an infant, who crawls to maturity. This first image gives way to a second, that of the sun (suggested by the "main of light"). "Main" is normally associated with the sea, thus linking the second quatrain with the waves of the first quatrain. The "main of light" suggests the brilliant daylight of noon when the sun has reached its zenith. The sun and the infant both "crawl to maturity". When they reach their highest point, they are "crowned"—here another image is being introduced. But all is not bright: "crooked eclipses" appear to overshadow one's glory. These crooked eclipses can signify the malignant forces which influence a man's life and fight against his glory. Since these forces were thought to have been decided on at the moment of birth, they bring us back to "nativity". The quatrain concludes with a description of Time as

---

[10] Stephen Booth, *A Reflection on Shakespeare's Sonnets* (New Haven and London: Yale University Press, 1969), pp. 227-228.

it "confounds" his gift. Time overthrows, confuses, destroys, demolishes and defeats us.

The final quatrain graphically etches the destructive power of Time:

> Time doth transfix the flourish set on youth,
> And delves the parallels in beauty's brow,
> Feeds on the rarities of nature's truth,
> And nothing stands but for his scythe to mow
> (Sonnet 60, lines 9-12)

Time really is the mean and hated destroyer of the bloom of youth—leaving people wrinkled and furrowed. It is like a wild animal devouring all in its path. Finally, Shakespeare provides us with the Father-Time image mowing everything with his scythe. Against such power Shakespeare places his couplet and the power of his poetry to withstand the forces of Time and confer immortality on his friend: "And yet to times in hope my verse shall stand,/Praising thy worth, despite his cruel hand." (lines 13-14)

Having built Time into such an immense force he empowers his poetry with an even greater might to outmanoeuvre the arch-enemy Time. His poetry will testify in future time to his friend's worth. Shakespeare's couplet quoted above succeeds in capturing his confidence in his poetry. Booth's interpretation of "in hope" to mean "time still to come" makes explicit Shakespeare's intention that his verse will last.[11] In Sonnet 65 Shakespeare's poetry is again presented as the might to be pitted against Time: "0, none, unless this miracle have might/ That in black ink my love may still shine bright." (lines 13-14). There is a contrast here comparable to the following lines in Sonnet 55: "But you shall shine more bright in these contents/ Than unswept stone, besmeared with sluttish time" (lines 3-4). In Sonnet 65 Shakespeare claims that his love will shine bright in black ink because of the miraculous power of his poetry.

In Sonnet 81 Shakespeare again confirms that he is not pre-occupied with his own posthumous fame. Instead he gives life to his friend through his poetry, thus enabling the friend to live on long after Shakespeare himself has been forgotten:

> Or I shall live your epitaph to make,
> Or you survive when I in earth am rotten.
> From hence your memory death cannot take,
> Although in me each part will be forgotten
> (lines 1-4)

---

[11] *Ibid.* p. 241.

These lines highlight again the difference between Shakespeare and
the Roman poets as do the following lines: "You still shall live—such virtue hath my pen—/Where breath most breathes, even in the mouths of
men" (lines 13-14). Shakespeare's poetry is a life-giving force reminiscent
of the Holy Spirit breathing life into his creatures.

In Sonnet 100 Time as the wielder of the deadly scythe appears again
and predictably at this stage poetry opposes him. Time quickly wastes life,
but Shakespeare's poetry is even swifter in renewing and prolonging life
than Time is in destroying it: "Give my love fame faster than Time wastes
life,/So thou prevent'st his scythe and crooked knife."(lines 13-14). He
also notes in the next sonnet (101) that it lies within his power as a poet:
"To make him much outlive a gilded tomb,/And to be praised of ages yet
to be." (lines 11-12). Sonnet 107 recalls Sonnet 55, reminding us of the
useless monument preferred by tyrants: "And thou in this shalt find thy
monument,/When tyrants' crests and tombs of brass are spent." (lines
13-14) in contrast to the guaranteed memorial of the friend to the end of
time. From this sonnet as well as from Sonnet 55 it is clear that Shakespeare's poetry will ensure the "life" of his friend until judgement day. He
will be remembered in all ages to the end of time.

Postmortem Immortality

There is another consideration that has been introduced here—the afterlife. On judgement day Shakespeare's friend will assume his own immortality—independently of his children and even of Shakespeare's poetry. This reference to an afterlife emphasises the importance to Shakespeare of defying the stranglehold of Time and Death. In challenging the
power of Death, Shakespeare would share Donne's sentiments[12] expressed
in these lines:

> Death be not proud, though some have called thee
> Mighty and dreadful, for thou art not so;
> For those whom thou think'st thou dost overthrow
> Die not, poor death, nor yet canst thou kill me.
>   (lines 1-4)

Life cannot end with the grave or judgement day as indicated in the
couplet of Sonnet 55. It is worth noting that Shakespeare clarifies his position on this in Sonnet 146. In addressing his soul, Shakespeare acknowledges that it will live on after the body's death. In Donne's words: "One

---

[12] *Holy Sonnets*, 6 (X). Cf. Chapter Seven

short sleep past, we wake eternally, And death shall be no more; death, thou shalt die."[13] Shakespeare urges us, therefore, to take more care of the soul than of the body. The body is likened to a fading mansion, with a short lease; hence, there is no point in taking pains to pamper the body. We should concentrate on the soul instead:

> Then, soul, live thou upon thy servant's loss,
> And let that pine to aggravate thy store;
> Buy terms divine in selling hours of dross;
> Within be fed, without be rich no more:
> (lines 9-12)

This is, of course, a religious view of immortality and the way to defeat death: "So shall thou feed on Death, that feeds on men,/And Death once dead, there's no more dying then." (lines 13-14) With this sonnet Shakespeare completes his exploration of the third way of achieving immortality and overcoming Death and Time as depicted in the sonnet sequence.

Some Comments

Of the three methods referred to by Shakespeare: (1) breeding—physical reproduction of oneself in children; (2) the immortalising power of his poetry; and (3) the power of the soul to attain eternal life, he is most successful in the forceful and thorough presentation of the power of his poetry to immortalise. The numerous references to the strength of his poetry and its ability to perpetuate the memory of his friend coupled with the powerful and varied images justify this conclusion. This theme is introduced quite early in the sequence and, even if the order of the sonnets as we know them is not the one intended by Shakespeare, the sheer frequency of its occurrence makes it a major theme. The grammatical arrangement used to present the power of his poetry as a strategy for defeating Time (which is quite different from that used in the "procreation group") gives this group of sonnets an intrinsic unity. As outlined earlier, David Kaula notes that the grammatical arrangement in the immortalising sonnets is "simple and decisive". He continues: "The pose of defiance appears to best advantage in Sonnet 55 ('Not marble, nor the gilded monuments') where after the three quatrains present a succession of six verbs preceded by the emphatic "shall", the tense is modulated in the couplet into a continuous present extending to the farthest limit of time: "So, till the judgement that

---

[13] *Ibid.* lines 13-14.

yourself arise,/You live in this, and dwell in lover's eyes." [14] The palpable power of his poetry exudes from such lines and makes this strategy the most successful of the three under discussion.

The first strategy is weaker for a number of reasons, some of which are mentioned by Shakespeare himself. First, it cannot reproduce the loved one fully as some of the traits of the child come from the spouse. Secondly, it does not guarantee perpetuity and is dependent on the loved one's child or children continuing the line by which time very little of the loved one's "beauty" is passed on. Thirdly, the grammatical construction used by Shakespeare makes it less convincing and attractive as a strategy than his poetry. As illustrated previously, Kaula observes that in the procreation sonnets the present beauty of the loved one is offset by the emphatic form of the future tense (confirming that the beauty shall be destroyed) and is often followed by "should" (he should preserve it) and finally by the conditional future expressed through "if": if and only if the loved one accepts Shakespeare's advice and has a child can Time's power be averted. This more involved grammatical structure seems to underline the difficulties and uncertainties of this strategy.

Since Shakespeare used the third strategy only at the end of Sonnet 55 and in Sonnet 146, it is not a well-developed one. He takes the theme up once more in his plays, for example in *Macbeth and Hamlet,* but in terms of its presentation in the sonnets it leaves one opting for the second strategy—the power of Shakespeare's poetry to win the war against Time. The fact that his poetry survived thus far and does not appear to be in imminent danger of disappearing is further testimony to Shakespeare's success.

It would be interesting to pursue these strategies further—and widen our enquiry—in the context of Charles Hartshorne's philosophy. Hartshorne has defended a version of immortality which he refers to as "objective immortality". It consists in "being remembered by God". Inasmuch as Hartshorne also refers to God as the eternal Poet, there are indeed shades of similarities between these two. However, unlike Shakespeare, Hartshorne has been critical of other philosophical interpretations of immortality, particularly the traditional concept of personal immortality. His own interpretation of immortality rests on certain metaphysical principles that have been questioned by others. These principles are: God as the recipient of values, the immortality of the past, and personhood understood as a series of events rather than a substantial self. He argues that these metaphysical principles, which maintain a non-dualistic psychicalist under-

---

[14] David Kaula. "'In War with Time': Temporal Perspectives in Shakespeare's Sonnets," *Studies in English Literature,* 3 (1963), p. 49.

standing of reality, have led him to reject the idea of post-mortem existence in favour of the doctrine of the retention of human existence in
God's memory.

Criticisms of Traditional Understandings of Immortality

In Hartshorne's view, one of the reasons for the doctrine of personal
immortality is the belief that final justification of the good can take place
only after death.[15] According to this belief, the good will ultimately be
rewarded while the evil ones will be punished. Thus, even if evil deeds
seem to reap rewards rather than punishments in life, it is held that this
imbalance will be rectified in the next world. Full justice will be meted
out, and the scales of justice will be tipped over in favour of the good and
the deserving.

Hartshorne takes issue with this interpretation; he disagrees with the
form of human immortality presented here and with the underlying understanding of God's goodness and justice. He firmly believes that this life is
our opportunity for doing good and for loving God and others. It is also
where due rewards and punishments take place. For Hartshorne the intrinsic value for good and disvalue of evil should motivate us, rather than the
fear of punishment or the hope of reward in the afterlife. He thinks that
this is a more appropriate understanding of God's love and justice. As he
puts it, "If love is not its own reward, then God is not love."[16] In the view
that he is criticising, God becomes simply the dispenser of awards and
demerits.

Yet Hartshorne's rejection of post-mortem rewards or punishments is
not a denial that the possible good or bad consequences of our actions will
outlast us. All he wishes to emphasise is that our reward is *now* while we
are performing the actions. Neither does Hartshorne deny the possibility of
a future reward, e.g. benefit to someone who survives us. But he points out
that what constitutes our reward in this case is this *present* aiming at something in the future. In one respect, the future good accruing to us will be
our reward; but it is one which we can enjoy only in anticipation as we
could be gone before it happens. In short, our participation in that good is
now rather than later. Thus, Hartshorne cannot accept the argument that
since many do not have a fair lot in this life, justice demands that they

---

[15] It should be pointed out that Shakespeare's acceptance of personal immortality is
not based on this ethical consideration.

[16] Hartshorne, *The Logic of Perfection and Other Reflections in Neoclassical Metaphysics* (La Salle: Open Court, 1962), p. 254.

should have another and better opportunity elsewhere. He adds that in any sphere there will be chance, hence good and bad luck due to creativity. The demand for justice, i.e. to each according to one's deserts, is not an ultimate axiom valid cosmically or metaphysically.

Hartshorne carries his criticisms further by attacking the doctrine of personal immortality itself, on which the belief in post-mortem rewards and punishment stands. According to him, his view on initial inspection may be seen as contrary to religious sentiment but upon closer examination the so-called rift may not now be as wide.[17] He has some harsh words for the doctrine of personal immortality, especially when it is closely linked with the notion of divine justice expressed as the apportioning of post-mortem rewards and punishments for human actions. He sees in it "substantial elements of irrationality, not in the sense of doctrines above reason but of doctrines below and contrary to it."[18] In an approving tone he quotes Berdyaev who refers to it as the "most disgusting mortality ever conceived".[19] Hartshorne looks on the doctrine of personal immortality as actually a rival to belief in God rather than a logical consequence of it since it seems to enshrine self-interest as ultimate.[20] The believer is led to expect an everlasting award in comparison with which nothing on earth would or could be as significant.

Hartshorne also finds fault with this doctrine because one cannot talk of an identical self reaping rewards or punishment. Here his criticism is based on his metaphysics. "Each momentary agent and sufferer," he says, "is numerically new, from which it follows that the I which now acts never can receive either reward or punishment, beyond the intrinsic reward or punishment of acting and experiencing as it does now. The account is immediately closed. Anything one demands for the future is demanded for

---

[17] Hartshorne, "Philosophy After Fifty Years," in P. Bertocci (ed.), *Mid-Twentieth Century American Philosophy: Personal Statements* (N.Y.: Humanities Press, 1974), p. 147.

[18] Hartshorne, "A Philosopher's Assessment of Christianity," in W. Leibrecht (ed.), *Religion and Culture: Essays in Honor of Paul Tillich* (N.Y.: Harper, 1959), p. 175.

[19] Hartshorne, "Religion and Creative Experience," *Unitarian Register and Universalist Leader,* 141 (1962), p. 11.

[20] Hartshorne, *Omnipotence and Other Theological Mistakes* (SUNY Press, 1984), pp. 97-99. For the ethical implication of this point, cf. his "Ethics and the Process of Living," in Jorge J.E. Gracia (ed.), *Man and His Conduct: Philosophical Reflections in Honor of Risieri Frondizi* (Rio Piedras, Puerto Rico: Editorial Universitaria, 1980), pp. 191-202; "Beyond Enlightened Self-Interest: a Metaphysics of Ethics" ch. 12 of his *The Zero Fallacy and Other Reflections in Neoclassical Philosophy* ed. Mohammad Valady (Open Court, 1997).

another, even though this other is termed 'one's self'".[21] Hartshorne adds that the concept of personal "substance" has been the backbone of the questionable theory of heaven and hell. Evidently, Hartshorne's counter-argument depends on the acceptability of his own interpretation of personal identity. To this point we shall return later.

Another form of immortality that Hartshorne considers is social immortality: ultimate value is preserved by posterity rather than by an individual who continues to exist after death. This is not unlike what Shakespeare has in mind with the first two strategies. But Hartshorne does not think that this form of immortality answers the quest for ultimacy either. Our acts will in a sense live on in future human beings (for example, in the readers of books which we may have written, the spectators of the buildings which we may have erected, or our children who will benefit from our efforts). These will furnish the actual or at least potential realisation of our future reality as individuals who have existed. But for Hartshorne this is an unsatisfactory solution to the quest for immortality. Since no one can know us fully while we live, more so will we be forgotten after our deaths. Many details about our lives are missed even by the closest of our contemporaries and not surprisingly by posterity. Generations are frequently almost wholly unconscious or unappreciative of the deeds of previous generations. The simple fact is that we, individually and collectively, forget. Our experiences seem to perish almost as fast as they occur because we fail to remember much about them. At any moment everything, except a tiny portion of our past life, is erased from our memories. If this is so now, future generations will hardly be better in this respect. Hartshorne asks, what will most of our lives mean to those who come after us, who will know little of these lives and care less?[22] Besides, there does not seem to be much evidence that humankind will continue forever. It is doubtful whether the human species is literally immortal even if species do last longer than individuals.[23] Over every generation hangs the apparently

---

[21] Hartshorne, "Religion in Process Philosophy," in J.C. Feaver and W. Horosz (eds.), *Religion in Philosophical and Cultural Perspective* (Princeton: D. van Dostrand, 1967), p. 264. See also: his "Toward a Buddhist-Christian Religion," in Kenneth K. Inada and Nolan P. Jacobson (eds.), *Buddhism and American Thinkers* (SUNY Press, 1984), pp. 1-13

[22] Hartshorne, *Reality as Social Process: Studies in Metaphysics and Religion* (Glencoe: The Free Press, and Boston: the Beacon Press, 1953), p.49.

[23] Hartshorne, "The God of Religion and the God of Philosophy," *Talk of God* (London: Macmillan, 1969), p.157. Hartshorne brings out the ethical implication of this point in his "The Ethics of Contributionism," in Ernest Partridge (ed.),

inevitable doom that theirs could be the last generation. When that happens, then the question of the ultimate value of our lives and deeds resur-
faces. Thus, even if one grants that our lives may leave their mark long
after we ourselves are gone, we nonetheless cannot suppose that humanity
would be capable of preserving for all time this monument of ours. To
suppose so is to ignore the known traits of humanity.

Hartshorne, therefore, sees the question of ultimacy or immortality as
pressing us toward the theistic solution.[24] After all, it is God, not humans,
who never dies. The fact of death reminds us that beings who are limited
in time cannot live forever. Deathless existence is God's prerogative.
Moreover, since God is the only knower whose knowledge is fully adequate and is thus able fully to grasp and evaluate the qualities, richness and
beauty of everything,[25] only God can be the final recipient of our
achievements and the ultimate beneficiary of our values. For this reason,
Hartshorne argues that values are permanent not as human but as divine
possessions.[26] Our achievements have eternal significance only if there is
an inclusive consciousness, such as God's, which enjoys and appreciates
their having occurred. God's continued existence and unsurpassable memory mean that God will cherish us no matter how long we may have been
dead. In acquiring us as we are on earth God acquires us forevermore. As
Hartshorne himself expresses it: "If we will have value in the memory of
friends and admirers who survive us, how much more can we have value
in the consciousness of God, who endures forever, and who alone can fully
appreciate all that we have been, felt or thought."[27] Hartshorne can therefore say that very literally we exist to enhance, and not just to admire and
enjoy, the divine glory. Ultimately, we are contributors to the ever-
growing divine treasury of values. Serving God means that our final and
inclusive end is to contribute to the divine life. Because of this, there is
something perpetual in each entity in that it will be preserved in God.[28] In

---

Responsibilities to Future Generations: Environmental Ethics (N.Y.: Promotheus
Books, 1981), pp. 103-107.

[24] Hartshorne, *A Natural Theology for our Time* (La Salle: Open Court, 1967), p.
57.

[25] Hartshorne, "A Metaphysics of Individualism," in G. Mills (ed.), *Innocence and
Power* (Austin: University of Texas Press, 1965), p. 145.

[26] Hartshorne, "Process Philosophy as a Resource for Christian Thought," in Le-
Frevre (ed.), *Philosophical Resources for Christian Thought* (Nashville: Abingdon, 1968), p. 48.

[27] Hartshorne, "The God of Religion and the God of Philosophy," p.156.

[28] Hartshorne, "The Dipolar Conception of God," *Review of Metaphysics* 21
(1967), p. 288.

Shakespearean language, God as the eternal Poet—rather than the poem itself—will preserve us forever.

God as Recipient of Values

To understand Hartshorne's theistic yet non-conventional version of ultimacy, it should be noted that for him reality contributes to God's actuality. God for Hartshorne is dipolar: God has an abstract aspect and a concrete aspect.[29] God's concreteness means that God is really related to us, affected by what we do and thus changed in actuality. Since the claim is made by Hartshorne that God's concreteness (which is relative) loves and genuinely becomes or acquires novel values, Hartshorne's God has relevance to human aspirations that an absolute and changeless deity cannot have. A God who cherishes us and is not once-and-for-all complete, but is ever enriched with new values can and will acquire values from the awareness of our experiences as these occur. There is no futility in our existence, Hartshorne consoles us, if indeed all human living as actually lived has passed into the imperishable reservoir of enjoyed experiences which is God's concrete actuality. Hartshorne's dipolar God is, as it were, "the cherisher of all achieved actualities". Hence, all of one's life can be a "reasonable, holy and living sacrifice to God".

The value of this "sacrifice" depends on the sort of life we have lived. We would be a poor gift to God if we lived a life that is characterised by a lack of generous openness to others or to the beauty of the world and the divine harmony pervading all seemingly insignificant things. How we conduct our lives will decide what God will remember of us. Hartshorne is quite graphic in his description: "One might say that we mold the picture that hangs in the living mansion. God will make as much out of the picture in beholding it as can be made, but how much can be made depends upon the picture and not merely upon the divine insight in seeing relations and meanings."[30] Thus, although the privilege of living everlastingly is not ours but God's, we can at least ensure that our lives have been well-lived within God's own life. In Hartshorne's philosophy then, the final significance of all we do is in the contribution our lives make to God, in whom all experiences once they have occurred, are perpetuated. Thus, it matters a great deal whether we have done well or not, or whether we have lived happy lives or not since in the final analysis it matters to God. Hartshorne

---

[29] Cf. Hartshorne, "Thoughts on the Development of My Concept of God," *The Personalist Forum*, XIV (1998), pp. 77-82.
[30] Hartshorne, *A Natural Theology for our Time*, p. 257.

adds that if we love God, then it matters to us now; we would care about what we do because of the impact we have on God.[31] According to Hartshorne then, our immortality is no other than *God's memory of us*.[32] Because God knows us adequately God can appreciate totally the worth of each moment of our lives. God, who does justice to all the beauty and value in the world, captures forever each passing moment. Because our memories are faint and selective we can never be in that position. Yet our forgotten experiences are not lost since they are additions to the experiences of God, the cosmically social and all-cherishing being, to whom all hearts—not only as they are but also as they have been—are open. Hartshorne describes the essential meaning of our immortality as "the everlasting transparency of our lives to the divine".[33]

A possible objection to Hartshorne's interpretation of our immortality is that it seems to enshrine God's memory of us rather than us. Hartshorne replies that this objection bares a secret egotism since it shows that what we have really wanted is to be the Immortal Person ourselves, or that we have regarded God, not as the end of ends, but as a means to our own ends, namely, the achievement of permanence. We wish, it would appear, to set ourselves up as immortal gods, rivalling God. As Hartshorne points out, "If we claim immortality for ourselves, then God is needed only as support for our self-fulfillment."[34] Hartshorne finds this blasphemous. On a more philosophical level, Hartshorne counters this objection to his position by arguing against the idea of an immortal "self" which is implied by this objection. In Hartshorne's metaphysics, as will be seen later, there is no substantial or underlying self, merely a series of experiences which comes to an end upon death but is retained in God's memory.

Because life is contributory, ultimately to God, Hartshorne admits that there is some truth in the doctrine of social immortality despite his reservations already noted earlier. It would be one-sided, he says, to contrast social immortality (the non-religious form of everlasting life) with theistic immortality (the kind he is espousing) for the two need not be regarded as incompatible. Instead, he redefines social immortality in theistic terms:

---

[31] Hartshorne, "Man's Fragmentariness," *Wesleyan Studies in Religion* 41 (1963-64), p. 23.
[32] This should be understood, not in the psychological, but in the metaphysical sense. It is really the retention of the past in present actuality.
[33] Hartshorne, "Religion in Process Philosophy," 1967, p. 265. Cf. also his, "God and the Meaning of Life," in Leroy S. Rouner (ed.), *On Nature*. Boston University Studies in Philosophy and and Religion, Vol. 6 (University of Notre Dame Press, 1984), pp. 154-168.
[34] Hartshorne, "Man's Fragmentariness," p.23.

God whose future is endless and who alone fully appropriates our ephemeral good is *the social being* who is neighbour to all of us. Social immortality, as Hartshorne sees it, is literal immortality in God as *the* neighbour. Since God alone is exempt from death and able to love all equally, God is the "definitive posterity".[35] If it is true that our abiding value is what we give to posterity, to the life that survives us, then the permanence of life's values cannot consist simply in what each of us does for our human posterity. In the long run, this must be God.

Supporters of Hartshorne's idea of a God who is sensitive to our needs and who treasures forever all our achievements have argued that such a God can be said to be truly sympathetic and personally related to us. But how adequate and consistent a conception of God is it in the context of Hartshorne's own interpretation of human immortality?[36] To clarify this question further and possibly answer it, let us first turn to another of the metaphysical principles which that interpretation makes use of.

Immortality of the Past

Hartshorne's interpretation of immortality is complemented by his doctrine of the immortality of the past which asserts that what once existed but now seems to have ceased to exist is not reduced to nothingness—this is a stronger claim than Shakespeare's personal conviction in the enduring power of his poetry. Hartshorne provides metaphysical support; namely, that, strictly speaking, something cannot become nothing. Once something has taken place, it cannot be undone; it continues to exist in another way. Hartshorne firmly holds that events do not cease to have status just because they are over. On the contrary, they become part of something else by becoming constituents of the events whose past they constitute. Nothing ceases to be once it has been actualised; instead, it becomes included in a new actuality. Pastness thus is not unreality since past events become part of the total reality.

---

[35] Hartshorne, "Beyond Enlightened Self-Interest: a Metaphysics of Ethics," in H. Cargas and B. Lee (eds.) *Religious Experience and Process Theology* (N.Y.: Paulist Press, 1976), p. 309.

[36] It should be noted that Hartshorne's concept of God is dipolar (which is different from the classical theistic idea of God). For a fuller discussion see S. Sia, *God in Process Thought: a Study in Charles Hartshorne's Concept of God* (Martinus Nijhoff, 1985). For critical responses, see S. Sia (ed.), *Charles Hartshorne's Concept of God: Theological and Philosophical Responses* (Kluwer Academic Press, 1989).

In Hartshorne's metaphysical system the past is regarded as inde-structible. Hartshorne holds that if the past were reduced to nothing at all, then propositions about it would be empty for they would have no refer-ents. The truth "about x" is impossible without x; if x had been obliterated, it would be meaningless to refer to it. As Hartshorne puts it: "Truth is a relational function; if a proposition about x is true, its truth consists in the relation between itself and x, if it is nothing at all, then so is the relation of which it is said to be a term."[37] Does Hartshorne then deny destruction? The answer here is a qualified one. Events or occurrences cannot be anni-hilated; things and individuals, however, can be. (Shakespeare's poetry may vanish; however, that he had written the poems never will.) But the annihilation of things and individuals consists not in the destruction or removal from reality of the events forming their histories up to the mo-ment of destruction but only in the prevention of additional events belong-ing to this history. That is, no more such events will be created. Hartshorne explains that people and trees and cities can be destroyed. But what this really means is that an event-sequence with a certain persistence of charac-ter and with peculiarly intimate relationships among the member-events may have a final member. Or to use one of Hartshorne's favourite meta-phors, that the book itself has existed is not destroyed just because the number of chapters has been limited due to the appearance of a last chap-ter. Neither is a life, properly seen as an event-sequence, turned into naught by virtue of the limited number of its experiences and behavioural occurrences.[38] In short, the past does not consist of unrealities or of noth-ing but of the very events which have happened.[39]

The past continues in existence by being preserved in the present. This is exemplified by human memory. For Hartshorne memory is one way that we know and retain the past.[40] But our memory is so feeble that the events that we remember are not fully preserved for us even if we do remember them. But the events we best remember are the ones most near-ly preserved as real. For instance, we can remember a certain wonderful moment so well that the beauty of it is almost fully embodied in the pre-sent by that memory.[41] For the past to be fully preserved, Hartshorne ar-

---

[37] Hartshorne, "The Logical Structure of Givenness," *Philosophical Quarterly,* 8 (1958), p. 310.
[38] Hartshorne, "Religion in Process Philosophy," p. 251.
[39] Hartshorne, "Duality versus Dualism and Monism," *Japanese Religions* 5 (1969), p. 59.
[40] Hartshorne, *Reality as Social Process*, p. 160
[41] This sentiment is well captured by Wordsworth in his poem "Daffodils", lines 19-24, *Wordsworth: Poetical Works* (Oxford University Press, 1969). He acknowl-

gues that there must be a perfect memory such as a divine memory. The past is contained in the present to the extent that it is retained absolutely in God. God's perfect knowledge means that all the past must still be before God without loss of any detail or quality. For this memory neither joy nor pain, once experienced anywhere in the world, can ever be wiped out.[42] Thus, Hartshorne finds support for the doctrine of the total indestructibility of the past in the supposition that there exists a divine memory. Since human memory, whether individual or collective, cannot contain all that has happened and since the past must be regarded as nevertheless real, Hartshorne turns to a memory which, by definition, meets the need to preserve all events. Experience shows that the past is deficiently continued in human memory, and yet the notion of truth seems to demand the persistence of past events in all their details about which there is truth. The only possible reconciliation of these two is to posit a memory that is able to perpetuate the past completely. According to Hartshorne, one senses the existence of such a memory—a memory which is perfectly conscious, clear, vivid and retentive—by contrasting it with one's own imperfect memory. Such a model memory would possess the whole quality of the past, all its joys and sorrows, contrast, harmony, and discord.[43]

Returning to the topic of human immortality, one can see that for Hartshorne the death of a human being then is not total annihilation—a consoling point for Shakespeare. While that human being's capability of acquiring more experiences has been curtailed, his or her past experiences continue to live on in God's memory. The true basis of that person's permanence is God's complete memory. In Hartshorne's view then, only an ideally perfect memory could constitute the adequate conservation of experience in full vividness and value. We can, in the profoundest sense, "live forever" if and only if we are cherished by an imperishable and wholly clear and distinct retrospective awareness which Hartshorne calls "the memory of God"[44].

---

edges how the daffodils cheered him up when he "wandered lonely as a cloud" but more importantly how his memory of this delightful sight will enable him to relive this pleasure again and again.

[42] Hartshorne, "The Divine Relativity and Absoluteness: a Reply to John Wild," *Review of Metaphysics* 4 (1950), p. 56.

[43] Hartshorne, "The Immortality of the Past: Critique of Prevalent Misinterpretations," *Review of Metaphysics*, 7 (1953), pp. 103-104.

[44] Hartshorne, "The Buddhist-Whiteheadian View of the Self and the Religious Traditions," *Proceedings of the 9th International Congress for the History of Religions* (Tokyo: Maruzen, 1960), p. 301.

What Hartshorne has to say on human immortality, therefore, implies that death is not the final end although it is "the fixing of the concluding page to one's book of life".[45] That there is death is not an indication that God does not love us despite the persistent feeling among many people that if God loves us God will not suffer us to be destroyed.[46] But, as far as Hartshorne is concerned, this cannot be true because death does not represent destruction but only the setting of a definitive limit. It is not the obliteration of what has existed. Thus, for him death does not militate against the belief in God's goodness.

While Hartshorne's arguments for the immortality of the past are persuasive, it is difficult nevertheless to understand how the past can be said to be retained in God's memory. John Wild, for instance, criticises Hartshorne for saying that the past is contained in the present through memory since this is really to destroy the distinction between the two. Noetic presence before the mind should not be confused with physical possession or inclusion. It is not really correct, Wild maintains, to assert that the past exists in the present because existence refers to physical presence. The kind of presence that is in question in the process of knowledge is noetic or mental. To have the past so present before the mind is not to give it physical presence or existence. Wild also points out that that which includes versus that which is included is evidently not the same as present versus past. Moreover, if pastness is simply being included as a part, then the present will also become past. He asks, "Where does the distinction between past and present lie then?"[47]

Another criticism of Hartshorne's claim that God immortalises all events by being included in God's memory is whether it is consistent in view of the fact that Hartshorne has changed his position regarding contemporary occasions. F.F. Fost first noted the problematic area into which this shift places Hartshorne. By relinquishing his earlier position concerning the mutual immanence of contemporary occasions and adopting the view that contemporaries are causally unrelated to one another, Hartshorne has undermined his doctrine that God literally includes all reality. Essentially, Frost's criticism is that part of the real world, that which is in unison

---

[45] Hartshorne, *The Logic of Perfection and Other Reflections in Neoclassical Metaphysics,* p. 253. Cf. also, Hartshorne, "The Acceptance of Death," in Forence M. Hetzler and Austin H. Kutscher (eds.), *Philosophical Aspects of Thanatology,* Vol.1 (N.Y.: MSS Information Corporation, 1978), pp. 83-81 and "A Philosophy of Death," *Ibid.* Vol. 2, pp. 81-89.

[46] See Chapter Seven.

[47] J. Wild, "A Review-Article: Hartshorne's *Divine Relativity,*" *Review of Metaphysics* 2 (1948), p. 71f.

of becoming with God, is not known by God. Hence, God cannot be said to be *all*-inclusive (and for that matter, all-knowing) since God can be said to know something only after it is past. In other words, the contemporariness of any event is outside God's knowledge.[48] Similarly, Jerry Clay Henson wonders whether Hartshorne can consistently claim that God's knowledge corresponds with reality and that all the objectives of divine knowledge are everlastingly preserved in the divine memory. Taking account of Hartshorne's view that to preserve past events is to preserve them as complete and past, Henson asks how that can be complete when the quality of presentness is lost. On the other hand, if entities are to be preserved in subjective immediacy, then they must continue as subject in process. This would in turn invalidate Hartshorne's notion of objective immortality. Henson's criticism is worth quoting here at some length:

> It is not at all clear how God might 'perfectly preserve' a person if God does not preserve that which makes the person who he is, namely, the integrating force which gives identity to the millions of discrete momentary occasions that the person *is*—his immediate awareness of himself as a self. Without such awareness how could one be 'himself', and how could one be preserved in *subjective* immediacy? ... does God experience my experiences or does God experience *my experiencing* of my experiences? [The latter would mean] that God also experiences *me*, my self-conscious subjective self. This would mean, however, that what persists beyond death is not just my heap of experiences, a billion or so discrete selves, but the full and complete self that I am in both concrete and abstract aspects.[49]

Henson thus creates a dilemma for Hartshorne: if personal experiences are perfectly preserved without loss, then subjective, self-conscious persons are also preserved. But Hartshorne disclaims this. If, on the other hand, only actual occasions are preserved, then something very significant is lost—self-conscious personhood. The preservation that Hartshorne talks of is therefore not really complete.[50]

One could defend Hartshorne against these criticisms by arguing that subjectivity must be said to lie outside the grasp of any kind of knower. Hence, even God should not be considered present in the subjectivity of actualities (or in the contemporariness of actual occasions). After all, in

[48] F. Fost, "Relativity Theory and Hartshorne's Dipolar Theism," in L. Ford (ed.), *Two Process Philosophers: Hartshorne's Encounter with Whitehead* (AAR Studies in Religion, 1973), pp. 95-96.

[49] J.C. Henson, "Immortality in the Thought of Charles Hartshorne," Ph.D. diss. Baylor University, 1975, p.124.

[50] *Ibid.* p.125.

personal relations—and we could possibly use this as an analogy for understanding God's relationship with us—there is always an element in the other person which escapes our knowledge of him or her. It eludes us, not because we are non-divine knowers but because this is the whole meaning of subjectivity. This is what constitutes the uniqueness of every person. Existentialists have rightly put much emphasis on this. There is a very important sense in which an individual is a world unto himself or herself and a centre of consciousness which no one may strictly penetrate. To say that this is outside God's knowledge is not to limit God's status. In this case, we would have to say that subjectivity or contemporariness means *that aspect which remains unknowable until it becomes actualised or is past.* Since in Hartshorne's metaphysics no reality is totally subjective or past, then no reality can be outside God's knowledge. That is to say, no reality in its actuality is *completely present or contemporary.* There is always an element of the past in it. Contemporariness is only *one* aspect of every actuality. God can still be said to be really related to us in knowledge, provided this is taken to mean *in their pastness.* But no actuality can be outside God even if one aspect of it is. In other words, it merely means a redefining of God's inclusiveness to mean "inclusion by knowledge", not the surrendering of it. This has to be done if Hartshorne is to answer the criticisms noted above.

Personal Identity

Earlier on it was noted that Hartshorne's doctrine of immortality assumes a certain understanding of personal identity. According to Hartshorne, any changing yet enduring thing has two aspects: the aspect of identity (what is common to the thing in its earlier and later stages) and the aspect of novelty. A being which changes through all time has an identical aspect which is exempt from change. It is in this sense immutable. However, this unchanging identity should not be confused with a substantial soul. For Hartshorne, personal identity is an abstract aspect. He writes: "The same-self ego is an abstraction from concrete realities, not itself a concrete reality."[51] This is not to say that it is unreal, but it is real within something richer in determination than itself. Hartshorne explains that the "I" spoken by me is distinct from the "I" uttered by someone else because there is a different referent of the pronoun in each case. In the same, though subtler, way the "I" which I say now has a different referent from

---

[51] Hartshorne, "The Development of Process Philosophy," in E.H. Cousins (ed.), *Process Theology: Basic Writings* (N.Y.: Newman Press, 1971), p. 56.

the "I" which I uttered earlier. The reason for the difference is that the pronoun "I" (or any of the personal pronouns) is a demonstrative and is context-dependent or token-reflexive; that is, the meaning changes each time it is used. There is, of course, an enduring individuality or a specific subject with definitive experiences. But each new experience which the subject undergoes means a new actuality for that subject. The persistent identity itself is abstract while the actual subject having these experiences is concrete. Thus, there is a new I every moment and the "I" really means not just "I as subject here" but also "I now". In short, spatial and temporal considerations are intrinsic to one's concrete reality. The concreteness of the subject is due to the society or sequence of experiences of which the subject is composed. The referent of "I" is usually some limited part of that sequence of experiences. As Hartshorne puts it, "Personal identity is a partial, not complete, identity: it is an abstract aspect of life, not life in its concreteness."[52] This is why it would be erroneous to hold that each of us is always simply the same subject or the same reality even if we must admit that we are the same individuals. We are identical through life as human individuals, but not so in our concreteness. Concretely, there is a new man or woman each moment. To recognise the sameness of that man or woman, we must disregard that which is new at each moment.

Hartshorne furthermore differentiates personal identity from strict identity. Identity in its strict meaning connotes entire sameness, total non-difference, in what is said to be identical. If x is identical to y, then "x" and "y" are two symbols but with one referent. The difference between them is only the symbols or the act of symbolisation, not in the thing symbolised. It follows that x does not have any property which y does not have and vice versa. Personal identity, on the other hand, is literally partial identity and therefore partial non-identity, the non-identity referring to the complete reality while the identity, to a mere constituent. Personal identity is the persistence of certain defining characteristics in a very complex reality which constantly changes.[53]

Peter Bertocci agrees with Hartshorne that identity is never a strictly logical identity as attested by personal experience since one is self-identifying unity-continuity in change. Nevertheless, he has reservations

---

[52] Hartshorne, "Beyond Enlightened Self-Interest: a Metaphysics of Ethics," p. 302.

[53] Hartshorne, "Strict and Generic Identity: an Illustration of the Relations of Logic to Metaphysics" in H.M. Kallen *et al.* (eds.), *Structure, Method and Meaning: Reflections in Honor of Henry M. Sheffer* (N.Y.: Liberal Arts Press, 1951), p. 26. See also his, "Personal Identity from A to Z," *Process Studies*, II (1972), pp. 209-215.

over Hartshorne's statement that "reality is the succession of units" (i.e. actual entities or experient occasions). In Bertocci's view, this statement cannot be rendered coherent with personal self-conscious experience. Instead he argues that he experiences himself as a unity, a self-identifying continuant who can recognise and recall his own experiences as successive. He writes, "There is nothing in my synthesis of successive moments. I am indeed active in any moment, but I am neither a collection of moments nor a 'synthesis'."[54] Bertocci is voicing a basic epistemological and ontological disagreement. He questions the validity of Hartshorne's doctrine that the present contains the past—this doctrine, it was noted, complements Hartshorne's interpretation of human immortality and forms the basis for his version of personal identity—because there does not seem to be an experiential basis for this. Simply put, the past does not come into the present for it is gone forever. When it comes to personal identity, therefore, one cannot say that one is *in* one's past, but only in one's present. "The burning, present experience is a *present complex unity* that is *able* to identify itself as changing and successive... In a present [experience] I recognise aspects I describe as past, but my present is never an accumulation of pasts (hidden, distinct, or clear)."[55] In short, Bertocci claims that one knows the past but this does not mean that the past itself exists.

Bertocci, it would appear, is equating experience with the substance theory. He himself wonders whether his present uneasiness with Hartshorne's theory is due to an obstinate residue of the psycho-logic of substantive metaphysics. In this respect, one could indeed ask whether Bertocci is justified in regarding the substantive theory as our experience of personal identity. After all, many others, notably the Buddhists, would have a different interpretation of their sense of personal identity. One suspects that the Western mind has been shaped mainly by Greek conceptions which make it easy for some Westerners to accept them as indeed *their* experience. Robert Neville does acknowledge this point. In his criticism of Hartshorne's account of continuity, Neville writes that Hartshorne's event pluralism which is intended to account for continuity does not articulate "the Western's sense of individual continuity".[56] Both critics accuse Hartshorne's theory of not having a basis in experience. What is surprising about their criticisms is that some have rejected the substance theory pre-

---

[54] P. Bertocci, "Hartshorne on Personal Identity: a Personalistic Critique," *Process Studies*, II (1972), p. 217.
[55] *Ibid.* p. 219.
[56] R. Neville, "Neoclassical Metaphysics and Christianity," *International Philosophical Quarterly*, X (1969), p. 56.

cisely because it does not seem to square with personal experience. The Buddha had rejected the Hindu doctrine of Self (although this is not the same as the substantial self) because he could only experience momentary, transitory states, which he regarded as constituting "the self". David Hume was critical of the classical notion of "soul" since according to him there was nothing in our experience to support it. The point at issue here is: which aspects of our experience can justifiably serve as the basis for philosophical thinking? The more crucial question then is: what exactly do we mean by experiencing ourselves as subjects? The answer to that question will shape our response to Hartshorne's theory of personal identity.[57]

Henson is of the opinion that Hartshorne has not really explored the possibility of a notion of self-identity that is not the same as the substantial self that he is critical of. He claims that Hartshorne "seems to be in danger of making selfhood, a concrete dimension of experienced reality, into an empty—hence unreal—abstraction".[58] Henson's question as to whether one cannot uphold a third alternative to the classical notion and to Hartshorne's interpretation of personal identity remains.

Some Observations

In a joint article, Lewis Ford and Marjorie Suchocki offer what they consider to be a Whiteheadian reconstruction of the notion of "subjective immortality".[59] Similarly, Jan Van der Veken undertakes a re-thinking of the meaning of "personal immortality" by reinterpreting Whitehead.[60] Hartshorne's own interpretation of human immortality likewise calls for another look since the issues raised by Hartshorne's critics point to certain unresolved aspects of his position. Given these difficulties (and ambiguities as when he says: "A conscious state of life cannot *become* an unconscious state of being dead. Consciousness is consciousness, unconscious-

---

[57] This topic is discussed in more detail in Ferdinand Santos and Santiago Sia, *Personal Identity, the Self and Ethics* (Palgrave Macmillan, 2007).

[58] Henson, "Immortality in the Thought of Charles Hartshorne," p. 142.

[59] Lewis S. Ford and Marjorie Suchocki, "A Whiteheadian Reflection on Subjective Immortality," *Process Studies* (1977), pp. 1-13. See also: Marjorie Hewitt Suchocki, "Charles Hartshorne and Subjective Immortality," *Process Studies*, XXI, 2 (Summer, 1992), p.121, and Randall Auxier, "Why One Hundred Years is Forever: Hartshorne's Theory of Immortality," *The Personalist Forum*, XIV (1998), pp. 109-140.

[60] Jan Van der Veken, "Talking Meaningfully about Immortality," in S. Sia (ed.), *Process Theology and the Christian Doctrine of God* (Petersham: St. Bede's Publications, 1986), pp. 95-108.

ness is unconsciousness, the one cannot *be* the other"[61] and "there is nothing impersonal about being remembered by God since there is no loss of
individual distinctiveness"[62] and presuming that any philosophical interpretation of human immortality has to be based on the way we experience
ourselves as subjects, Hartshorne could be more open to the possibility of
personal immortality. In fact, one can even make use of his own distinction between concreteness and abstractness to pave the way to such an
openness.

Hartshorne's view supports the belief *that there must be immortality*
as borne out by his discussion on the immortality of the past. This is the
abstract aspect of immortality, a partial description of it. To specify the
form of immortality beyond this very general and abstract description of it
is to raise the question of the concreteness of immortality. To designate the
concrete form of immortality is to stretch beyond the limits of metaphysics, understood as the search for the general traits of reality. By relying on
this distinction one can at least leave open the question of personal immortality or of any other kind of immortality. Because metaphysically one is
not in a position to show the validity of a claim to personal immortality
(which is really the essence of Hartshorne's objections) does not mean it
can be discounted. It seems Hartshorne himself senses this as he accepts
that personal immortality is not an absurd notion, only that he cannot vali-
date it in his metaphysics.[63]

The reason why Hartshorne should be more open to the traditional notion of personal immortality is that his doctrine of immortality does not
really answer the human quest for ultimate meaning. We are referring to
what has traditionally been described as "metaphysical evil". Is it sufficient to calm the *Angst* experienced by human beings confronted by the

---

[61] Hartshorne, *Omnipotence and Other Theological Mistakes* (SUNY Press, 1984),
p. 32.
[62] Hartshorne, *Wisdom as Moderation: a Philosophy of the Middle Way* (SUNY
Press, 1987), p. 62.
[63] Hartshorne believes that it is more certain that there can be no subtraction. That
there can be no addition, however, he is less sure, saying that personal survival
after death with memory of personal life before death is "hardly an absurdity'" He
finds that the analogy to a butterfly with its succession of bodies, while remote and
implausible, is not necessarily strictly inapplicable. What looks to him like a genuine impossibility is the view that there can *never* be any end, that the chapters of
our book will be infinite in number. Cf. his *Logic of Perfection and Other Reflections in Neoclassical Metaphysics,* p. 253. My reading of Hartshorne on this point
is that he is really indefinite about the validity of personal immortality. He is inclined to deny it, as has been noted, because he wants to argue that human fragmentariness means temporal as well as spatial limitedness.

threat of death and even utter destruction that the ultimate meaning of our existence is to live a life that will be well remembered by God?[64] Granted that Hartshorne's doctrine forces us to be more God-centred rather than anthropocentric in our search for ultimate meaning, has he not ignored this deep-seated existential concern? Hartshorne claims that we should accept our finitude: we are humans limited in space and time. But do we not transcend that finitude somehow? In becoming aware of our finitude have we not in a way transcended our limitations? Otherwise, we would not know that we are limited. In the very act of raising the question regarding the ultimate meaning of human existence, are we not somehow pointing to the possibility of its ultimate reality beyond Hartshorne's doctrine of "being remembered by God"?[65]

Hartshorne is definite in his rejection of post-mortem rewards and punishments. But this is really to deny the idea of ultimate justice, whatever one may say regarding the concrete form of post-mortem rewards and punishments (which as was already indicated is outside the grasp of metaphysics). In his philosophy Hartshorne accepts the notion of ethical responsibility. But full justice is not and cannot be meted out in this life, not even in the way Hartshorne presents it. Is justice not an ultimate value?[66] It seems that it is precisely the need to explain justice *ultimately* that has led many theists to posit post-mortem rewards and punishments and not, as Hartshorne believes, egotistic reasons. Hence, God is described not only as good but also as just. Hartshorne appears to acknowledge this point when he writes: "While I have the notion that the theory of heaven and hell is in

---

[64] John Polkinghorne makes the following observation: "I would go beyond the Kantian assertion that belief in God, and in an afterlife, is necessary in order to confirm the moral order of the world, to the claim that the integrity of personal experience itself, based as it is in the significance and value of individual men and women and the ultimate intelligibility of the universe, requires that there be an eternal ground of hope who is the giver and preserver of human individuality...." *Belief in God in an Age of Science* (New Haven and London: Yale University Press, 1998), pp. 21-22.

[65] Polkinghorne correctly remarks: "I cannot think that mere remembrance, such as process theology's notion of our lives contributing to the filling of the reservoir of divine experience, is an adequate account. It confuses the preservation of the past with the perfection of the future and it gives a diminished description of God's love for Abraham, Isaac, and Jacob, for you and me." *Ibid.* p. 23.

[66] Our reservation on this point is related to Hartshorne's solution to the problem of evil. If evil is the unwelcome result of the clash of creativities and there is no resolution of this "unfortunate situation" after one's death, then it could encourage the attitude of "making the most of the present situation"—and not always in the positive sense.

good part a colossal error and one of the most dangerous that ever occurred to the human mind, I also think that it was closely associated with
certain truths and that it requires intellectual and spiritual effort to purify
these truths from the error."[67] Since Hartshorne's own version of human
immortality does not adequately explain this need for ultimate justice—
which we maintain is the truth behind the doctrine of post-mortem rewards
and punishments—one should indeed purify but not dismiss the doctrine
of personal immortality.

---

[67] Hartshorne, *The Logic of Perfection and Other Reflections in Neoclassical Metaphysics*, p. 254.

POSTSCRIPT

"WHERE DOES IT ALL END?": THE QUEST FOR ANSWERS

> "..we arrive where we started
> And know the place for the first time."
> —T.S. Eliot "Little Gidding,"

> "We were all born under the sign of the question-mark, Michael.
> And that's how we end, too...Questions, questions!"
> —Thomas Kilroy "Christ Deliver Us"

By way of a postscript, let us follow some fictional characters whom we had met previously in the various chapters of this book: Professor de los Reyes, Professor Malachowski, Richard, Rodrigo, Enrique, and Aisling. Each had a set of questions about the challenges of life and had embarked on his or her own particular quests in life. Let us note what they have learned about the challenges of life and the quest for answers:

Professor de Los Reyes: The Source of the Question[1]

Indeed Enrique held Professor Luis de los Reyes in high esteem. And it was very satisfying to the professor. After all, as a father he regarded it as his moral duty to provide him with a role model. Brought up in a strict regime of family ties, he wanted to be able to pass on his to son what he himself had inherited from his father. No, not just the material things but more importantly, some answers to his questions.

His own father had impressed on him that while money, a good reputation and indeed success made life easier to manage, living a true human life was something else. It meant paying attention to the deep impulses within us which none of these things could adequately cater for. His father had learned this lesson in the crucible of life rather than in any academic pursuit. That important lesson found its way into the then young de los

---

[1] M.S. Sia, *Those Distant Shores* (forthcoming).

Reyes' mind. But unfortunately his father had died before they had the opportunity to explore that truth more fully.

It was for that reason that Luis de los Reyes decided that he would take up a career pursuing that truth. He turned to philosophy because after all it was the love of wisdom. And that, he thought, was how he could develop even further what his father had wanted to teach him. After all, what his father had communicated to him was an insight into life. Now what he craved was the deeper meaning of that insight. If he gave it his full attention, if he made it his life-long quest, if he devoted his energy investigating this truth, it would make him a truly wise man. And he believed that it would perpetuate the memory of his unschooled but educated father.

Professor de los Reyes was searching not just for answers but the answer to life. No, not so much the origins of life. He could leave that to the scientists. But does life have any meaning at all? He always felt that the answer to that question would dictate how he, or anyone else for that matter, would live their lives. For whatever meaning we discover about human existence would throw some light on the kind of activities that we should seriously engage in. Yes, his father was right. If all that there is to life is garnering as much material possession, or being at the top, then he could not see why anything else would matter. But his father had talked about human impulses that lie deeper than our craving for the goods of this world. He even had hinted that he meant more than just the human desires for food, drink and sex.

Somehow the young Luis de los Reyes had felt that his father's untimely death had left him wandering about in Plato's cave. He had managed to be freed from the shackles and even to turn around from the wall. When he did, he realised that the attraction of money, success and pleasure were like those shadows on that wall, beckoning and convincing him and so many others that these were indeed the reality of life. But why were they just mere shadows? What was that fire that was casting those shadows and at the same time, as he turned around, enabled him to see them as such? And why do so many of us remain in the shadowy world? How he missed his father as a guide towards the sunlight that was now filtering through his world.

He had read in the Upanishads that in our pursuit of wisdom we need a good teacher. He often wondered whether his father could have done that or whether he needed to turn to academic scholars for some of the answers. One thing he was sure of was that he would live up to that ideal as far as his relationship with his own son, Enrique, was concerned. But how would he do that? Communicating lofty ideals to young minds was indeed a challenge. Start too soon, and you lose them. Do it much later and you still lose them. There has to be a right time, a timely event.

So what is it that truly mattered for humans? His father had mentioned human impulses. So Luis turned to Aristotle for some kind of an answer. And sure enough, to this great surprise Aristotle seemed to have devoted a lot of time discussing the very thing that his father had pointed out. As

Luis delved deeper into the *Nicomachean Ethics*, he could see that the great question regarding our ultimate goal as humans is tied up with other intriguing questions: Who are we truly? What does it mean to be a human being? What is it that distinguishes us as humans? What is it that humans, because they are humans, are really searching for? As he read Aristotle's work (or at least the lectures attributed to him and edited by his nephew), he could almost hear his father's voice. No, it is not pleasure, nor fame, nor material goods. It is not even virtue. All these we need and should appreciate of course. But they are means to an end, to something much more fundamental. Was that human impulse that his father had been talking about comparable to what Aristotle meant by the human desire for happiness? He had wondered whether his father had ever heard of Aristotle. Or was Aristotle simply disclosing what any thinking person already knows? Aristotle had referred to that human characteristic in terms of rationality. Unlike any other creatures, according to the great Greek philosopher, only humans are endowed with rationality, and that rationality shows itself in the fact that only humans have intellects and free will.

Great stuff, Luis had commented. Perhaps Aristotle and his father were deep in conversation now.

But Luis balked at Aristotle's conclusion as to what that human impulse was driving us towards. It can't be just "thinking of thinking", Luis commented. Surely that is not the true destiny of human beings, he wondered. It sounds so cold, so detached, so "unhuman" even if Aristotle insisted that it is what makes us closer to the gods. Surely, there is more to it than Aristotle's answer to the question that he was asking.

In his philosophical studies Luis came across another philosopher who was in fact concerned about the same thing that he was. Thomas Aquinas, who had devoured Aristotle, as it were, pursued the answer further. That great medieval thinker had insisted that there is more to human existence than just developing ourselves fully as rational beings. Something was missing in Aristotle's account, Aquinas had pointed out. That is why he had claimed that Aristotle was not wrong, just that his account was incomplete. Aquinas had maintained that making use of the very tool that we have as human beings, which is what Aristotle did, would be inadequate. It was a good tool but insufficient to really provide us with the true answer. It made Aquinas fall back on his Christian faith. Human reason needed to turn on something else.

Luis envisioned that human reason falling back on its own resources would be like the question mark. Turning back leaves it as a question. It needs to straighten out, to be an exclamation point. It has to have the element of surprise. It has to be surprised by a disclosure of God. Perhaps that is why Aquinas believed that the human impulse was not just driving us towards our full development, but it was also a tug from God towards God.

Is this what Augustine had meant when he wrote that the human heart is restless until it rests in God? Prof Luis de los Reyes had wondered.

Professor Malachowski and Richard:
In Pursuit of the Question:[2]

'Professor Malachowski, Professor Tanaka, Dr. Linden. I introduce Dr. Jennifer Sidney and Dr. Richard Gutierrez to you. I leave you now to get to know each other better.' Professor van der Riet then went to the door since the doorbell rang again to announce other new arrivals.

As the group became better acquainted, Richard learned that Professor Malachowski was a professor of philosophy from Lublin in Poland and was particularly interested in meeting Richard since he too was writing something on the problem of evil, but from a process philosophical point of view. Dr. Tanaka, a professor of education from one of the universities in Japan, was on a flying visit, as it were. He said that he was spending his sabbatical in England since he was working on a comparative study of educational systems in the world. Dr. Linden had come from the Netherlands to attend a conference being held at Leuven. She belonged to the theology faculty of one of the state universities in that country. After a while, it was not surprising that Dr. Linden and Jennifer should break away from the group to chat about common interests in theology.

Richard tried to circulate so as to meet as many individuals as possible. And it was a lively gathering, helped no doubt by the generous amounts of drink being poured by their solicitous host. Richard was impressed at how international the gathering truly was. He introduced himself to a professor from Ghana, then to another one from Sweden. An academic from Argentina joined Richard and a professor from Spain as they were conversing about their common heritage.

Most of the evening, however, Richard found himself talking to Dr. Malachowski. He found Dr. Malachowski very critical of Thomistic philosophy, the school of thought that informed his own perspective on the problem of evil. In contrast he had only a vague idea of process philosophy, which the more senior professor was very interested in. All Richard knew was that it was a contemporary movement in philosophy associated with Whitehead and Hartshorne and had been influential particularly in theology. Instead of entering into a debate about the subtleties of their respective philosophical schools of thought, however, the two talked about how they approached the problem of evil.

As they discussed their specific approaches, Richard disclosed the difficulty he was experiencing in completing his work. Somehow there was an important factor missing in his scholarly research, he confided to Dr. Malachowski.

'I feel that I'm working on a solution without knowing what the real problem is,' remarked Richard after they had retreated to the corner of the spacious dining room to give themselves some room away from the others.

---

[2] M.S. Sia, *The Fountain Arethuse*, pp. 103-108.

Richard kept swirling the contents of his brandy glass. It was particularly welcome, given the chilly temperature outside.

'That sounds strange. We philosophers are supposed to be able not only to evaluate the merits of each argument but also to clarify the issues.' The professor looked Richard in the eye. 'You are talking about the proper starting point for our philosophising, aren't you?'

'Possibly. But I don't just mean articulating what the philosophical issues in a problem are.' Richard tucked his left hand under his right elbow. 'Take human suffering, for instance. A very concrete reality if ever there was one. I've worked on this topic for some time now and yet when I am faced with the challenge of talking to someone who's just lost a loved one, or an individual who has just been through a disaster, I'm lost for words. Surely, we philosophers should be able to say something meaningful in situations like that. Maybe it's me. Maybe it's not philosophy that is at fault here.' Richard retrieved his left hand and slipped it into his trouser pocket.

'But do you expect philosophy to say something meaningful in this situation?'

'Yes, since the study of philosophy is meant to provide us with wisdom. But I sometimes get the impression that what we philosophers have become concerned with is knowledge and more knowledge.' Richard paused, not knowing how his remarks would be accepted.

'Go on, I'm listening,' the older professor, who took a sip from his glass of Beaujolais, was encouraging.

'We sometimes blame the sciences for accumulating all this information and math for juggling with figures and becoming too abstract in the whole process. And yet aren't we doing the same thing? I know of some philosophers who regard the problem of evil, for instance, as an intellectual puzzle. They get a lot of kicks from solving problems which are of their own making. In the end one could ask what that has to do with life.'

'Wait now. Are you talking about the problem of suffering or of philosophy as a problem?' interrupted Dr. Malachowski. 'Are these not separate issues?'

'That's precisely *the* problem. We philosophers are so fond of being clear about the issues that we start classifying reality.'

'But how can you expect to address the issues adequately if you have not clarified them? That *is* important, as you know.'

'True, but sometimes we do lose the real issue as we dissect, as it were, what we perceive to be the problem. I remember my Asian colleague once quoting Mencius, who said that what one dislikes in clever men is their tortuosity. I'm probably taking the words out of context, but I can't help seeing their relevance. And I remember being intrigued by her reference to Chuang-tzu, who disdained all the philosophical disputations carried on during his time. And we're still doing it today.'

'I'm not familiar with Chinese philosophy, but there is something in Whitehead's *Adventures of Ideas* that I was reading just this morning.' Dr. Malachowski, placing the forefinger of his left hand across his lips as if to recall the appropriate passage, knit his eyebrows. 'He was alerting us to what is lost from speculation by scholarship. He says, in speculation there is delight and discourse while in scholarship there is concentration and thoroughness. Of course, Whitehead claims that for progress both are necessary.'

'I believe that we have lost the "feel" of the problem because of all our disputations, as Chuang-tzu I suppose would put it, although I too don't know much about him except through my colleague.'

'But that is not the domain of philosophy, at least as commonly understood.'

'Exactly, we have left out an important aspect of the problem in our philosophising.'

'And what is that?' quizzed the professor.

'The element of life. The importance of experience. The necessary connection between our thinking and our living.'

There was some laughter from another part of the house, but the two philosophers engrossed in their conversation ignored it. 'And how does that relate to the problem of suffering that you mentioned earlier on?'

'That we need a different way of describing the problem. Philosophy shouldn't attempt a solution until it has done justice to the reality of suffering. It's much too abstract to do that. At least the way philosophical thinking has become.'

'And how do you propose to do that?' inquired the Polish professor.

Before Richard had a chance to respond, a third voice joined them. 'I see you two are discussing an area of common interest.' It was Professor van der Riet with a bottle of wine in his left hand and a decanter of brandy in the other. 'I fill up your glasses first. You are not driving, yes? And I introduce you two to Dr. Fuentes from the Philippines. He is here—sent by his bishop—on sabbatical.'

Richard and Dr. Malachowski shook Dr. Fuentes's hand. Much to their delight, they realised that his field was also in philosophy. 'You know, that was what we had just been talking about,' remarked Dr. Malachowski. He then summarised what he and Richard had been discussing.

Dr. Fuentes was quickly on the scene. 'Who was it who said—I think it was Heidegger—philosophers are reducing reality to a mentally fabricated axiomatic project. I can understand your situation.' Dr. Fuentes, who was about ten years older than Richard, looked at him. 'Although my difficulty with the way philosophy generally handles the problem of evil is that it is seen too much as a theodicy. Too much attention is given to the challenge of atheism. Don't you agree?' He turned his head in the direction of Dr. Malachowski, who nodded. 'And so we are expected to provide a coherent and credible resolution of how God can be defended as almighty *and* all-good when there is so much evil and suffering around us.'

Richard's face must have registered some surprise—after all, that was exactly what he was working on here in Leuven—since Dr. Fuentes quickly added, 'Oh, don't get me wrong. That is still an important issue. But you know, for us in the Philippines—and I'm sure that it is true in Latin America too, from what I have read of liberation theology there—the important question is not theodicy but idolatry.'

More laughter from another part of the room. But Dr. Fuentes continued, 'Like you, I've been wrestling with the starting point for our reflections on this important subject. But I ask myself, why do philosophers not sometimes reckon with the fact that many people continue to believe in God despite their suffering? Granted that one may need to scrutinise the reasons that these believers come up with for their continued belief, isn't it strange that we do not focus on the concept of God that lies behind their belief? Perhaps it is very different from the way philosophers have portrayed God to be and has consequently led to the so-called problem of evil. It seems to me that the existence of evil is challenging us to reformulate our descriptions of God.'

'How would you state the problem of evil then?' asked Dr. Malachowski, whose interest was aroused since his leanings towards process philosophy made him pursue a remarkably similar line of inquiry. It was good to hear somebody coming from a different background, making the same point.

'What kind of God can we continue to believe in, given the presence of so much undeserved suffering?' came Dr. Fuentes's ready reply.

The glass of orange juice which Dr. Fuentes had been drinking was now empty so he gently set it on top of the nearby drinks cabinet, thus providing himself with the opportunity to gesticulate for emphasis.

'The danger for us is that in our attempts to defend God, as it were, we could be perpetuating idols, rather than the true God. Christianity is part of our Filipino culture'—with those words he pounded his breast with his fist—'just as it is in Latin America; but our complaint is that the concept of God which we have inherited from the past is not only inadequate, but worse, it could also be responsible for supporting the structures which maintain the status quo, which in turn results in the misery, poverty and degradation of our people.' Dr. Fuentes ticked these off with his fingers.

Richard was very attentive. He wanted Dr. Fuentes and Dr. Malachowski to elaborate more on this issue, but since two others attached themselves to the group there was no opportunity to continue the conversation. After all, this was a social, not a seminar. It was just that it was so natural for the philosophers not to shed their professional gown, so to speak. But he made a mental note to contact the two philosophers again. Perhaps not all was lost with his research.

The rest of the evening Richard enjoyed chatting with the other guests. He managed to exchange a few glances with Jennifer, who was certainly quite popular with several of the guests.

Professor Malachowski and Richard:
The Significance of the Quest[3]

Richard had reached the Spanish quarter when he heard a voice call out to him: 'Good morning, Dr. Gutierrez. Do you remember me?'

'Well, of course, Professor Malachowski. It's great to see you again. Do you have your accommodation around here?'

'Yes, the university got us one of those fabulous houses, right here in the Begijnhof.' His house, timber-framed and with clay walls, was in Middenstraat. 'And you?'

'I'm staying in one of the apartments in the building beside Schappenstraat.' Richard's apartment was near the gatehouse which the French Republic had demolished in 1798 so as to connect the beguinage with the town. Only the frame of the gate remained.

'Isn't this a magnificent location? So peaceful. It certainly encourages one to be reflective, doesn't it? When I go for a walk inside the compound, I try to imagine what it was like for the Beguines to live here. They must have spent a lot of their time in quiet meditation. This place seems to have been built for that purpose. But tell me, are you going anywhere in particular?'

'Not really, I wanted to clear my mind. I thought the air would help. I was trying to do some writing on my manuscript, but I'm afraid that nothing would come. I've made no progress since our last conversation.'

'Well, why don't you join me then? I'm out for some exercise. A habit, and a good one at that, which I formed when I was in America a few years ago. Why don't we take up where we left off the last time?'

Richard hesitated. He had not come out for an academic seminar. In fact, it was the last thing he had intended. Anyway, he was more concerned about what was happening to him personally than he was with his research. But his respect for the professor got the better of him. He did want to talk to him again about his manuscript, but at some future day when he was more prepared. This was like being put on the spot and being asked to don his academic hat. But he had been asked, so he may as well talk about it. This time he did not rehash his difficulty about finishing his manuscript on the problem of evil. Instead, without his knowing it, he found himself telling the professor what happened that evening after the social when he went for a late night/early morning stroll to the center of Leuven. He repeated to this learned man the questions which buzzed in his mind about academic life.

'You know, Richard—shall I call you that?—it seems that you're grappling with a much wider problem about what we academics do. To outsiders, our job is teaching, and that's easy enough to understand since they

---

[3] *Ibid.* pp. 176-185.

can see us inside the classroom in front of our students. Others will probably accept that we also engage in research, although that is less tangible.'

The professor smiled knowingly as they turned around since they had come to a dead end.

'I'm sure you will have met people who are really bothered about what all this research means since, until there is some published work, there doesn't seem to be much evidence. Particularly in philosophy. Even some administrators don't see that. They always want the finished product, so to speak.'

This time it was Richard's turn to smile, nervously, as his Dean's words reverberated in his mind.

'And then there are the cynics. Confronted with the published work, they appear shocked. Astonished.' And Professor Malachowski became rather dramatic. 'You mean after all that time, money and effort, *this* is the result? they utter in dismay. Like the conclusion that reason is so limited that we could not possibly describe reality in its entirety. I remember talking to somebody in America who said that he could have told me that for nothing! Needless to say, he was the kind of gentleman who was results-oriented, as you put it over there. But what's it really that we do as academics? Academia is not just a profession. It is a way of life, but what is it really? Is that the real question you're asking, Richard?'

The Polish professor and Richard had been treading the cobbled walks of the Spanish quarter. Richard couldn't help feeling that it was very much like the Lyceum of Aristotle. The Peripatos and all that. It was as if the professor were Aristotle and he, one of the students walking around the Lyceum, debating, questioning, criticising, in search of the truth. It was Greek philosophy being relived or maybe restaged. Just as well they were not moving in a circle. That would have been too much for the professor's results-oriented acquaintance. It would have invited the comment that that was what philosophers did—talk in circles. Their dialogues never came to any hard conclusions.

'Part of it, I think, Professor. In some ways I wish I really knew. Somehow it has something to do with not losing touch with concrete life.' Richard noticed that the professor did not suggest that he call him by his first name. The hierarchy was clearly established. Was that the case in ancient Athens?

'I remember from our previous conversation about your difficulty. Despite all the research and the writing that you had done on your topic, you always felt that you have no convincing answers to give when faced with the reality of evil. Is that right?'

'Correct.'

'Now you seem to be saying that academic life, particularly the scholarly part of it, is moving you away from what you regard as concrete life to something that is of importance only to a few. Do you believe that we've lost the true purpose of the academic task? You know, when you made the distinction between wisdom and knowledge.'

'Do you think that there is some truth in that, Professor?' A good strategy. When a philosopher asks you a question, ask another one. That shifts the burden. He never liked it though when he was asking the question and a student would retort by putting up another question. It always sounded as if the student was biding for time. A cheap shot, but sometimes it worked.

The professor welcomed the question. In fact, it led him to a pet topic of his. 'Definitely. In his *Adventures of Ideas* Alfred North Whitehead makes that very same point. He makes a distinction between speculation and scholarship.'

Richard smiled as he recalled the professor having referred to it before.

Professor Malachowski continued. 'Speculation, he says, is what makes you wonder at the world around you. It's characterised by delight and enthusiasm for the concreteness of life. Scholarship on the other hand demands concentration. Scholarly work requires us to be thorough, to be exact as to what's correct and what's not correct, to be consistent. Whitehead claims that Plato speculated. He had great insights into reality but he was not a systematiser. There is a passage in that book which says that if one converted Plato into a respectable professor by providing him with a coherent system, he would find that Plato is most inconsistent. I'm paraphrasing, of course. For progress, we need both, Whitehead tells us.'

'Would Whitehead say that the pursuit of wisdom is what speculation is all about while the acquisition of knowledge is what scholarship is all about?'

'I suppose he would.'

'Why do we need both?'

'Because we need to develop our insights, to strengthen them. But we also need to keep our feet on the ground. Otherwise we could be talking about theories that have no bearing on concrete life...there's that phrase again.'

'I'm beginning to think, Professor, that I'm not ready for the second part. I don't want to lose the first.'

Richard was not expecting the professor's answer.

'On the contrary, Richard, perhaps you have gone beyond that distinction. Without knowing it, you may have understood what Whitehead really meant.'

The professor and Richard continued with their conversation as they walked further in the direction of the sports grounds of the university of Leuven. They walked past the Faculty Club, previously the infirmary of the Begijnhof but now a splendid restaurant where people dined in style, and continued on past the Begijnhof Congreshotel. They went through the tunnel under busy Tervuursevest, a refuge from the danger and roar of the traffic.

After a few minutes they found themselves in the well-used sports grounds. The huge building to their right had a large swimming pool and an indoor basketball court. To their left was a cafeteria which served not only the sports enthusiasts but the general public as well. There was something about the cliéntele which showed that somehow they were all connected with university life. But as they both concluded, it would be hard to find someone in Leuven who had nothing to do directly or indirectly with the academic institutions here.

As they drew close to the running fields, they passed by the tennis courts. There was only one brave twosome playing tennis. On the other hand, there were a good few individuals running around the tracks, all trying to keep fit. It probably was early in the season for serious training.

Their conversation surprisingly turned to Chicago. It must have been the previous cold weather, although as Professor Malachowski pointed out that was nothing compared to what he had experienced in that large American city. He felt very much at home there because it was as cold as Poland in the winter! Richard had studied there so he knew what the professor meant. They talked about the beautiful walk along Lake Shore, commented on the performance of the Cubs, described the impressive downtown with one of the world's tallest buildings and reminisced about events in Chicago. It was a relaxing conversation as they exchanged experiences.

On the way back, they decided to look inside the gymnasium. There was a basketball game going on. The teams were not professional ones, but it was still an exciting game. There was a lot of cheering as the two teams tried to outdo each other. But there was also a lot of friendly rivalry. Richard was enjoying himself, possibly because there was a lot of spontaneity in the game. The teams were under no pressure to excel, they were playing for fun. And he and the professor shared in that pleasure.

Richard couldn't help comparing it to the basketball games he used to watch back home. The statistics were blinding as figures were presented on what the average scoring was for each player, the number of rebounds, assists, etc. Even an enjoyable game had become a science. The spontaneity was lost in the quest for excellence. Do we always have to be the best? he wondered. But best at what? He was reminded of what the professor had told him about Whitehead's distinction between speculation and scholarship. Even in sports, the need for development, refinement and perfection robbed the occasion of pleasure. The spirit of competitiveness took over.

As Richard continued with his musings, uninterrupted by the professor, who was thoroughly enjoying the game, it dawned on him what Jennifer meant to him. She represented a side of academia that he was now questioning. She was constantly striving for excellence. And she was succeeding. Her scholarly reputation was certainly growing and met with a lot of admiration, including Richard's. But her devotion to such excellence had ignored life itself: the challenges, the simple joys, the ordinary results. Her life was too focused on one aspect. And now it was starting to shatter.

No, Richard was looking for more. He wanted to be able to face life itself. And life itself was not always demanding of a particular kind of excellence. Jennifer's kind of inspiration was not what he was looking for.

Back in his apartment Richard pondered on his leisurely walk with the professor from Poland. It had turned out to be somewhat of an eye-opener although the professor probably had not intended it to be. He had merely introduced the topic of Richard's research as a way of sparking off the conversation. He wanted to continue where they had left off. After all, it was very natural for two academics to discuss their scholarly work, particularly in this case since they were interested in the same area. They were even working on the same problem but from different perspectives. But their exchange led them to talk about life itself. The professor unsuspectingly left the door ajar for Richard to explore the topic himself. In the professor there was no gap between life and his academic pursuits. He naturally went from one to the other.

But what really made the conversation with Dr. Malachowski of particular significance for Richard was his discovery of what had led the professor to study the problem of evil in depth. It was not merely scholarly interest. Nor did he, unlike Richard, stumble into the topic as it were. No. Dr. Malachowski had an intriguing story to tell.

The Polish professor was the son of two victims of the concentration camp in Majdanek in Poland. His story moved and probed Richard's mind as the professor narrated how he had had to struggle to survive after his parents died in that camp. But it was the professor's reason for turning to philosophy that goaded Richard even more. Having survived such a tragedy and grown up with that painful memory, Dr. Malachowski had searched for answers to the question of why such an evil situation could possibly exist. It was so atrocious that it baffled any rational explanation. The professor needed to find some answers; he was not merely juggling intellectual puzzles. His academic pursuit was rooted in existential concernWhat was also interesting was that, despite offers to more prestigious positions in other universities, Professor Malachowski chose to stay in Lublin. His reason was that he wanted to be as close as possible to the source of his philosophising. He regularly visited the Majdanek camp, which was only a few miles from his university. For him that was *the situation* that spurred on his philosophising. It was the *font* which fed his craving for answers.

………

That was why he listened to and was very sympathetic to Richard. This young philosopher sensed what he had long been searching for. He wished he could offer a convincing answer. But that was why he was in Leuven. He would not allow philosophy to let him down. Maybe there was another kind of philosophy, born out of concrete experiences like his. He had met one of the professors from Mercier University when he gave a talk at his university in Lublin. This professor, a specialist in process philosophy, invited him over to Leuven so that he could study the philosophy of Whitehead. Dr. Malachowski was not optimistic. But he was willing to give it a try. After all, it would give him a chance to follow up on his personal-academic pursuit.

And that was what really impressed Richard. Academic work should not be an escape route as had been the case with Jennifer, he thought. It is not merely a profession which one could put aside after a day's work. As Dr. Malachowski put it, it is a way of life. Or it should be. Not in the sense that there is nothing else that one does, but talk and write as a scholar. That would be obnoxious. But one's academic work should come from one's experiences. That was what was missing in his own research work. It was meant to be scholarly—but should it be divorced from daily life? That was the big difference between Dr. Malachowski's work and his, although both of them were working on the same topic. On the other hand, perhaps his peers would dismiss Dr. Malachowski's work as not scholarly enough. Richard doubted whether it would bother the senior professor, who had after all already established himself in the field of the philosophy of religion. For him the present work was a culmination of his search for truth, probably a different kind of *opus magnum* that he would be more proud of.

But could he, Richard, an untenured assistant professor, afford to change his approach to his research? And yet could he afford to be dishonest with himself since he really was bogged down with the so-called academic research that he was doing? He knew that he had to prove his scholarship. What should he do?

Rodrigo and Enrique: Life and its Challenges[4]

Rodrigo looked down at the foamy trail the ferry was leaving behind. Just like the shores of Ireland earlier on, it too was disappearing into the darkness. In the far distance, there was not even a trace of it. Rodrigo thought that somehow it was symbolic of how ephemeral life can be. A few minutes earlier, the forceful churning of the water had produced such powerful results that one would have expected them to last that little bit longer. Instead, the foam soon quickly dissipated back to its watery origins. It only had a few minutes to stand out, to acquire a different status, to enjoy its freedom. Sooner rather than later, it was indistinguishable from the sea itself.

It was just like the waves he had been watching earlier—or should not have been watching, as he was well aware. (Fortunately, right now the sailing was so smooth it seemed like the ferry was gliding on the water.) Those waves at the harbour would build up into a white crest, relish their momentary high status, only to roll over and back into the sea. And the sea would take them back, just like a parent pulling at an errant child. But then they would try again, tugging at the mother sea's restraints and attempt to break loose once more. And once again they would be reined back, sometimes with the accompanying sound of a slap. Inevitably a time comes where there is peace again, where calm reigns, and the mother sea and the waves become one. The waves have, as it were, come home. And the gentle ebbing of the seawater becomes more like an invitation to any beachgoer to immerse himself or herself in the comforting caresses of the water.

He too was returning—back to where it had all started, Dumpao beach in Guiuan. He recalled T.S.Eliot's lines: "..we arrive where we started/ And know the place for the first time."

And he wondered how he would re-act.

It was time to go inside. The air was definitely much colder. Time to join the other passengers. In a journey such as this there were other ways of passing the time besides rummaging through one's memories.

He turned to see whether Enrique was still there. He was; and when he caught his eye, he moved towards him.

'I'm going in now,' he informed Enrique. 'It's gone cold out here. Want to have something to drink?'

'Good idea, it'll make us warm.'

The two fellows headed for the cafeteria in the ferry, laughing because they said almost at the same time: 'I'm dying for a cup of tea!' Ireland's influence had seeped into their drinking habits. It was a good context for swapping stories about their stay in Ireland.

Neither, however, referred to what they had been thinking about while standing on the deck. It was as if those thoughts were precious because they were private. To share them would be to lose their significance.

---

[4] M.S. Sia, *Those Distant Shores* (forthcoming).

For both had been thinking of another journey—a more significant one—a voyage in the waters of life. And those waters can be, and had been, even more tumultuous.

Aisling: Lessons from Nature[5]

Spring had definitely arrived. The cold, sometimes biting, winds were long since gone. Everywhere there was new life sprouting—out of the ground as well as from seemingly dead branches and twigs. Leuven was turning green, ready to shed off all the burden of the gray winter months. True, it had not been a bad winter. Snow this year had fallen only a couple of days and even then it was a mere sprinkling, lasting on the ground for only about an hour. Right now, the flowers, impatiently peeping out, were anxious to display their best colors. The birds which had made the park their home were once again chirping, alerting passers-by to the oncoming beauty of the months ahead. Lovers did not want to be left out either, as more and more of them strolled, leisurely enjoying each other and the slightly warmer weather.

In some ways nature in spring is like Leuven itself coming to life after the night before when everything had been closed. There would be some stirrings, tentative at first as if the town were still coming to terms with the day. It could be the garbage collectors making their rounds. Then there would be the early risers moving hurriedly in different directions, a few at first then growing larger and larger in numbers. The shops would raise their shutters. An odd shopkeeper might even appear, pulling out a couple of shelves or sweeping the front part of the shop. Traffic would initially be light but as the minutes ticked by, more and more cars would fill the narrow streets. Then, of course, the bicycles, the school buses and the students. Only after a while does Leuven really come to life. The town would be waking up just as nature now was in the process of coming back to life.

There is always something vibrant about waking up, whether it is nature, Leuven or in general. It always signals a fresh start. Like the dawn of a new day. It makes one want to look forward rather than backwards. As if it is cajoling you into thinking that whatever happened in the past, there is yet another chance. Perhaps life is but a series of such beginnings. And we make it cumbersome when we burden it with the ever increasing weight of the past. Waking up, the beginning of spring, a town facing a new day stir up anticipation. Each gives one hope. Maybe that is how we are meant to live—and nature provides numerous examples.

....

---

[5] M.S. Sia, *The Fountain Arethuse*, pp. 202-203, 273.

The park was much more beautiful now with the tall trees covered in leaves. Aisling and Philip had frequented that park. But at that time, the trees were bare, and although leafless trees have their own rugged beauty, the new growth in the trees was much more pleasant to see. She tried to describe the images which were conjured up in her mind as she watched nature awakening. And she talked of the wealth of imagery in Robert Frost's poem *The Birches* and quoted Hopkins's remarks about the grandeur in creation.

'You seem to see beauty everywhere, Aisling, even in bare trees.'

'Because it's there, isn't it? It's difficult to see it now since the trees have their leaves. And it's the leaves that give the trees their beauty in the spring. But in the winter, when the cold weather makes you wrap yourself up, nature unveils the beauty of the trunks and of the branches of the trees. It's as if Mother Nature wants to remind us that the leaves, the externals, aren't the only things about nature that can be admired. The inner beauty that's hidden in the spring and summer and autumn comes out on its own in the winter. We don't always see it. And even when it's really there we don't always appreciate it.'

Professor Malachowski: The Quest for Answers[6]

Professor Malachowski was spending his last evening in Leuven, enjoying a sumptuous meal in the company of Professor van der Riet. Tomorrow he would be taking the train to Aachen, from where he would be switching to the train for Bonn since he had an invitation to speak in the afternoon to the Philosophy Department of the university there. He then planned to spend a few weeks in Germany, afterwards a week in Liechtenstein, before returning to his native Poland.

'So, Piotr, would you say that it was a fruitful stay in Leuven for you?' inquired Professor van der Riet.

'I believe so, in fact more than I had expected,' came the reply.

'You mean, you have become a convert to process thought,' teased his Belgian host professor.

'Not so fast, André,' Professor Malachowski teased back. 'You are not out to win converts, are you?'

The two eminent professors laughed heartily. Professor Malachowski had come to Leuven specifically to research on process philosophy, in which Professor van der Riet was a recognised expert.

'I must confess, I find it fascinating. But there are still a number of issues, and I mean a good number, about which I would have to quarrel with you process people. One of these days I will record my objections in print. Perhaps you and I can dialogue further.'

---

[6] *Ibid.* pp. 267-268

Professor Malachowski then proceeded to elaborate on the real reason why he believed that his stay had exceeded his expectations. As he reminded his Belgian counterpart, his search for an adequate philosophy to make sense of a life that had been marred yet nurtured by the bitter experiences of the past had led him to Leuven to read up on process thought. But what he was beginning to appreciate, in his advanced years, was that the search itself, *the process*—Professor Malachowski couldn't resist the pun—was the more important thing.

Unknown to Richard, with whom he had had a number of conversations following their walk, the younger academic's questions had sparked off a new inquiry for the senior professor. Professor Malachowski was beginning to turn to the question rather than to the answer. He wondered whether the questions we ask about life should not remain as questions. They should continue to unsettle us and not dry up because we have become comfortable with 'the truth'.

Maybe, he thought, that is what is wrong with human nature. Or, maybe that is the truth about human nature. From one point of view, we have been condemned to be seekers after an elusive truth. From another point of view, that it is our privilege. For we can ask, we can wonder. We can journey. And the quest for the answer becomes the answer itself. Leuven had been a welcome oasis in that journey—which he now believed would go on and on.

APPENDIX A

LITERATURE AND PHILOSOPHY: A WHITEHEADIAN NEXUS

"Surely philosophy is not other than sophisticated poetry."
—Montaigne

Literature and Philosophy: an Uneasy Relationship

Despite the famous wish of Plato to banish poets from the Republic and the ancient quarrel between poets and philosophers, there has always been a close, if at times tense, relationship between the art of poetry and the act of philosophising. Western philosophical tradition, at least in its dominant form, may not be as keen, compared to the Asian philosophical heritage for instance, on regarding literature in general and poetry in particular as a rich source of philosophical insight. In fact, many would maintain a certain distinction, with clearly described features, between what is literary and what is philosophical. In certain quarters of European philosophy, which insists on criticism, depth and comprehensiveness, there is a rather negative attitude towards poetry. Heidegger in his essay "What are Poets For?" bemoans the fact that philosophers consider a dialogue with poetry as "a helpless aberration into fantasy".[1] This rather negative attitude can be traced back to Plato, the great European philosopher. As Whitehead puts it, the emergence of the critical discontent with the poets is exemplified by Plato.[2]

---

[1] Heidegger does warn that scholars of literary history consider the dialogue to be "an unscientific violation of what such scholarship takes to be the facts". Cf. his *Poetry, Language and Thought,* trans. Albert Hofstadter (N.Y.: Harper & Row, 1971), p. 96. For a helpful anthology on this topic, see Hazard Adams (ed.), *Critical Theory Since Plato* (Harcourt Brace Jovanovich Publishers, 1971).

[2] A.N. Whitehead, *Adventures of Ideas* (N.Y.: Macmillan, 1961), p. 12. See also, Lok Chong Hoe, "Plato and Aristotle: Their Views on Mimesis and its Relevance to the Arts," *Φιλοσοφια* 36, 2 (May 2007), pp. 119-140.

Nonetheless, there has also been an acknowledgement by some European philosophers that Plato's understanding of poetry *vis-à-vis* philosophical thinking was too restricted. Much poetry contains a great deal of philosophical insights; and some philosophical writings, in so far as these are the works of well-respected philosophers, are in genres which are more literary. (One can readily recall the writings of many of the existentialist thinkers.) Romanticism, which upholds spontaneity, emotion and individuality, arose in reaction to the perceived inadequacy of the kind of theoretical reason upheld by the Hegelian system. The Romantics felt that poetry provides the most adequate path to truth. In the essay cited above, Heidegger maintains that the course of the history of Being will lead thinking into a dialogue with poetry. Gadamer's recent book, *Literature and Philosophy in Dialogue*, promotes that exchange of views between literary writers and philosophers.

The relationship between literature (particularly poetry) and philosophy appears to be an issue in contemporary European philosophical debates, especially in the context of philosophical hermeneutics. Paul Ricoeur's conviction that there is always a Being-demanding-to-be-said (*un être-à-dire*) which precedes our actual saying prods him on to the poetic uses of language. Towards the end of *Being and Time* Heidegger had stated that the propositional form in which he had been writing was not really adequate to capture his thought. (It is an observation reminiscent of Kierkegaard, who refers to a mode of communication in which the writer uses all the artistic means at his disposal to awaken the reader to what can only be indicated, not stated.) The later Heidegger becomes more specific. Pre-occupied with language as the "house of Being", he pointed to the inextricable connection between our conception of the world and our language: language alone brings beings as beings into the open for the first time. Maintaining that poetic language is the purest form of language speaking, he considers that in poetic language, language speaks itself (*Die Sprache spricht*) and unfolds its true essence. The essence of poetry is "the founding of truth" (as Heidegger understood it). He had confidence in poetic language's ability to evoke the nature of things whereas he had grave reservations about the form of writing that he had himself adopted. In fact, he regarded the poet, whose "projective saying" enables new aspects of Being to reveal themselves, as the true philosopher.[3]

---

[3] See, among his other writings, *Poetry, Language, Thought,* trans. Albert Hofstadter (N.Y.: Harper & Row, 1971) and *On the Way to Language*, trans. Peter D. Hertz (N.Y.: Harper & Row, 1971). Heidegger maintains that the purity of poetic language is such that it is not important to know anything about the poet or the origins of the poetic work. Poetic language which reveals the essence of being, and

Whitehead, for his part, regards literature (and poetry in particular) as a concrete expression of experience and a source for philosophical thinking. Here Whitehead manifests his closeness, even if rather implicit, not only with the rich European literary-philosophical tradition, but also with the concerns of European philosophers cited above. There is an interesting passage which provides some insight into Whitehead's understanding of the relationship between poetry and philosophy. In his *Modes of Thought,* he writes: "Philosophy is akin to poetry. Philosophy is the endeavour to find a conventional phraseology for the vivid suggestiveness of the poet. It is the endeavour to reduce Milton's 'Lycidas' to prose, and thereby to produce a verbal symbolism manageable for use in other connections of thought."[4] And in another work, *Adventures of Ideas,* he acknowledges that what philosophy does is to build on what is a strong foundation, explaining that philosophy expresses "flashes of insight beyond meaning already stabilised in etymology and grammar."[5]

Modes of Experience and Language

Here we should like to suggest how the dialogue between literature and philosophy can be grounded in Whitehead's thought. In doing so we also hope to indicate why the methodological task of preserving the concreteness of experience, specifically in literature, is an important one for philosophical reflections.

Whitehead regards the word "experience" as "one of the most deceitful in philosophy".[6] Nonetheless, he maintains that what philosophy describes or discloses through the system of general ideas is "our experience". This means that for him the primary datum for philosophical analysis is none other than subjective experiencing. This "subjectivist bias" is for Whitehead an ontological principle (referred to as "the reformed sub-

---

not ordinary language, is the truly original manifestation of human language. Reference to Heidegger here is not meant to be an agreement with his methodology as will be evident in what follows in the main text. While Heidegger's dissatisfaction with philosophical discourse leads him to poetic language, what is being claimed here is that poetry and other literary forms are a valuable *source* for philosophical thinking.

[4] A.N. Whitehead, *Modes of Thought* (Cambridge University Press, 1938), pp. 49-50. On this point, cf. Robert E. Doud, "A Whiteheadian Interpretation of Baudelaire's Poetry," *Process Studies,* XXXI, 2 (Fall-Winter, 2002), pp. 16-31.

[5] Whitehead, *Adventures of Ideas,* p. 291.

[6] A.N. Whitehead, *Symbolism: its Meaning and Effect* (Cambridge University Press, 1928), p. 19.

jectivist principle"). As he puts it, "Apart from the experiences of subjects there is nothing, nothing, nothing, bare nothingness."[7] Insofar as it is an ontological principle, experiencing is not, as is commonly understood, limited to human experiencing. Whitehead rejects any sharp distinction between humans and other beings, living and non-living. To make such a sharp distinction, according to him, is too vague and hazardous.[8] He therefore universalises experience, extending it to all realms of reality.

What makes human experience distinctive is that it includes thinking. But thinking itself does not constitute the generic nature of human existence since humans live even when asleep and are unconscious. Whitehead regards thinking as derived from sensation; however, not in the sense in which that is interpreted by the sensationalist theory of the empiricists, who maintain that "perception is the conscious entertainment of definite and clear-cut sensa".[9] According to Whitehead, experience cannot be identified with clear, distinct and conscious entertainment of sensation, explaining that the unborn child, the baby in its cradle, or one in the state of sleep, and so on have a vast background of feeling which is neither conscious nor definite. He explains, "Clear, conscious discrimination is an accident of human existence. It makes us human. But it does not make us exist. It is of the essence of our humanity. But it is an accident of our existence."[10] On the other hand, the structure of human experience discloses the structure of reality itself. As he puts it, "We construct the world in terms of the types of activities disclosed in our intimate experience."[11] One can find therefore in descriptions of human experience what Whitehead

---

[7] A.N. Whitehead, *Process and Reality*, corrected ed. by David Ray Griffin and Donald W. Sherburne (The Free Press, 1978), p. 167.
[8] A.N. Whitehead, *Science in the Modern World* (Cambridge University Press, 1926), p. 79, also his, *The Function of Reason* (Oxford University Press, 1929), p. 5.
[9] Whitehead, *Adventures of Ideas*, p. 228.
[10] Whitehead, *Modes of Thought*, p. 116. In *Function of Reason*, Whitehead explains, "The equating of experience with clarity of knowledge is against the evidence. In our own lives, and at any one moment, there is a focus of attention, a few items in clarity of awareness, but interconnected vaguely and yet insistently with other items in dim apprehension, and this dimness shading off imperceptibly into undiscriminated feeling. Further, the clarity cannot be segregated from the vagueness. The togetherness of the things that are clear refuses to yield its secret to clear analytic intuition. The whole forms a system, but when we set out to describe the system direct intuitions play us false. Our conscious awareness is fluctuating, flitting, and not under control. It lacks penetration. The penetration of intuition follows upon the expectation of thought. This is the secret of attention." p. 62.
[11] Whitehead, *Modes of Thought*, p. 115.

refers to as factors which also enter into the descriptions of less specialised natural occurrence.[12]

Whitehead describes every occasion of experience, human or otherwise, as dipolar; that is to say, it has an aspect of subjectivity and another aspect of objectivity, an aspect of process and another aspect of permanence.[13] "It is mental experience integrated with physical experience. Mental experience is the converse of bodily experience."[14] His reformed subjectivist principle is thus a claim that the final fact is a subject experiencing objects which in turn are determined subjects. Subject and object are thus regarded as interlinked in the same final fact. This claim amounts to a rejection of the extreme realist position of the sensationalist principle of the empiricist tradition which holds that "the primary activity in the act of experience is the bare subjective entertainment of the datum, devoid of any subjective form of reception."[15] As Whitehead explains it, experience is not purely a private qualification of the mind. He adds that "if experience be not based upon an objective content, there can be no escape from a solipsist subjectivism."[16] Accordingly, he affirms that "the world within experience is identical with the world beyond experience"[17] and that what Descartes discovered on the side of subjectivism "requires balancing by an 'objectivist' principle as to the datum for experience."[18]

---

[12] Whitehead, *Adventures of Ideas*, p. 237.
[13] Dipolarity is a metaphysical principle in both Whitehead's and Hartshorne's metaphysical systems.
[14] Whitehead, *Function of Reason*, pp. 25-26.
[15] Whitehead, *Process and Reality*, p. 157.
[16] *Ibid.* p. 152.
[17] Whitehead, *Adventures of Ideas*, p. 293. On page 268 and the following pages, Whitehead discusses the dichotomy within the objective content of an occasion of experience in terms of "appearance and reality".
[18] Whitehead, *Process and Reality*, p. 160. The following passage is a particularly helpful summation by Whitehead: "An occasion of experience is an activity, analysable into modes of functioning which jointly constitute its process of becoming. Each mode is analysable into the total experience as active subject, and into the thing or object with which the special activity is concerned. This thing is a datum, that is to say, is describable without reference to its entertainment in that occasion. An object is anything performing this function of a datum provoking some special activity of the occasion in question. Thus subject and object are relative terms. An occasion is a subject in respect to its special activity concerning an object; and anything is an object in respect to its provocation of some special activity within a subject. Such a mode of activity is termed a 'prehension'. Thus prehension involves three factors. There is the occasion of experience within which the prehension is a detail of activity; there is the datum whose relevance provokes the origination of this prehension; this datum is the prehended object; there is the subjective form,

Turning now to human experience itself, Whitehead describes two modes of experience, independent but each contributing its share of components into one concrete moment of human experience.[19] He calls the clear, conscious, sensory mode "perception in the mode of presentational immediacy". But this mode of experience is based upon and derived from a more elemental form of experience, which is vague and unconscious and which he calls "perception in the mode of causal efficacy".[20] The mode of causal efficacy, which Whitehead describes as heavy and primitive, dominates primitive living organisms.[21] He explains that in human experience, this elemental form of perception is exhibited by what he terms "withness of the body": "it is this withness that makes the body the starting point for our knowledge of the circumambient world."[22] Senses are specialisations of the withness of the body: "we see with our eyes, we do not see our eyes" while our body is "that portion of nature with which each moment of human experience intimately cooperates."[23] For this reason Whitehead maintains that it is difficult to determine accurately the definite boundary of one's body and that it is very vaguely distinguishable from external nature.[24] He regards the body as united with the environment as well as with the soul.[25] Causation then, as far as Whitehead is concerned, is not an a priori category within the mind alone, as in Kant, but an element in experience. The notion of causation arose, in his view, because mankind lives amid experiences in the mode of causal efficacy.[26] Thus the elemental form of perception is causation, it being an element of the very structure of reality.

Whitehead defines the mode of presentational immediacy, the other mode of experiencing, as "our immediate perception of the contemporary external world, appearing as an element constitutive of our own experience."[27]

---

which is the affective tone determining the effectiveness of that prehension in that occasion of experience. How the experience constitutes itself depends on its complex of subjective forms." p. 226.

[19] In *Symbolism*, p. 20, Whitehead actually mentions three modes, the third being "the mode of conceptual analysis".

[20] Whitehead, *Function of Reason*, pp. 78-79.

[21] Whitehead, *Symbolism*, p. 52.

[22] Whitehead, *Process and Reality*, p.112.

[23] Whitehead, *Modes of Thought*, p.115.

[24] *Ibid.* p. 114.

[25] *Ibid.* p. 161.

[26] Whitehead, *Process and Reality*, pp.166-167.

[27] By "presentational immediacy" Whitehead explains that he means what is usually termed "sense perception" but not as having exactly the same connotations as that term. Cf. *Symbolism*, p. 25. He maintains that "presentational immediacy is

It expresses how contemporary events are relevant to each other while preserving a mutual independence.[28] In this mode, contemporary things are "objectively" in our experience. No actual thing is objectified as such but only an abstraction. Among these abstract entities are those called sense-data; for example, colours, sounds, tastes, touches, and bodily feelings.[29] Compared to the mode of causal efficacy, presentational immediacy leads to knowledge that is vivid, precise, and barren. It is also to a large extent controllable at will; that is to say, that one moment of experience, through various modifications, can predetermine to a considerable extent the other characteristics of the presentational immediacy in succeeding moments of experience.[30]

---

only of importance in high-grade organisms, and is a physical fact which may, or may not, enter into consciousness. Such entry will depend on attention and on the activity of conceptual functioning, whereby physical experience and conceptual imagination are fused into knowledge," (p. 19) and that "the reason why low-grade purely physical organisms cannot make mistakes is not primarily their absence of thought, but their absence of presentational immediacy." p. 24. Also for most events, he presumes that their intrinsic experience of presentational immediacy is so embryonic as to be negligible. "This perceptive mode is important only for a small minority of elaborate organisms." p. 29.

[28] Whitehead, *Ibid.* p. 19. He cites the main facts about presentational immediacy to be: "(i) that the sense-data involved depend on the percipient organisms and its spatial relations to the perceived organisms, (ii) that the contemporary world is exhibited as extended and as a plenum of organisms, (iii) that presentational immediacy is an important factor in the experience of only a few high-grade organisms, and that for the others it is embryonic or entirely negligible," p. 26.

[29] *Ibid.* p. 30.

[30] Whitehead provides a useful summary in the following passage: "…the intervention of any sense-datum in the actual world cannot be expressed in any simple way, such as mere qualification of a region of space, or alternatively as the mere qualification of a state of mind. The sense-data, required for immediate sense-perception, enter into experience in virtue of the efficacy of the environment. This environment includes the bodily organs. For example, in the case of hearing sound, the physical waves have entered the ears, and the agitations of the nerves have excited the brain. The sound is then heard as coming from a certain region in the external world. Thus perception in the mode of causal efficacy discloses that the data in the mode of sense-perception are provided by it. This is the reason why there are such given elements. Every such datum constitutes a link between the two perceptive modes. Each such link, or datum, has a complex ingression into experience, requiring a reference to the two perceptive modes. These sense-data can be conceived as constituting the character of a many-termed relationship between the organisms of the past environment and those of the contemporary world." *Ibid.* pp. 62-63.

The fusing of these two modes into one perception is called by Whitehead "symbolic reference". He explains that in symbolic reference "the various actualities disclosed respectively by the two modes are either identified, or are at least correlated together as interrelated elements in our environment," the result being "what the actual world is for us, as that datum in our experience productive of feelings, emotions, actions, and finally as the topic for conscious recognition when our mentality intervenes with its conceptual analysis."[31] This linking of the two modes, which leads to human symbolism, shows that there are common structural elements since they are perceptions of the same world. However, there are gaps, which means that their fusion is indeterminate. Whitehead adds that "intellectual criticism founded on subsequent experience can enlarge and purify the primitive naïve symbolic transference."[32] He contrasts symbolic reference with direct recognition insofar as the latter is "conscious recognition of a percept in a pure mode, devoid of symbolic reference."[33] As a matter of fact, however, there is no complete ideal purity of either perceptive experience without any symbolic reference.[34] Error may arise in symbolic reference inasmuch as direct recognition may disagree in its report of the actual world. In symbolic reference mental analysis is rather at a minimum. On the other hand, it compensates for this in its imaginative freedom.

Symbolic reference precedes conceptual analysis, but the two promote each other. One may be inclined to associate symbolic reference with mental activity, but Whitehead holds that it is a matter of pure convention as to which of our experiential activities we term "mental" and which "physical" since, as we have already noted, for Whitehead there is no proper line to be drawn between the physical and the mental constitution of experience. Moreover, much of our perception is subtly enhanced by a concurrent conceptual analysis. There is no conscious knowledge without the intervention of mentality in the form of conceptual analysis.[35] Symbolic reference is a datum for thought in its analysis of experience. Our conceptual scheme of the universe should generally and logically be coherent with it and should correspond to the ultimate facts of the pure perceptive modes. But when this does not happen, we then should revise

---

[31] *Ibid.* p. 21.
[32] *Ibid.* p. 35.
[33] *Ibid.* p. 22.
[34] *Ibid.* p. 64.
[35] *Ibid.* p. 23.

our conceptual scheme to retain the general trust in the symbolic reference, while accepting as mistaken definite details of that reference.[36]

Whitehead also defines symbolic reference as "the organic functioning whereby there is transition from the symbol to the meaning," when some components of experience, i.e. symbols, elicit consciousness, beliefs, emotions, and usages, respecting other components of its experience, i.e. meaning. It is "the active synthetic element contributed by the nature of the percipient."[37] Symbolic reference is, as Whitehead defines it in another context, "the interpretative element in human experience".[38] In this sense, symbolic reference is related to language. In language we have a fundamental type of symbolism: "The word is a symbol, and its meaning is constituted by the ideas, images and emotions, which it raises in the mind of the hearers."[39] But in addition to the bare meaning, words and phrases carry with them an inclusive suggestiveness and an emotional efficacy associated with the way they had been used in history.[40] Whitehead explains this point: "A word has a symbolic association with its own history, its other meanings and with its general status in current literature. Thus a word gathers emotional signification from its emotional history in the past; and this is transferred symbolically to its meaning in present use."[41] He maintains that the whole basis of the art of literature is "that emotions and feelings directly excited by the words should fitly intensify our emotions and feelings arising from contemplation of the meaning."[42]

Given the above consideration by Whitehead on experience and our expression of that experience, what Whitehead has to say on literature is particularly relevant: "It is in literature that the concrete outlook of humanity receives its expression. Accordingly it is to literature that we must look, particularly in its more concrete forms, namely in poetry and in

---

[36] *Ibid.* p. 64.

[37] *Ibid.* p. 9.

[38] Whitehead, *Process and Reality*, p. 73.

[39] Whitehead, *Symbolism*, p. 2.

[40] *Ibid.* p. 79.

[41] *Ibid.* p. 99. In *Adventures of Ideas*, p. 5, Whitehead actually points out that there is no "mere knowledge" since knowledge is always accompanied by emotion and purpose.

[42] Whitehead, *Symbolism*, pp. 98-99. There is a certain vagueness in symbolism. Compared to direct experience which is infallible in that what one has experienced has been experienced, symbolism is very fallible "in the sense that it may induce actions, feelings, emotions, and beliefs about things which are mere notions without that exemplification in the world which the symbolism leads us to presuppose." *Ibid.* p. 7.

drama, if we hope to discover the inward thoughts of a generation."[43] We have already noted that he holds that the ultimate appeal is to experience, and now he adds his reason why he puts much stress on the evidence of poetry: "My point is, that in our sense-experience we know away from and beyond our own personality, whereas the subjectivist holds that in such experience we merely know about our own personality."[44] Whitehead points out that one function of great literature is to evoke a vivid feeling of what lies beyond words.[45] Literature manages to combine what Whitehead considers to be a curious mixture of "tacitly presupposing analysis, and conversely of returning to emphasise explicitly the fundamental emotional importance of our naïve general intuitions."[46]

It is interesting to compare Whitehead's observations with the poet Goethe's comments on poetry. Goethe holds that it is reality that provides, as it were "the points to be expressed". According to him, reality is the kernel. It also supplies the motive.[47] And Goethe's advice to the poet is: "Only have the courage to give yourself up to your impressions, allow yourself to be delighted, moved, elevated; nay, instructed and inspired for something great: but do not imagine all is vanity, if it is not abstract thought and idea."[48] As he reflects on his own role as poet, Goethe has this to say:

> It was in short not in my line, as a poet, to strive to embody anything *abstract*. I received in my mind impressions, and those of a sensuous, animated, charming, varied, hundred-fold kind—just a lively imagination presented them; and I had, as a poet, nothing more to do than to round off and elaborate artistically such views and impressions, and by means of a lively representation so to bring them forward that others might receive the same impression in hearing or reading my representation of them.[49]

Although in a different context, the novelist-philosopher Iris Murdoch makes a similar observation regarding literary modes of expressing our concrete experiences. She points out that literary modes are an everyday occurrence: they are naturally close to ordinary but reflective life. She remarks that we are beings who constantly use words, employing language

---

[43] Whitehead, *Science and the Modern World*, p. 106.
[44] *Ibid.* p. 125.
[45] Whitehead, *Modes of Thought*, p. 7.
[46] *Ibid.* p. 6.
[47] This text is included in Hazard Adams' anthology, *op. cit.*, p. 514.
[48] *Ibid.*
[49] *Ibid.* p. 515.

to make interesting what is originally dull or incoherent. Thus, we are immersed in a literary atmosphere, where we live and breathe literature. We all are, as she describes us, "literary artists". Literature or art of any sort emerges because of "the desire to defeat the formlessness of the world and cheer oneself up by constructing forms out of what might otherwise seem a mass of senseless rubble."[50]

The Role and Significance of Literature

As will have been observed by now, for Whitehead, literature is a way of capturing the concreteness of experience, and thus is a fertile source for philosophical reflections inasmuch as philosophical thinking arises from our experiences. In addition, the poetic rendering of our concrete experience, according to him, reminds us that "the element of value, of being valuable, of having value, of being an end in itself, of being something which is for its own sake, must not be omitted in any account of an event as the most concrete actual something."[51] By "value" he understands the intrinsic reality of an event. It is an element that permeates through and through the poetic view of nature. He illustrates this point by referring to the nature-poetry of the romantic poets, which he regards was a protest not only on behalf of the organic view of nature, but also against the exclusion of value in the description of reality. As he puts it rather succinctly, "The romantic reaction was a protest on behalf of value."[52]

Whitehead furthermore notes the significance of literature in general in its description of nature. Citing the works of Wordsworth, in particular, he compares the poet's view of nature with the strained and paradoxical view which modern science offers to us: "Wordsworth, to the height of

---

[50] Iris Murdoch, *Existentialist and Mystics: Writings on Philosophy and Literature* (London: Chatto & Windus, 1997), p. 6. Murdoch maintains that despite the fact that philosophy and literature are so different, they are both truth-seeking and truth-revealing activities. They are cognitive activities, explanations. She adds that "how far re-shaping involves offence against truth is a problem any artist must face." p.10. For Whitehead, philosophic truth is to be sought in the presuppositions of language rather than in its express statements. He maintains that this is why philosophy is akin to poetry in that both of them seek to express that ultimate good sense which we term civilisation. "In each case there is reference to form beyond the direct meaning of words. Poetry allies itself to metre, philosophy to mathematical pattern." *Modes of Thought*, p. viii. See also, Martha Nussbaum, *Love's Knowledge* (N.Y.: Oxford University Press, 1990).
[51] Whitehead, *Science and the Modern World*, p. 131.
[52] *Ibid.* p. 132.

genius, expresses the concrete facts of our apprehension, facts which are distorted on the scientific analysis. Is it not possible that the standardised concepts of science are only valid within narrow limitations, perhaps too narrow for science itself?"[53] Wordsworth's view can be a helpful corrective on how humans should relate to and deal with nature.

Whitehead bemoans the over-emphasis on the intellectual, an attitude that he considers prevalent in the learned world. Such an attitude, he claims, "sterilises imaginative thought, and thereby blocks progress."[54] Similarly, the Irish poet W.B.Yeats remarks in a rather forceful fashion: "By reason and logic we die hourly, by imagination we live."[55] Whitehead reminds us that all productive thought has resulted from and developed because of the poetic insight of artists, or by the imaginative elaboration of schemes of thought capable of utilization as logical premises[56] while philosophical thought has created for itself difficulties by dealing exclusively in very abstract notions.[57] In this connection, what Whitehead has to say about the advance of ideas is particularly significant:

> Now, so far as concerns beliefs of a general character, it is much easier for them to destroy emotion than to generate it. In any survey of the adventure of ideas nothing is more surprising than the ineffectiveness of novel general ideas to acquire for themselves an appropriate emotional pattern of any intensity. Profound flashes of insight remain ineffective for centuries, not because they are unknown, but by reason of dominant interests which inhibit reaction to that type of generality.[58]

From Literature to Philosophy

Whitehead, however, points out that "the language of literature breaks down precisely at the task of expressing in explicit form the larger generalities—the very generalities which metaphysics seeks to express."[59] One then needs to go further than literary language to philosophical language which uses reason. Whitehead regards reason as a factor in experience, one that directs and criticises the urge towards the attainment

---

[53] *Ibid.* p. 118.
[54] Whitehead, *Modes of Thought*, p. 59.
[55] Quoted in J.M. Cocking, *Imagination: a Study in the History of Ideas* (London & N.Y.: Routledge, 1991), p. viii.
[56] Whitehead, *Process and Reality*, p. 9.
[57] *Ibid.* p.18.
[58] Whitehead, *Adventures of Ideas*, p. 220.
[59] Whitehead, *Process and Reality*, p.11.

of an end which has been realised in imagination but not in fact.[60] He adds that "the essence of Reason in its lowliest forms is its judgments upon flashes of novelty, of novelty in immediate realisation and of novelty which is relevant to appetition but not yet to action."[61] Explaining further his point, he states that:

> In its lowliest form, Reason provides the emphasis on the conceptual clutch after some refreshing novelty. It is then Reason devoid of constructive range of abstract thought. It operates merely as the simple direct judgment lifting a conceptual flash into an effective appetition, and an effective appetition into a realised fact.[62]

Whitehead assigns to reason, and thus to philosophy, the task of understanding and purging the symbols on which humanity depends.[63]

As we have already noted in our discussion of the modes of experience, Whitehead maintains that consciousness itself does not initiate the process of knowledge. Rather, we find ourselves already engaged in it, "immersed in satisfactions and dissatisfactions, and actively modifying, either by intensification, or by attenuation, or by the introduction of novel purposes" but that "after instinct and intellectual ferment have done their work, there is a decision which determines the mode of coalescence of instinct with intelligence."[64] Here reason acts as "a modifying agency on the intellectual ferment so as to produce a self-determined issue from the given conditions."[65] Reason has a tremendous effect in selecting, emphasising, and disintegrating data.[66] In this sense one can say, according to Whitehead, that thought is mainly concerned with the justification or the modification of a pre-existing situation.[67] While all knowledge is conscious discrimination of objects experienced, this conscious discrimination—to return to the point already discussed earlier—is "nothing more than an additional factor in the subjective form of the interplay of subject with object.... All knowledge is derived from, and verified by, direct intuitive observation."[68]

---

[60] Whitehead, *Function of Reason*, p. 5.
[61] *Ibid.* p.15.
[62] *Ibid.* p.18.
[63] Whitehead, *Symbolism*, p. 8.
[64] Whitehead, *Adventures of Ideas*, p. 58.
[65] *Ibid.*
[66] *Ibid.* p. 127.
[67] *Ibid.* p. 140.
[68] *Ibid.* p. 227.

Whitehead also insists that it is the business of rational thought to describe the more concrete fact from which abstract thought has been derived.[69] Literature, which conveys meanings through rich and concrete images, powerful metaphors and engaging analogies, is a fertile field for philosophical reflections, which with the aid of reason, make such literary language more explicit. Philosophy for Whitehead is intended to regain an undivided world, to think together all aspects of reality. Its aim is to disclose "a complete fact" in all its scientific, aesthetic, moral, religious, etc. aspects. His well-known definition of speculative philosophy is: "the endeavour to frame a coherent, logical, necessary system of general ideas in terms of which every element of our experience can be interpreted."[70] Whitehead states that the rationalists failed to disclose a complete fact because of their chief error of overstatement.[71] They overstated abstraction and landed in a dogmatic fallacy. Whitehead understands as a function of philosophy "to harmonise, refashion, and justify divergent intuitions as to the nature of things"; he then argues that philosophy must "insist on the scrutiny of the ultimate ideas, and on the retention of the whole of the evidence in shaping our cosmological scheme. Its business is to render explicit, and—so far as may be—efficient, a process which otherwise is unconsciously performed without rational tests."[72] Philosophy makes the content of the human mind manageable by adding meaning to fragmentary details, by disclosing disjunctions and conjunctions, consistencies and inconsistencies.[73]

Moreover, Whitehead regards philosophical reflections as ongoing. Philosophy is an "endeavour", an "essay"—an adventurous attempt or search. As Whitehead so often puts it, "Philosophy is the search for premises. It is not deduction."[74] It is not surprising then that he describes philosophy as "descriptive generalization"[75] inasmuch as it should describe, rather than explain, reality. He is critical of traditional philosophy which explained things and whose preoccupation was on the principles which constitute the concrete things, thereby ignoring the very concreteness of reality.[76] Whitehead also uses the term "imaginative generalization" to

[69] *Ibid.* p. 239.
[70] *Ibid.* p. 285; also, Whitehead, *Process and Reality*, p. 3.
[71] Whitehead, *Process and Reality*, p. 11.
[72] Whitehead, *Science and the Modern World*, p. ix.
[73] Whitehead, *Modes of Thought*, p. 67.
[74] *Ibid.* p. 105.
[75] Whitehead, *Process and Reality*, pp.15-16.
[76] Whitehead, *Adventures of Ideas*, p. 143.

refer to philosophy[77] highlighting the point that by an imaginative leap the philosopher attempts to capture those aspects of reality which logical technicalities cannot reach.[78]

The following passage sums up Whitehead's conception of the philosophical task in the context of what has been said so far:

> Philosophy is the critic of abstractions. Its function is the double one, first of harmonising them by assigning to them their right relative status as abstractions, and secondly of completing them by direct comparison with more concrete intuitions of the universe, and thereby promoting the formation of more complete schemes of thought. It is in respect to this comparison that the testimony of great poets is of such importance. Their survival is evidence that they express deep intuitions of mankind penetrating into what is universal in concrete fact. Philosophy is not one among the sciences with its own little scheme of abstractions which it works away at perfecting and improving. It is the survey of sciences, with the special objects of their harmony, and of their completion. It brings to this task not only the evidence of the separate sciences, but also its own appeal to concrete experience. It confronts the sciences with concrete fact.[79]

In our philosophical discussion about our experience of reality, Whitehead reminds us of a 3-fold distinction of what we need to keep in mind: "(i) our direct intuitions which we enjoy prior to all verbalisation; (ii) our literary modes of verbal expression of such intuitions, together with the dialectic deductions from such verbal formulae; (iii) the set of purely deductive sciences, which have been developed so that the network of possible relations with which they deal are familiar in civilised consciousness."[80] He warns us that the chief dangers in philosophy are dialectic deductions from inadequate formulae which exclude direct intuitions, such as those found in literature.[81]

---

[77] Whitehead, *Process and Reality*, p. 7.

[78] *Ibid.* p. 6.

[79] Whitehead, *Science and the Modern World*, p. 122.

[80] Whitehead, *Adventures of Ideas*, p. 177.

[81] *Ibid.* pp. 177-78. Whitehead refers to what he calls "third chapter of evidence" delivered by language, which concerns "meanings beyond individual words and beyond grammatical forms, meanings miraculously revealed in great literature." *Ibid.* p. 291.

APPENDIX B

SUFFERING AND SURRENDER IN THE MIDST OF DIVINE PERSUASION: A DISCUSSION OF THE SIAS' APPROACH TO THE CHALLENGE OF SUFFERING AND EVIL

BY ALIMAN SEARS

We take it in stride when we hear Lady Macbeth proclaim that while giving suck to an infant she may, "while it was smiling in my face, Have pluck'd my nipple from his boneless gums, And dash'd the brains out", but such depravity is real: in the United States about 600 children are killed each year by their mothers[1] Evil seems to be ubiquitous. And evidence for the human propensity toward evil is overabundant, as are accounts of evil (murder) in the animal world.[2] If a caring God exists, why is there so much evil and suffering in the world? Furthermore, do human beings have a responsibility to abate evil? If so, what is the nature of evil and how may evil be nullified?

In this essay we will examine how we might transpose our traditional thinking and *dissolve* the "problem of evil" instead of trying to *solve* the problem of evil along traditional lines. We will examine an underlying theme in Marian and Santiago Sia's novel *The Fountain Arethuse* (hereafter: *Arethuse),* and see that this theme is a transformed version of the traditional approach to the problem of evil. Instead of dealing with the question of the existence of divinity, the Sias ask, "What kind of God can we continue to believe in, given the presence of so much undeserved suffering?"[3]

---

[1] LyallWalson, *Dark Nature: A Natural History of Evil* (London: Hodder & Stoughton, 1995), p. 175, .Also see William Shakespeare,*Macbeth* (I, vii, 56·-8).
[2] For example, see Frans De Waal„*Peacemaking Among Primates* (Cambridge,MA: Harvard University Press, 1989). Also see Jane Goodall, *The Chimpanzees of Gombe* (Cambridge,MA: Harvard University, 1986).
[3] Marian Sia and Santiago Sia, *The Fountain Arethuse: a Novel set in the University Town of Leuven* (Lewes, U.K.: The Book Guild, Ltd., 1997), p. 107.

It turns out that the kind of God we can continue to believe in bodes well with the religious comportment of "surrender", and that this comportment is the path that leads towards dissolving the problem of evil.

The basis for the Sias' novel is the Whiteheadian/Hartshornean approach to philosophy and theology, called "process philosophy" or "process theology". Before writing the novel *Arethuse* the Sias had written an academic book, *From Suffering to God: Exploring our Images of God in the Light of Suffering,* and this earlier text explores some of the very same questions raised in *Arethuse,* but from a more scholarly point of view.[4] In addition to examining the problem of evil in general, this essay will trace common themes in the two books and explicate the underlying theodicy in *Arethuse.* I will also show the connections between *Arethuse* and the Hartshornean idea of God and divine power. In Charles Hartshorne's conceptual scheme, God is not the sole cause of creaturely actions and is therefore not solely responsible for evil. As the writings of Alfred North Whitehead and Hartshorne show, this implies nothing less than a reconception of divine power as traditionally conceived. This reconception leads to different approaches (I will explicate three such approaches) to the problem of evil, and it also leads to a revised interpretation of our relation to divinity. Since God does not control human actions, it follows that humans have the responsibility to "surrender", so as to bring God's power into the world and thus help abate evil in the world.

The Recovery of Reason

Present-day thinking about theology and religion distances humanity from its own spiritual roots. Thus, before we examine the above issues in detail, let us first turn our attention to the need today to recover the use of reason in the portrayal of divinity, with the hope that it may become clear that the domain of theological investigations is important for all persons: theistic, agnostic and atheistic.   .

Modern thinking deprecates the power of reason. In this age of Nietzsche, Heidegger *et al.,* deconstructive postmodernism indicts theologians and philosophers of religion with practising onto-theology, and with presuming that reason can yield truth. Pope John Paul II laments that "There is the distrust of reason found in much contemporary philosophy, which has largely abandoned metaphysical study of the ultimate human questions in order to concentrate upon problems which are more detailed

---

[4] For reviews, see Theodore Walker, "Reviews of *From Suffering to God,* and *The Fountain Arethuse," Process Studies,* 28, 1-2 (1999), pp. 147-149.

and restricted, at times even purely formal."[5] Abandonment of the ultimate questions happens not because of the unintelligibility of the thinking underlying theology or metaphysics, but because of the inability of the modernistic, narrow, scientifically-oriented conception of reason that is currently in vogue. Talking about God entails opening up this narrow notion of reason and letting reason regain its ancient ground of "robustness". This is a recovery of the reason used by Plato, Socrates and Aristotle, the reason that starts in wonder and is open to all human experience and activity, the reason imbued with a teleological ethos, the reason of thinking and of feeling. Whitehead laments that "Philosophy has been haunted by the unfortunate notion that its method is dogmatically to indicate premises which are severely clear, distinct, and certain; and to erect upon those premises a deductive system of thought."[6] Modernistic reason has narrowed the domain of philosophical and theological thinking.

In contrast, the expanded reason of *constructive postmodernism* can wlden the domain again. Against *deconstructive postmodernism,* a construction of worldviews and knowledge is still needed today, but the reconstruction should be launched from a broader platform than tradition allowed in the past. The new reconstruction should take into account the whole of human experience. The question is: can we account for *all* human experience in a coherent way? This widening of parameters is called *constructive postmodernism,* and it cuts across traditional battle lines (of, for example, empiricism/rationalism and realism and idealism). The path of investigation is shaped from a wider platform: the investigation of reality is shaped by literature and the arts as well as science and theology—all realms are respected. Constructive postmodernism is a creative synthesis of pre-modern, modern and postmodern intuitions.[7] An important part of these intuitions is our felt, pre-thematic or pre-reflective experiences in the world.[8] Constructive postmodernism expands the domain of investigation by giving credence to feeling and action in the world as well as to thinking.

---

[5] Pope John Paul II, *Fides et Ratio*, Papal Encyclical, September, 1998., p. 56.

[6] Alfred North Whitehead, *Process and Reality: An Essay in Cosmology*, corrected edition by David R. Griffin and Donald Sherburne (N.Y.: the Free Press, 1978), p. xi.

[7] David Ray Griffin (ed.). *The Reenchantment of Science: Postmodern Proposals* (Albany, N.Y.: SUNY Press), 1988), p. xi.

[8] Causality is a felt prereflective experience. All persons feel the present as causally influenced by past events. Even those sceptics that verbally deny causation cannot efface the prereflective belief in real causation. See John B. Cobb Jr. and David Ray Griffin, *Process Theology: an Introductory Exposition* (Philadelphia: The Westminster Press, 1976), p. 31.

In terms of theology, this expanded view may show us that nearly everyone already has an image or idea of God, and that we already use reason to deal with that image, and finally that it is thus possible to change that image. Regarding religionists, even those who appeal to Mystery about perplexing theological matters at a minimum pre-reflectively believe in contending with the divine in a logically coherent manner (that is, even negative theology has a logic). Regarding those with an atheistic mindset, the word "God" has meaning for atheists, because an atheist must have a definite idea of what he or she rejects.[9] This assumed definition of God, naturally, profoundly shapes a person's stance towards divinity and spirituality. Childish or incoherent notions of divinity often breed atheism. If we already have an idea of God, it is possible to refine and evolve that idea.

Recovering the power of reason may let us participate in the spiritual dimension of human existence which we pre-thematically feel is part of us. It is important to recover reason and engage in this constructive postmodern search for intelligibility because people in general already have the resources to engage in a deeper spiritual existence, but traditional viewpoints currently distance people from that awareness. Holding the narrow materialistic or sensationistic worldview, or even a traditional theistic worldview, may further today's nihilistic attitude wherein notions of religion and spirituality are either absent or only theoretically operative in our day-to-day lives. And so, by re-examining traditional theism in the light of the Whiteheadian/ Hartshornean reconception of divine power, a shift in human awareness towards a deeper spirituality may occur; religious persons may see and feel more deeply the basis of their spirituality and shift into an ecumenical realm characterised by an appreciation of the mystical dimension. In turn, the agnostic and even atheistic worlds may shift towards the process theistic point of view wherein spirituality may come alive. It is this process theistic point of view that we examine through a consideration of *Arethuse* and *From Suffering to God.*

---

[9] Marian Sia and Santiago Sia, *From Suffering to God: Exploring our Images of God in the Light of Suffering* (London: the Macmillan Press, 1994), p. 1

Arethuse and *From Suffering to God*

Arethuse and *From Suffering to God* both sprang from within the philosophical and theological horizon offered by the Whiteheadian/ Hartshomean synthesis of pre-modern, modern and postmodern intuitions. Both books attempt to communicate that reason can be used in the search for God by reconstructing a world-view from a multifaceted theme: the Whiteheadian/Hartshornean "event ontology". They seek to communicate issues related to process metaphysics and process theology: *Arethuse* in a literary mode, and *From Suffering to God* in an academic mode. Santiago Sia has stressed that it is important to develop a methodology followed in process thought that takes seriously the role of concrete experience in thinking, and is inclusive of literary and poetic insights as a basis for abstract thinking.[10] Recovering the use of literary and poetic insights is part of the purpose of *Arethuse*. Sia has likewise stressed the importance of making process ideas more readily available through using literary modes of presentation.[11] At the same time, *From Suffering to God* argues for the need to develop those insights philosophically.

From Suffering to God makes connections between literature, theology and philosophy. It points out that conventional religious attitudes—the traditional concept of God and the traditional formulation of the problem of evil—lead directly to atheism for many people today, but that, if those attitudes are shifted, belief and faith may emerge instead of atheism. Using the thinking of Hartshorne, the book outlines the role of human reason in thinking about God, and explores notions of God as Co-Sufferer and as Liberator. It takes as its starting point the observation that some people live in bleak situations but continue to believe in "the God of Life", to use a phrase coined by Gustavo Gutierrez, noted Latin American liberation theologian. Rather than suffering being a route to atheism, knowledge of God can deepen or even arise in the midst of suffering. According to the authors, "Whereas atheism, given the presence of considerable misery and evil in the world, protests against belief in God, [our] aim is to give due regard to the experiences of many people who

---

[10] Santiago Sia, "Concretising Concrete Experience: a Discussion Paper on a Possible Task for Process Thought in Europe," Paper presented at a conference on "The Future of Process Thought in Europe", Lille, France, 1 April 1997, p. 4. See also Santiago Sia, "Process Thought as Conceptual Framework," *Process Studies*, 19, 4 (1990), pp. 248-255.

[11] On this score see some of the early and entertaining essays by Whitehead such as "The Clerk of the Weather," *Cambridge Review* 7, 10 (February 1886) and "Davy Jones," *Cambridge Review*, 7, 12 (May 1886), pp. 311-312.

continue to believe in God despite suffering, impoverishment and oppression. But unlike traditional theism, this work starts not with a developed concept of God but with reflections on the experience of suffering and asks what it can disclose about God."[12] Therefore, although the book addresses the problems of suffering and evil, it is not a theodicy in the traditional sense of a purely logical vindication of belief in God.

Arethuse grew spontaneously from the soil of these issues, and was written after the Sias completed writing *From Suffering to God*. Set in the university town of Leuven, Belgium (where the Sias actually wrote *From Suffering to God)*, *Arethuse* offers original responses to perplexities faced by people in the throes of everyday life. Fictitious scholars from around the world, thrown into the hub of university life in Leuven, grapple with their lives and with their disciplines. We see how philosophical assumptions shape the decisions and attitudes of the characters: the senseless death of Sean O'Shea, the husband of a young literature lecturer (Aisling O'Shea) from Ireland, results in Aisling's enmity for an uncaring God. How can God let this happen? Moreover, Richard Gutierrez, an American philosophy instructor desperately seeking tenure, arrives in Leuven and questions the relationship between his intellectual commitment to Thomistic philosophy and his lived experience of the everyday world: what relevance does an academic inquiry into *the problem of evil* have for real people undergoing real suffering? Finally, an eminent Polish philosopher, Piotr Malachowski, turns to process philosophy as he tries to come to grips with the abominations suffered by his family in the Nazi camps of World War II: given the depravity of the Nazis and the suffering of his parents in the camps, how can we countenance the reality of a caring God?

With this said, we may now explore the underlying process theodicy in *Arethuse* through an analysis of, and reflections on, some of the events and characters.

Is God to Blame?

Aisling O'Shea, the young English literature lecturer from Ireland, has received a grant to study postmodernism and literature at the Mercier University in Leuven, Belgium. Accompanying her is her six-year-old son, Philip. Aisling is carrying the burden of raising Philip alone. Her husband, Sean, was a fellow teacher at Aisling's university in Dublin. The two met while doing their graduate work and, as they delved deeper into literature,

---

[12] Sia and Sia, *From Suffering to God*, p. 10.

she English and he the Classics, their relationship deepened. They were married and enjoyed a full life in Dublin until, when Philip was just a year old, Sean was senselessly killed by a drunk driver. This crushed Aisling— her world had utterly collapsed and she almost gave up.

At one point in the novel Aisling is recalling an event that took place five years before her arrival in Leuven when she, Sean, and the one-year-old Philip had just returned to Dublin from a leisure-filled vacation in southern Spain. As soon as they arrived back home in Dublin, they received a phone call saying a friend's one-year old child had been in an accident and was in a critical condition at a local hospital. Sean immediately dropped everything and went to the hospital to console the parents, Patrick and Eileen, in their difficult time. This is an example of a practical response to human suffering: rather than going to the hospital and trying to explain anything or provide answers for the parents, Sean simply sits in solidarity with them, thus sharing their burden. Meanwhile, Aisling stayed at home unpacking suitcases and caring for the baby:

> It was almost 11:00 in the evening when Aisling heard a car pull up on the driveway. While waiting for Sean she had unpacked their suitcases, fed the baby and put him back to sleep. She had been restless throughout. Bad news like that always unsettled her. She breathed a sigh of relief. 'Thank God, he's back,' she muttered.
>
> The doorbell rang. Did he forget his keys? She wondered. Sean was so anxious to be of some comfort to their friends in their moment of pain he must have forgotten them. She hurried down the stairs ... She opened the door.
>
> It was the Gardaí
>
> 'Mrs Aisling O'Shea? I'm afraid that we have some very bad news for you. Can we come in?' The two Gardaí removed their caps and followed Aisling, who had gone pale.
>
> There had been an accident, the Gardaí explained ... Sean did not have a chance. He died instantly, while the other driver managed to pull himself out of the wreck.[13]

The Gardaí reported that Sean had spent a few hours sharing in the suffering and difficulty with Patrick and Eileen. Simply his presence, rather than any words, provided tremendous comfort for the parents.

After the Gardaí left that night, Aisling went through stages of bewilderment, denial and finally anger. In her bewilderment she sobbed uncontrollably in the midst of a vacuous feeling. She dragged herself around the house throughout this agony, going from room to room fleeing the com-

---

[13] Sia and Sia, *The Fountain Arethuse*, pp. 46-47.

plete emptiness pressing in upon her. When she finally realised it was not a nightmare her denial turned into a seething anger at God:

> She could feel her muscles tense up. She was clenching her fists, as she wanted to strike hard, really hard, at whoever was responsible for this. Not just the driver, but whoever allowed that situation to happen. Blast any community that does not prevent such things! Curse those barmen who keep selling drinks to those who are already too drunk to decide for themselves. Where are those parents who did not instill responsibility into this driver, even if they had to *beat* it into him? The pain he was causing her was unforgivable. Curse ...
> '*God, why did you let this happen?*' Aisling cried out. 'We had always been taught to love you and trust in your goodness. This is not good, this is wrong. Then why, with all your power, did you not prevent the accident? Just a few minutes more and Sean would have missed the other driver.' She was angry with God, angry because, unlike Sean who had tried to take care of Philip, God was not caring enough for the likes of Sean and her. God seemed in fact to be toying with them, giving them a happy life, only to snatch it away now. 'God, how can you do this? Why do you do this?'....*What kind of God was this?*[14]

The bewildered Aisling was in pain partly as a result of her notion of an all-perfect, all-powerful, and all-controlling God, a belief from her childhood. In *From Suffering to God,* the Sias delineate some of the theological background involved in this traditional conception of God's power, and in juxtaposition offer a Hartshornean or process view. On this view, God does not fully control the actions of creatures because creatures enjoy true freedom, therefore the blame does not rest solely with God as Aisling imagines. When Aisling asked, *What kind of God was this?* she was asking a crucial question. Since our ideas of God can only be humanly constructed notions if our experience contradicts our notion of God, we have to question and challenge that received or traditional idea of God. I suspect atheists become who they are because they reject an inadequately cultivated concept of God, not because they disbelieve in God *per se*.[15] Rather than blaming God for injustices, we should look to ourselves and our societies, for we are truly free creatures. To be truly free entails accountability; if we are accountable because we are truly free then we cannot blame God. Hartshorne says, "The creatures must determine something of their own actions, and to this extent the supreme capacity to in-

---

[14] *Ibid.,* p. 52.
[15] Sia and Sia, *From Suffering to God,* pp. 1-2.

fluence others cannot be power unilaterally to determine the details of reality."[16] God and creatures co-create in a social manner, with God leading the way.[17] On this scenario, Sean and the people around him (the drunk driver, the bartenders, the parents of the drunk driver and so on) are all partly responsible for his death; God is not the sole cause. On Hartshorne's view, God sets the limits of the universe by way of the natural laws and this only means that the arena creatures have to operate in is advantageous and ordered in the long run rather than risky and chaotic. But some risks are necessarily involved.[18] "God provides creatures with such guidance or inspiration as will optimise the ratio of opportunities and risks ... while setting the best or optimal limits to freedom."[19] Given this view, Aisling is wrong in blaming God.

Instead of claiming that God causes evil, Hartshorne asserts that the root of evil in the world is the clash of decisions made by free creatures, and this is bound up with Hartshorne's conviction regarding the nature of *creativity*. Creativity pervades all of reality. It is the basic notion in Hartshorne's interpretation of causality. All processes atomic, biological, social and so on, are creative in some sense. Creativity lies in the nature of all things that they may enter into a complex and creative unity with other things.[20] On Hartshorne's view, elements from the past enter into the constitution of the entity being shaped in the present, and these acts contour or condition the present, but they do not *determine* the present because any coming together always involves some creativity:

> Causes, including God as Supreme Cause, never determine the effect in all its details. While a cause is necessary in the sense that there can be no effect without a cause, it does not follow that the event will take place in precisely the way it is predicted, even when all the necessary causes are present. All one can say is that it may take place. There will be *an* effect but it will not be a fully detemlinate effect. Because every effect has a creative

---

[16] *Ibid.*, p. 52

[17] Note that "co-creation" is not an omnipotent God sharing power with creatures. An omnipotent God sharing power may be "traditional free will theism" and is a position that opposes process theism. For (at least) 10 problems with traditional free-will theism, see David Ray Griffin, *Evil Revisited: Responses and Reconsiderations* (Albany, N.Y: SUNY Press, 1991), pp. 16-22.

[18] See Charles Hartshorne, "A New Look at the Problem of Evil," in F.C. Dommeyer (ed.), *Current Philosophical Issues: Essays in Honor of Curt John Ducasse* (Springfield, Ill.: Charles C. Thomas, 1966), pp. 209-210.

[19] Sia and Sia, *From Suffering to God*, p. 131.

[20] Whitehead, *Process and Reality,* 21,

aspect it is never literally anticipated.[21]

Today's scientists, especially given the findings in particle physics, are also encountering this statistical notion of causality, even in terms of the actual laws of physics themselves.[22] Because of (among other things to be discussed) this unknown element of creativity and the harmonisation or lack of it that result from free choices, evil sometimes occurs The night Sean died, he and others made certain free decisions about driving a car. There are virtually hundreds of small decisions made at the time of driving and at other times that ultimately affect the probability of a person getting into an accident or not; for example, route taken, speed, physical condition of one's body, physical upkeep of the car, as well as various decisions by other persons, such as decisions made by the drunk driver, his friends at the pub, the employees of the pub, the police and the societal stance regarding drunk driving. Hartshorne stresses also, that chance plays a role in the probabilistic notion of causes, because the degree to which free decisions harmonise is partly due to chance. God persuades entities along the most harmonious path, but God does not eliminate freedom or chance in the process: "Through the laws of nature God puts restrictions within which the lesser agents can effectively work out the details of their existence. These limits ensure that universal creativity does not end in universal chaos and frustration. But because of chance, there will still be elements of chaos and frustration; but they remain subordinate to the general order and harmony."[23] The root of all tragedy in the world, then, is the clash of free creaturely creativity.[24]

Some classical theists, however, vehemently retain the notion of a traditionally omnipotent God and are uncomfortable with the scenario of co-decision or co-creation between God and humans. But by maintaining the idea of an utterly omnipotent God, theists fuel an atheistic argument that God as creator and administrator of everything is thus responsible for eve-

---

[21] Sia and Sia, *From Suffering to God*, p. 135.

[22] See an essay by a widely-respected physicist regarding the postulation that physical laws evolve, Walter Thirring, "Do the Laws of Nature Evolve?" in Michael P. Murphy and Luke A. J. O'Neil (eds.), *What is Life? The Next Fifty Years* (Cambridge University Press, 1995), p. 131f.

[23] Sia and Sia, *From Suffering to God*, p. 133.

[24] Because of their particular approach, some process theologians (particularly Hartshorne) have been cited with overlooking heinous or monstrous evil. For an attempt to address this issue, see the declaration of "Demonic Evil" in Griffin, *Evil Revisited*, pp. 31-40, wherein the demonic is defined as creativity that diverges strongly from the divine creative aims in a violently destructive way.

rything in the world. The traditional view that God imposes an omnipotent will on the world, and that the will of creatures carries little weight, spawns the atheistic conclusion that because evil exists a good God cannot exist. Hartshorne says:

> Sometimes I think this should be shouted from the housetops: the most famous,and probably the most influential, atheistic argument implies a misconception of the idea of divine power, a misconception that does not exalt God but really degrades Him to the level of a tyrant unwilling or unable to inspire and permit in others any genuine decision-making.[25]

The questions for classical theism are: What problems could God *possibly have,* being supremely and eternally secure, with participating in co-creation with truly free creatures? Is it possible to have an unequivocally meaningful universe without creatures who make unequivocally free decisions? Hartshorne thinks not. The radical absurdity of such a meaningless universe came crashing down on Aisling the night of Sean's death because, in her case, the absurdity stemmed from her notion of an omnipotent and all-controlling God. Hartshorne maintains, "No worse falsehood was ever perpetrated than the traditional concept of omnipotence. It is a piece of unconscious blasphemy, condemning God to a dead world, probably not distinguishable from no world at all."[26] Aisling was *literally feeling* this absurd, dead world, and was suffering from that feeling.

God as *Actually* Caring

Another aspect of Aisling's suffering over the death of her husband is that she had difficulty finding solace in God given her assumption that God is perfect and impassible and therefore cannot sympathise with creatures. If God is all-controlling and removed from our personal situation, and makes decisions by an unknown logic about what happens in the world, one possible reaction is Aisling's reaction: feelings of profound abandonment. Classical theism holds that God is perfect and impassible, therefore God cannot feel passion, disappointment or sorrow. Anselm wanted to deny any passion in God, yet concomitantly he wanted to sustain the notion of a compassionate God. To solve this dilemma, Anselm held that "God is compassionate in terms of our experience, but not so in

---

[25] Charles Hartshorne, "Can We Understand God?" *Louvain Studies,* 7, 2 (1978), pp. 75-84.
[26] Charles Hartshorne, *Omnipotence and Other Theological Mistakes* (Albany, N.Y.: SUNY, 1984), pp. 17-18.

terms of God's being. While we experience the effect of God's compassion, God does not."[27] The questions here become: Is such one-way help possible? If God does not *actually* care and feel for us in our suffering, then where is our comfort? It seems that classical theism demands that humans somehow ignore the normal biological and psychological necessities of human existence.

Tradition reports that Jobn Wesley's dying words were, "The best of all is this, that God is with us." If God is truly "with us" God would be compassionate with us and share in our sorrows. In Chapter Three of *From Suffering to God,* the Sias consider another aspect of the process theistic notion of God: a God "with us" is, in some sense, a Co-sufferer. They explore this idea by using the analogy of a practical response to human suffering, namely, the comforting of victims by joining in immediate and unconditional solidarity with them. In *Arethuse,* this response is well illustrated. Sean does this by immediately going to the hospital to console his friends, Patrick and Eileen, in their moment of need, even though his personal situation requires his presence at home. The burden of the suffering parents is greatly eased even though Sean spends little time actually *talking* to Patrick and Eileen. The parents share their fears by telling Sean some of the details of the accident their son was in, and Sean simply listens, taking on the burden, and sits quietly in solidarity with them for some time. This is co-suffering. The knowledge and the feeling that other people *truly care* about us in moments of suffering can intensely ease our burden: given our psychological make-up, this may be the only way that any entity (including God) can help ease suffering. In times of crisis, barriers between people fall and real sharing takes place, with therapeutic results. If God does not suffer with us in solidarity and, as Anselm claims, is only *apparently* and not really moved by our plight, it is hard to see how such a being can ease our suffering. Something is amiss with Anselm's God if that God only causes us to feel that God is compassionate, while the reality is that God is not compassionate.

Surrender and God's Persuasive Power

Sean's death tore Aisling apart and left her abandoned and without hope, but eventually she was able to surrender that hopelessness and move on. Prior to that point, however, the nights were long and lonely and the days filled with hardship. She was mistaken for an unmarried mother; she experienced people's prejudice and hate towards her; and she suffered the

---

[27] Sia and Sia, *From Suffering to God,* p. 135.

humiliation of single men taking her for "a poor weak thing that sorely needed the protection of stalwart men like themselves". All this made her bitter, but "she knew that simply fighting back in rage and bitterness was not going to end the misery and frustration that she was experiencing. She was being hurt by others, and she was helping them hurt her even more by being bitter and angry ... She was contributing to the seeming absurdity of life."[28] The God she was taught to believe in, one who oversees and controls everything, was no longer a God she could believe in. In a dialogue with Richard Gutierrez, the American philosopher on a sabbatical in Leuven, Aisling admits that she lost her faith: "It was the very idea of paying homage to a God who couldn't care less about me. Why should I care about *that* God?"[29] Unknown to Aisling, her loss of faith in *that* God was the first step towards her "surrendering" and eventual ability to move ahead with her life in the midst of a new faith. We will return to Aisling's situation after we elucidate our particular notion of surrender.

What is meant by "surrender"? Process thinking posits that God acts from within creatures and provides for each entity a persuasive lure of feeling that leads the creatures in the most harmonious direction contingent upon their particular present and past situation. Religion or spirituality then must be about feeling this divine lure in ourselves. The idea of "surrender" as a religious comportment centres upon the fact that reality is too complex. to fathom with our discursive reasoning process. William James quips that moralists often prescribe intense use of the will in observance of religious or ethical law, but that it "only makes them two-fold more the children of hell they were before".[30] Continually trying to second guess something as complex as human existence may lead to severe frustration. Instead, James recommends self-·surrender, and by this he means giving up an attitude of responsibility, and taking on an attitude of indifference; by doing so the very things that one thought one was surrendering are in fact gained. Although I have the greatest respect for James, nevertheless surrender as he describes it may be further nuanced because surrender as a spiritual comportment is different from apathy, renunciation, or passivity. If one merely resigns effort because the path is too difficult, or if one's surrendering is contingent upon receiving some grace or guidance, then the self is still at the centre of awareness. Being concerned about the self, naturally, is *antithetical* to self-surrender. Surrender requires thrusting oneself into the middle, into that "no-man's land" of both doing and not

---

[28] Sia and Sia, *The Fountain Arethuse*, p. 276.

[29] *Ibid.* 277.

[30] William James, *The Varieties of Religious Experience: the Study in Human Nature*, with an Introduction by Martin E. Marty (N.Y.: Penguin books, 1985), p. 110.

doing, of both activity and passivity.[31]

In a manner of speaking, one must surrender without attempting to surrender. "Surrender" as used here is a perplexing concept, more akin to concepts found in eastern religion and philosophy. Again, surrender does not mean abdication, disempowerment or resignation, but quite the contrary. Surrender is the capacity to set aside worries, immediate goals and desires, to make room for action in the moment. Surrender means letting go and not acting—but it also means struggling with what Whitehead would likely call "the remainder of things". In surrendering one waits for the myriad of circumstances to arrange themselves so that with one small adjustment the whole falls into place. Three examples are helpful here. First, in order for an athlete to win a contest, surrendering the goal of winning may empower him/her to perform at the maximum capacity and with spontaneity: surrendering enables the mind and the body to be free so as to render the crucial act at the crucial moment. Second, a business owner should surrender the immediate success of his/her business so as to operate impartially within the folds of novelty and spontaneity. This surrender is the essence of negotiating risk in the business world. Third, some martial artists are able to "become" their opponent: through surrendering their own will they feel the prereflective will of their opponent, thereby feeling the mode of attack at the same time that their opponent feels that they should initiate an attack. This then enables them to meet the attack and foil it spontaneously. In all three of these examples the person does not simply give up—they "surrender". In fact, surrender somehow *intensifies* the quest or the activity.

Surrender as a comportment is found in traditions such as Quietism and

---

[31] There are overtones here of William Desmond's philosophy of "the between". Desmond articulates a fourfold sense of being: univocal, equivocal, dialectical and metaxological. On pain of over-simplification, we note that the univocal sense of being puts the emphasis on simple sameness and sweeping unity; the equivocal breaks out of this unity to do justice to diversities which cannot be mediated; the dialectical tries to mediate equivocity and overcome the equivocal difference, but sometimes dialectic may be too self-involved because its mediation reorganises and fundamentally changes what it reconciles. Thus, the metaxological sense of being avoids the reduction of dialectical subordination: it lets the other three senses of being, even if they repudiate one another, live in a dynamic interrelationship. There is no closure here, nor is there simply a free play of capacities. The metaxological between is complex and full of harmonies and tensions as is our notion of "surrender". Surrender is in-between activity/passivity, in-between light/dark, and not quite grey either. Regarding this four-fold sense of being, see William Desmond, *Desire, Dialectic and Otherness: An Essay on Origins* (New Haven, CT: Yale University Press, 1987).

Taoism. Regarding the latter, "Tao" signifies "Way" or "Path". Taoism is characterised by opposites in harmonious interaction, and one such pair of opposites forms the concept of doing and not-doing, or "non-action". *Wu-wei* in Chinese means "non-action" or "non-doing". However, it does not mean total passivity or inactivity. A person implementing the *wu-wei* in his/her life surrenders and simplifies, and relies on proper timing to resolve the situation into a harmonious resolution. In Taoism *wu-wei* is regarded as the secret to a happy and harmonious life, for through non-action all things can be accomplished:

> Learning consists in daily accumulating;
> The practice of Tao consists in daily diminishing.
> Keep on diminishing and diminishing,
> Until you reach the state of No-Ado [non-action].
> No-Ado, and yet nothing is left undone.[32].[1]

Accumulation and learning are certainly necessary for human lives, but at some point we must surrender that learning and "unlearn" so as to foster spontaneity, non-interference and the capacity to let things take their natural course when necessary. To apprehend the "vague beyond" one must shake free from learning.[33]

But non-doing and non-interference, like surrender, do not mean removing oneself from the world of daily action and living (as for example an ascetic or hermit often does); rather it means acting from within a stance of being guided. Lao Tzu says "keep on diminishing and diminishing", which implies that one has in fact learned about things in the past, enabling diminishment now to occur. Thus non-doing happens from *within* learning and doing. Lest we think that this diminishing results in an abandonment of our duties, he immediately states the other side of the opposition, "yet nothing is left undone". When one attains the state of non-doing then life has been simplified so that there is the time, the awareness and the mindfulness to bring to fruition all relevant questions and tasks one is faced with.[34] Through surrender it is possible to discern, via human feel-

---

[32] Lao Tzu, *Tao Te Ching*, translated by John C.H. Wu and edited by Paul K. T Sih (N.Y.: St. John's University Press, 1961), p. 69.

[33] Alfred North Whitehead, *Modes of Thought* (Cambridge University Press, 1938), p. 8.

[34] Yet, at the same time, surrendering is not something one "does" or "accomplishes". For example, *hsü* in Chinese Taoism means "emptiness" or "purity" wherein one becomes at peace with the Tao: in tranquillity the self is transcended. Contemplative Taoists attain *hsü* by stilling their thought processes and passions, and some practise for many years; but they are denounced by other Taoists as at-

ing, the most intense and harmonious path for one's daily life. Since that path is through the lived world, which includes others and the physical environment, this intensity and harmony is not solely personal, it permeates the *Lebenswelt*. Sean was being guided away from the accident that eventually took his life: had he surrendered enough to heed that guidance, perhaps he would not have been in the wrong place at the wrong time.

Surrendering is a form of struggle, struggling in the middle while concomitantly letting go of the outcome of the struggle. Aisling's surrender was her struggle with the dissonance produced in her by challenging the experiences she faced in relation to Sean's death, and by the ramifications of those experiences in relation to her religious beliefs. In Aisling's case, when she was finally able to surrender the bitterness and sadness caused by Sean's death and by other people's prejudice towards her, she was liberated and felt she also had to surrender her paradoxical notion of an all-controlling God. When one examines human experience in the midst of suffering, three alternatives may emerge: acceptance that God somehow causes unjust suffering, or atheism, or revision of the concept of God.[35] Notice that Aisling asked why she should care about *that* God. She surrendered her externally-based faith in that God, the all-controlling God of religious tradition. It is vital to note that she did not become an atheist, or an agnostic; rather, she occupied those in-between spaces of the middle— between theism, atheism and agnosticism. After Sean's death she still had faith, but faith in *what?* An awareness emerged from within her prereflective faith as she discovered a God who has the power of "persuasion". Aisling's faith deepened in the midst of her suffering through her surrender.

How did this happen? Aisling tells Richard that her infant son Philip showed her the meaning of persuasive power. Aisling had two gifts: an underlying prereflective faith and Philip. These gifts brought about a beneficial change in her attitude from remorse and bitterness about Sean's death to courage and acceptance. Richard asked her about the change in her attitude from bitterness to courage and acceptance:

> 'And what brought about the change?'
> 'Philip.'

---

tempting to strive after something that is beyond human possibility. Rather, the latter Taoists hold, if one attains *hsü*, it "simply happens". We may say it happens because the effort to attain it was actually an obstacle to the attainment. Negotiating the obstacle is surrender.

[35] Regarding the debate over the issue, see Chapters One and Four in Sia and Sia, *From Suffering to God*. Also see Hartshorne, "Can We Understand God?"

'Philip? You mean he suddenly spoke and told you to shape up?'
'Yes!'
'[Philip] got up and spoke in a loud voice. No, seriously, it was not as
spectacular as that But have you ever thought of the power of the helplessness of a baby? ... In your [philosophy] books that's probably a contradiction ... I always tell the students during one of my lectures that I would bet
that no matter how interesting somebody's lecture may be, if somebody
brought a helpless baby into the lecture hall, everyone's attention would be
directed to that cooing baby. There's power in that It's a different kind of
power. It doesn't dominate, it attracts.,. It doesn't threaten, it influences.'
        'You must forgive me, but I don't see the connection between that and
God.'
        'I don't blame you. [Coming to this realization] took me a long time ...
The whole thing made me wonder what made me blame God. Well, I had
been taught that God could do everything. So God could have prevented
the accident. But the accident still happened. But what if God were like the
helpless infant, like Philip a few years ago!'
        'God, a helpless infant? And to think that I've been defending God's
almighty power in my research!'
        'But it doesn't make God any less powerful. Only that it's a different
kind of power.'[36]

Aisling explains that she had been blaming God for Sean's death, but
the fault was with the drunk driver and the causal chain of human decisions and actions. God does not solely control everything, and thus is not
solely responsible for everything. She realised that as a mother she had
certain responsibilities towards her infant, and that she, not God, was li-
able for fulfilling those responsibilities. A question then arose in Richard's mind regarding the efficacy of this kind of persuading power:

        'And how does that tie in with the way you describe power?'
        'That God, because God has chosen to share the responsibility, appeals
to us to exercise that responsibility. God doesn't force us. Just as a helpless
baby does not and cannot. But when a baby looks up to you, you know
through those teary eyes or smiling face, the baby is exerting an influence
on you.'
        'Doesn't that make God weak?'
        'Is someone weak who enables you to do something? Is a teacher less
powerful for inspiring others to accomplish more? Is a poet or an artist any
less effective than a tyrant? Is a Muse irrelevant?'[37]

---

[36] Sia and Sia, *The Fountain Arethuse*, pp. 277-278.
[37] *Ibid.* pp. 278-279.

Richard questions this notion of power, and thinks that persuasive power may be weak, but Whitehead and Hartshorne hold that it is the most effective power in the universe. On a personal level our actions are based on persuasive power in that our mind mainly *persuades* our body to act. On a social level, a CEO, a politician or an administrator cannot *efficiently* cause much of anything; it is only through persuasive power and thus the *free decisions of the ones being persuaded* that the politician is successful. Thus, persuasive power is wider in scope than direct efficient power. Because God works through the fabric of reality in an ubiquitous manner (throughout all space and time), God's persuasive power is not a limited form of power extant in, for example, creatures such as ourselves with bodies living in three-dimensional space for a few million years. God's persuasive power is far beyond this. God persuaded the evolution of all matter and energy from a chaotic state at the beginning of the universe into the order and harmony that has resulted in the natural world and intelligent beings such as ourselves. This is immense power, exerted over an immense period of time, with results that some call surprising and others call miraculous. Creation is so marvellous and complex that we have been trying to discern the nature of that order and harmony for millennia, and no doubt will continue trying to do so (this is the very quest of philosophy, science and religion). Richard arrived on the scene approximately 15 billion years late with a tiny sphere of influence, a small amount of persuasive and efficient causal power (the latter is due mainly to his two hands and two legs that enable him to manipulate his immediate physical surroundings) and he thinks the persuasive power of God may be weak! It is these very categories that are giving Richard trouble in his research about the problem of evil. Because he is thinking in classical terms Richard is running directly into a dead-end when confronted by the traditional idea of God's power and how it relates to suffering in the concrete world.

Persuasive Power: Malachowski Opens a Space

In a dialogue between Richard and Professor Malachowski, Richard makes explicit the implicit difficulties with his own approach to the problem of evil. In addition, the content of the dialogue itself points to a more robust approach to the problem of evil, an approach that is pursued in the academic book *From Suffering to God*.

For the past three years Richard has been working on a book (his first) dealing with evil, and has made little progress in the preceding year. He is under pressure and is suffering from anxiety in the attempt to finally finish the book, because its completion is important as he is applying for tenure at his university in the United States.. He is hoping for inspiration while at Mercier University in Leuven so he can finish writing the last chapter. Richard is discussing the problem regarding his research with the Polish professor Piotr Malachowski, who started on a philosophical and theological search for meaning after the death of his family in the German concentration camps. Professor Malachowski traversed philosophy and theology, and after many years was led to the process philosophical point of view where he hopes to find a way to make sense of appalling suffering and evil. The underlying feeling is that Richard is frustrated because his solution to the problem of evil, using the traditional Thomistic approach does not speak to the experience of the suffering people he has encountered in his daily life.

Richard's approach to the problem of evil is along discursive lines, and may be characterised as the traditional or "generic" problem of evil.[38] Below, we see Richard alluding to those who see the problem of evil as a logical puzzle, and he is referring to this approach. Richard himself takes this generic approach but is becoming suspicious of his own thinking.

By using a synoptic Whiteheadian view, Professor Malachowski is able to help Richard pin down the reasons why he has become uncomfortable with his approach and why his research is not proceeding. Similar to Sean taking on the burden and co-suffering in silence with his friends at the hospital, Professor Malachowski does not lecture Richard or give him ready-made solutions to his problem. A dialectic, familiar to those with experience in clinical psychology, occurs in this dialogue wherein the older more experienced Professor Malachowski opens intellectual and interpersonal "space" for Richard's frustrations. In a sense Malachowski "lures" Richard into discovering the solutions himself. I will first briefly explicate this five-step dialectical process (A to E below) and then follow with an example from the dialogue.

(A) Richard shares. Richard has a problem that is weighing on his feelings, and he shares his burden with Professor Malachowski.
(B) Professor Malachowski feels and intensifies Richard's problem. Because Malachowski is aware on a deeper level, and aided by the synoptic view of process ought, he is able to feel the source of Richard's frustration. However, the professor does not "solve" the problem, but instead *reshapes* the problem and thematises it for Richard. This enables Richard

---

[38] This problem results from maintaining simultaneously that (1) God is omnipotent; (2) God is omnibeneficient; and (3) evil exists. These three assertions taken together, unqualified and or undenied, must necessarily result in a logical contradiction.

to see and feel the nature of the problem more clearly so that Richard's own consciousness can attack the problem directly. The claim here is that this approach actually enables Richard to be more aware of his own thoughts and feelings.

(C) Professor Malachowski opens himself to genuine listening. He opens up to Richard by engaging in real listening. He encourages Richard to talk by stepping back and leaving the space and freedom for Richard to say whatever he needs to. Put another way, Professor Malachowski truly cares.

(D) Richard begins to answer his own questions. Because of this help, Richard is able to bring to light some aspects of solutions to his problem. Where do these aspects come from? They come from Richard, because the source of questions also harbours the answers to those questions: "a question bears with it an implicit answer, no matter how vague it may be when the questions are asked. For if the questioner had no knowledge at all of the answer, he or she would not be able to raise the questions in the first place."[39] Questions and problems crop up against the background of implicit knowledge and the task of the helper or the teacher is to lure the questioner or student into bringing that implicit knowledge to the foreground themselves.

(E) Malachowski points the way forward. Finally, and only in the end, Malachowski uses ideas from process thought to show Richard that possibilities exist for thinking along more fruitful and fundamental lines.

Let us see how these five factors are at play in a dialogue from *Arethuse.* The passages are lettered (A to E, keyed to the elements above) in the dialogue so as to differentiate the elements more easily:

(A) ...Richard disclosed the difficulty he was experiencing in completing his work. Somehow there was an important factor missing in his scholarly research, he confided to Dr. Malachowski. 'I feel that I'm working on a solution without knowing what the real problem is,' remarked Richard ...

(B)(C) 'That sounds strange. We philosophers are supposed to be able not only to evaluate the merits of each argument but also to clarify the issues.' The professor looked Richard in the eye. 'You are talking about the proper starting point for our philosophising, aren't you?'

(A) 'Possibly. But I don't just mean articulating what the philosophical issues in a problem are.' Richard tucked his left hand under his right elbow. 'Take human suffering, for instance. A very concrete reality if ever there was one. I've worked on this topic for some time now and yet when I am faced with the challenge of talking to someone who's just lost a loved one, or an individual who has just been through a disaster, I'm lost for words.

---

[39] Sia and Sia, *From Suffering to God*, p. 19.

> Surely we philosophers should be able to say something meaningful in sit-
> uations like that…..
> *(B)/(C)* 'But do you expect philosophy to say something meaningful in this
> situation?'[40]

Malachowski is opening the problem up for Richard and bringing out elements of Richard's own feelings and thoughts about the problem of evil, while Malachowski temporarily sets aside his own concerns and ideas. In the novel we already know that Malachowski *does* believe that philosophy should say something meaningful about human suffering. This is clear because the genesis of Malachowski's philosophising lies in trying to find meaning in the suffering and death of his parents in the Nazi camps; his quest is not a purely intellectual one but also an existential one.[41] But instead of immediately using his own experience and arguing that philosophy should say something meaningful about human suffering, Malachowski surrenders his own point of view by asking Richard if *he* (Richard) thinks philosophy should say something meaningful regarding the problem of suffering.

Next, continuing the dialectical exchange, Richard states that philoso-phy should say something meaningful about human suffering, and cau-tiously shares his worries with the professor that philosophy focuses too much on knowledge and too little on human experience. Again, Mala-chowski makes an effort to stimulate Richard's thinking:

> *(B)/(C)* 'But do you expect philosophy to say something meaningful in this
> situation [regarding suffering]?'
> *(A)* 'Yes, since the study of philosophy is meant to provide us with wis-
> dom. But I sometimes get the impression that what we philosophers have
> become concerned with is knowledge and more knowledge.' Richard
> paused, not knowing how his remarks would be accepted.
> *(C)* 'Go ahead, I'm listening,' the older professor, who took a sip from his
> glass of Beaujolais, was encouraging.
> *(D)* 'We sometimes blame the sciences for accumulating all this informa-
> tion and math for juggling with figures and becoming too abstract in the
> whole process. And yet aren't we doing the same thing? I know of some
> philosophers who regard the problem of evil, for instance, as an intellectual

---

[40] Sia and Sia, *The Fountain Arethuse*, p. 104.

[41] For example, instead of accepting teaching positions at more prestigious univer-sities, Professor Malachowski chooses to stay in Lublin, Poland, because the Ma-jdanek camp is physically close to his university. The actual camp is the situation that stimulates his philosophising and the font that feeds his craving for answers.

puzzle. They get a lot of kicks from solving problems which are of their own making. In the end one could ask what that has to do with life.'
(B) 'Wait now. Are you talking about the problem of suffering or of philosophy as a problem?'.... 'Are these not separate issues?'
(D) 'That's precisely *the* problem. We philosophers are so fond of being clear about the issues that we start classifying reality.'
(B) 'But how can you expect to address the issues adequately if you have not clarified them? That *is* important, as you know.'
(D) 'True, but sometimes we do lose the real issue as we dissect, as it were, what we perceive to be the problem. I remember my Asian colleague once quoting Mencius, who said that what one dislikes in clever men is their tortuosity.'[42]

It seems as if Richard is telling (or enlightening) Professor Malachowski that philosophy is too abstract, too classificatory and so on, but it is important to realise that Malachowski already believes this. Richard is coming to grips with the facts that philosophers are too fond of classification and abstraction, and that they lose sight of the real issues through dissection; but this deeper awareness is being lured out of Richard via the conversation. With the next comment, however, for the first lime Malachowski uses process philosophy and hints at a possible solution to Richard's problem. He says that both formal analysis *and* speculative delight are required in contemplating the major questions. The implication is that Richard has to widen his viewpoint considerably instead of conceiving philosophy as either formal or informal, creative or analytic. Richard has to surrender his dichotonomous attitude about what philosophy is, and occupy the arduous middle between speculation and scholarship. Malachowski says:

> *(E)* ...there is something in Whitehead's *Adventures of Ideas* that I was reading just this morning.' ... 'He was alerting us to what is lost from speculation by scholarship. He says, in speculation there is delight and discourse while in scholarship there is concentration and thoroughness. Of course, Whitehead claims that for progress both are necessary.'
> *(D)* 'I believe that we have lost the "feel" of the problem because of all our disputations....'
> *(B)* 'But that is not the domain of philosophy, at least as commonly understood.'
> *(D)* 'Exactly, we have left out an important aspect of the problem in our philosophising.'
> *(C)* 'And what is that?' quizzed the professor.

---

[42] Sia and Sia, *The Fountain Arethuse*, pp. 104-105.

(D) 'The element of life. The importance of experience. The necessary connection between our thinking and our living.'
(C) And how does that relate to the problem of suffering that you mentioned earlier on?'
(D) 'That we need a different way of describing the problem. Philosophy shouldn't attempt a solution until it has done justice to the reality of suffering. [But] It's much too abstract to do that. At least the way philosophical thinking has become.'[43]

Recall the events just before the car accident that ended Sean's life: Sean's practical response to the suffering of his friends at the hospital was to shoulder their burden in silence, and similarly here we see Malachowski take on Richard's problems by being "silent", by opening an interpersonal space for Richard; Malachowski provides a lure. This opening of space is akin to Malachowski exercising persuasive power. Richard now knows he must reconnect to concrete experience to do justice to the reality of human suffering. Richard seems to feel this because he says, "we need a different way of describing the problem", but he cannot actually surrender his classical approach just yet. Richard is still stuck at the level of the logical analysis of the "generic problem of evil".[44]

Different Approaches to the Problem

It is useful at this stage to make a distinction between three approaches to the question of evil and divinity. These three approaches are (1) a traditional theodicy or logical defence, (2) what I call a "robust theodicy", and (3) what I call a *theopraxical* approach.

The popular and traditional approach to the problem (the approach alluded to as purely formal and insufficient even by the present Pope) is a theodicy or logical defence. This is a purely theoretical defence wherein the theist defends against the atheistic charge that the proposition "God is omnipotent and all-good" is logically inconsistent with the proposition "evil exists". Leibniz coined the term "'theodicy" (with his book entitled *Théodicée,* from the Greek *theo-dike). Dike* signifies "order" or "right" and thus one way to think of what a theodicy does is that it attempts to

---

[43] *Ibid.* pp. 105-106.
[44] See David Basinger and Randall Basinger, "The Problem with the 'Problem of Evil'," *Religious Studies*, 30, 1 (1994), pp. 89-97, wherein it is suggested that the "generic" approach to the problem of evil is becoming unfruitful polemic that allows both theists and atheists to hide in the shadows of ambiguous argumentation. The generic or purely logical defence should be surpassed for a more substantial debate.

make God right or make God conform to an order. In the spirit of ensuring order, the important point for a traditional theodicy is that the argument make logical sense and little weight is given to the plausibility or ramifications of the argument. Many theists, for example Alvin Plantinga,[45] argue that it is wholly sufficient to provide a defence of this sort.

But our friend Richard in *Arethuse* is beginning to have misgivings about such an approach and is leaning towards a fuller point of view that may be characterised as a "robust theodicy". Examples of such theodicies are the works of, among others, Hartshorne, David Ray Griffin and Barry L. Whitney.[46] Today's world needs a full or robust theodicy that is more holistic in scope as opposed to past eras where a logical vindication of God was sufficient because belief in God was widespread. Griffin points out that in the past the traditional idea of God was not called into question even in the face of the evils of the world because belief was woven into the fabric of society. But today biblical criticism has changed our stance towards the authority of the Bible, and thus abstract approaches to the issue of evil and suffering are inadequate.[47] Griffin also says, "In our situation, the theologian needs [using Hartshorne's phrase] "global argument", the purpose of which is to show that a theistic interpretation can illuminate the totality of our experience, including the experience of evil better than nontheistic interpretations."[48] Process theodicy involves reconceiving the notion of God's power, but this reformulation is not undertaken solely as an answer to the problem of evil, rather for a broad range of reasons that have to do with reconceiving our entire worldview in a constructively postmodern way: God's power is reconceived so as to explain coherently the relation of religion to the evolutionary origin of our world, to explain contradictions in scripture, to explain miracles (some of these may be better explained as paranormal or psi events) and to explain the diversity of religions.[49] Part of this theistic reformulation involves acknowledging new findings in physics and the other sciences. In a holistic way, the robust

---

[45] For example, see Alvin Plantinga, "Reply to the Basingers on Divine Omnipotence," *Process Studies*, 11, 1 (1981), pp. 25-29, *passim*; and Alvin Plantinga, *God, Freedom and Evil* (London: George Allen & Unwin Ltd., 1975), pp. 7-73.

[46] For example, see David Ray Griffin, *God, Power and Evil: a Process Theodicy* (Philadelphia: Westminster Press, 1976) and David Ray Griffin, *Evil Revisited: Responses and Reconsiderations* (N.Y.: SUNY Press, 1991). Also see Barry L. Whitney, *Evil and the Process God*, Toronto Studies in Theology, volume 10 (N.Y.: The Edwin Mellen Press, 1985).

[47] Griffin, *God, Power and Evil*, p. 256.

[48] *Ibid.*

[49] *Ibid.* pp. 3-4.

theodicy is supplied with substance from other fronts also undergoing constructive reformulation.

We find a differently situated approach in *From Suffering to God* and in *Arethuse.* The element of *praxis* becomes important. This third approach I call a *theopraxical* one. It is not enough to produce a logical vindication, or even an expanded or more holistic theoretical framework. An important ramification of establishing that holistic theoretical framework is the realisation that the question of God and of evil is partly an empirical question because God acts through empirical reality. The "argument" regarding God and evil also extends into the realm of *praxis* or worldly action. Co-suffering and surrender (as a religious comportment) are important behaviours in addressing the evils and problems in the world.

From Suffering to God focuses less on the theist-atheist debate (that is, the questions of God's existence or non-existence) and more on the human practical response to suffering. Because the *theopraxical* approach is not burdened by the elements of the theist-atheist debate, it can address the issues of God and evil in a more comprehensive way. For example, *From Suffering to God* starts with the practical response of *believers* to the problem of suffering and then explores theological and philosophical issues implicit in those *already theistically-oriented* responses. This stance permits the Sias to move farther into the issues and effectively suggest that since *all* free creatures participate in creating evil in the world in some sense, even if they are not explicitly aware of it[50], it is therefore the duty of all free creatures to *alleviate* the sufferings of others.[51] The *theopraxical* approach acknowledges that an important part of dealing with the problem of evil involves personal action in the world.

The idea of praxis comes across clearly in *Arethuse* with the attitude of Dr Fuentes, a liberation theologian from the Philippines. Instead of questioning the existence of God, he questions the traditional idea of God and moves directly into the ramifications or implications as regards acting in the world. Dr Fuentes is a seminary professor of philosophy sent to Leuven by his bishop for a sabbatical and he personifies the approach towards the problem of evil taken in *From Suffering to God* and in many liberation theologies. Going back to the dialogue in *Arethuse,* Richard and Dr Mala-

---

[50] An important element of western religious clemency entails asking forgiveness for "sins of omission" and sins caused without the knowledge of the person (for example, see the Roman Catholic Act of Contrition). This element fits well with Hartshorne's view that the clash of free creativities sometimes produces evil effects unknown to the creatures.

[51] For arguments regarding our duty to alleviate the suffering of others, see Sia and Sia, *From Suffering to God,* Chapter Seven.

chowski are joined by Dr Fuentes. After Malachowski has summarised what he and Ricbard had discussed regarding the problem of suffering, Dr Fuentes directly responds, and he cuts across the traditional lines of the debate:

'Who was it who said—I think it was Heidegger—philosophers are reducing reality to a mentally fabricated axiomatic project. I can understand your situation.' Dr. Fuentes, who was about ten years older than Richard, looked at him. 'Although my difficulty with the way philosophy generally handles the problem of evil is that it is seen too much as a theodicy. Too much attention is given to the challenge of atheism. Don't you agree?' He turned his head in the direction of Dr. Malachowski, who nodded. 'And so we are expected to provide a coherent and credible resolution of how God can be defended as almighty *and* all-good when there is so much evil and suffering around us.... *The important question is not theodicy but idolatry.*'[52]

Dr Fuentes has a different approach to the problem of evil, one forged in the hot furnace of experiences under an oppressive political regime. He is not concerned with fighting against atheism and with defending God's almighty power in the face of atheistic arguments. He notes that such an approach is indeed an important aspect of the problem, but what is more important is that people are suffering and being told, ludicrously, that it is "in God's controlled and controlling plan" for them to suffer horribly. They are taught that their suffering is God's punishment Worse, they are told that human beings simply cannot know why God *is* choosing to cause their babies to be born tubercular and their young children to starve to death, while God chooses health and happiness for those in the more economically-developed nations. But Dr Fuentes does not believe God is choosing this, and is concerned that the government (and even the churches) are perpetrating a horrific evil themselves by handing down a notion of God that is idolatrous. Dr Fuentes says, "The danger for us is that in our attempts to defend God, as it were, we could be perpetuating idols."[53] He claims that the main question surrounding the problem of evil is not whether God exists, but "What kind of God can we continue to believe in, given the presence of so much undeserved suffering?"[54]

In addition, Professor Malachowski is concerned about praxis or dealing with the real world, He has been asking the same questions about the nature of God because of his experience with the concentration camps of World War II. The genesis of his philosophical search was the reality of

---

[52] Sia and Sia, *The Fountain Arethuse,* p. 106 (emphasis mine)
[53] *Ibid.* pp. 107-108.
[54] *Ibid.* p. 107.

Recall the ε
practical respon

the human suffering in the concentration camp, and his philosophising is kept alive by his physical visits to the camp. As mentioned above, he had the opportunity to further his career at a distinguished university, but refused the appointment because it entailed leaving Poland. The camp at Majdanek was the source of his philosophising:

> Truth stared him in the face as he meditated on the events which led to the death of his parents. As he wandered about the camp, a routine that he religiously followed, looking in distress at the piles of shoes of the former inmates, as he dodged the wire fence that had trapped his parents and several others in a pitiful existence, as he imagined the bitterness and the frustration that reduced humans to mere skeletons, he often asked why, why did such evil things happen? Why was suffering perpetrated by evil people?[55]

Some sufferers feel abandoned by God, but many feel their faith deepened. Why is their faith deepened? Malachowski searched theology, then philosophy, and ended up seriously questioning the traditional notion of God. The idea of a God who had to be defended in the face of suffering may not be a God worthy of worship. A good question is: What kind of God is God? The answer implicit in the Sias' novel but explicit in their scholarly book, is that the process notion of God is a persuasive God who truly co-creates with creatures. And further, God needs no defence because truly free creatures make decisions that sometimes result in evil, and God never coerces creatures.[56]

---

[55] *Ibid.* p. 103.

[56] A technical digression may be helpful here. In Whitney, *Evil and the Process God,* it is suggested that the Hartshornean position that God acts solely persuasively needs more clarification because Hartshorne can be interpreted as holding that God must act coercively in certain cases such as imposition of physical law. Thus, Whitney raises the issue of whether God's power may be a mixture of persuasion and coercion (pp. 99-114). He suggests in a preliminary way that God's lure may be persuasively effective to a degree that is directly correlated to the creature's openness to it; the more open we are, the more persuasive (and thus coercive) God is (pp. 12 and 130). This is intriguing, and I further suggest that a radical openness to the lure means not more coercion but more freedom, and that rejection of the divine lure leads to coercion and "purification". In other words, being consistently radically open to the divine lure means that eventually more order and harmony is prehended from the past and this means a richer initial aim (thus more viable choices in self-constitution) and thus more freedom. On the other hand, a radical rejection of the lure means eventually more chaotic data are extant in the past, and thus are inherited from the past, and this results in a "purification" of the past in present behaviour (something akin to a spiri-

Nature Alive: towards a Different Conception of God

The different approaches to the problem of evil and God entail a novel concept of God. If *theo-dike* signifies the attempt to make God right or make God conform to an order, then the "robust theodicy" and the *theo-praxical* approaches above are both truer to "theodicy" or *Théodicée* than a traditional theodicy because both approaches necessitate modifying the inherited concept of God. Ideas of God, whether they be directly received in a revelatory sense, or wrought by the hands of theologians and philosophers, are humanly-constructed notions.[57] Thus it makes sense that, if our inherited notion of divinity is paradoxical when confronted with manifest experience (such as the experience of evil), we amend that notion of divinity.

As mentioned earlier, most persons have a prereflective idea of God. There seems to be good reason to turn to this prereflective idea because God need not be conceptualised in the traditional manner as an utterly spiritual, transcendent, omnipotent, omniscient being in a separate heavenly reality fully controlling the material world. There is hope for those of us who have an intuitive inkling about the religious life, but are confused about the traditional idea of God. The process idea of God, as set forth by Whitehead and Hartshorne (and others), is examined in the Sias' novel and scholarly book. The books delineate an alternative notion of God that squares with human intuition. On this view, God is a persuasive force congenital in reality rather than a controlling being external to reality.

Today, given the microscope, biology, mathematics, quantum physics and so on, we know that in principle there is little difference between plant life, animal life and human life. "All life is either unicellular or multicellular, and a cell is a living individual which in a certain measure determines its own activities in response to stimuli from without."[58] Further, entering the realm of matter, given the findings of twentieth-century science, the concept of dead, inert matter does not do justice to new scientific

---

tual/psychological crisis or the mystic "Dark Night"). The past comes back to haunt (parallel to eastern notions of karma). Regarding the continuous rejection of the lure and thus the inheritance of more and more chaotic data, initial aims would be meagre and thus the degree of coercion high; that is, the entity has little choice in the attempt to maintain complexity of experience or order of experience.

[57] Hartshorne holds that divine revelation cannot be directly received in an infallible manner, which implies that revelation is partly human construction. See Hartshorne. *Omnipotence and Other Theological Mistakes*, p. 37

[58] Charles Hartshorne, *Creative Synthesis and Philosophic Method* (London: SCM Press Ltd., 1970), p. 49.

discoveries. Thus, the first step to a new conception of God is to realise that not only humans, animals and plants are alive, but also, in a sense, all of nature is "alive". All of reality, in a sense, experiences. "An occasion of experience which includes a mentality is an extreme instance, at one end of the scale, of those happenings which constitute nature."[59] For the most part, the world consists of primitive experience or aboriginal consciousness, or *life*. Scientists tell us that plant life (for example, algae) developed from inorganic matter some three billion years ago. It stretches credulity to believe that some sort of enigmatic or mystical transformation suddenly took place in history that resulted in life or animate matter—the appeal to Ockham's razor results rather in the belief that the conditions for life and consciousness are congenital in reality in the first place: nature is alive. Even among physicists, there is wide agreement that there must be some kind of "primitive choice" at the quantum levels of reality.[60]

Considering that all of nature is alive allows us to extend the notion of sentience upwards, to the world and the universe as a whole, and this leads to a new concept of God. On the physical level, the British chemist James E. Lovelock and the American biologist Lynn Margulis formulated the "Gaia hypothesis" wherein the Earth's matter, air, oceans and land surface from a complex system which can be seen as a single living organism. This might be a wild hypothesis to some, but it helps us expand out thinking about the nature of our world. Expanding this "Gaia" notion upwards and fitting it into a more philosophical framework lead to the Platonic or Plotinian *World Soul*. Again generalising up from this hypothesis we arrive at the whole cosmos as a single, feeling reality, or God. Consider Hartshorne's analogy where the soul is to the body as God is to the world:

> The body is a *society* of billions of cells, each a highly organized society of molecules and particles or wavicles. At a given moment each of us, *as* a conscious individual, is a single reality; but our body is no such single reality. Each white blood corpuscle is a tiny animal.... Similarly, God's cosmic body is a society of individuals, not a single individual. The world as

---

[59] Alfred North Whitehead, *Adventures Of Ideas* (New York: The Free Press, 1967), p. 184.
[60] Psychicalism (or panpsychism, or panexperientialism, or the event ontology of process thinking) is being considered today in relation to a reformulation of the fundamental principles of nature, particularly in the field of particle physics. See the works of David Bohm in David Ray Griffin (ed.), *Physics and the Ultimate Significance of Time: Bohm, Prigogine, and Process Philosophy* (Albany, NY: Stale University of New Yolk Press, 1986); also see Griffin, *The Reenchantment of Science,* and Roger Penrose, *Shadows Of the Mind: A Search for the Missing Science of Consciousness* (London: Vintage Press, I 995), pp. 393-421.

an integrated individual is not a "world" as this term is normally and properly used, but "God". God, the World Soul, is the *individual integrity* of
"the world", which otherwise is just the myriad of creatures.[61]

If we accept Hartshorne's analogy, then we may feel God's cosmic
body because we are a part of it. This is not a Hegelian move, or a bringing of God into presence. The move here is more fundamental than these
because it calls into question the very assumptions upon which we build
our world-view in this scientific epoch. In this epoch we think in dualistic
terms that engender a schism between nature and life, between humanity
and God, between mind and matter. Hartshorne and Whitehead aim to
close the ontological, epistemological and psychological gaps between
humanity and God. But Hartshorne does not unite them with a *pantheism*.
It is our habitual thinking which declares that God is either utterly external
to the universe or utterly immanent. Rather, Hartshorne's position is one
of *panentheism* which is midway between the traditional view of God being the wholly independent and universal cause of the universe and the
traditional pantheistic view wherein God simply *is* the universe. In Hartshorne's view, God is inclusive of the world, but not solely inclusive of the
world. God is also something more: a unifying factor. This is similar to the
way that the human soul is inclusive of the body—yet the soul is also
something more: a unifying factor. When we escape the confines of traditional thinking and instead think about God and creatures bound together
in co-creation, the problem of evil and responsibility gets transformed—
possibly *dissolved.*

Conclusion

As Richard said, there is a necessary connection between our thinking
and our living. One of the keys to escaping the confines of the philosophy
and the theology of our epoch, and thus dodging at least the brunt of the
blow of the *problem of evil,* is to expand our world-view and conceive of
God as acting persuasively from within in a co-creative process, and realising that the problem of evil does not involve exonerating God but rather
re-examining God and the nature of God's power in relation to ourselves.
Breaking out of the strictures of thinking and moving into the frontiers
of incorporating feeling and intuition into a world-view does not mean
abandoning rationality. On the contrary, it means regaining the original
ground of reason in all its "robustness". Overcoming the schism between
the so-called "material" and so-called "spiritual realms" means seeing the

---

[61] Hartshorne, *Omnipotence and Other Theological Mistakes*, p. 59.

connections between literature, philosophy, the sciences and theology. Mending the material/spiritual schism in awareness means realising that the ground of literature, philosophy, the sciences and theology is the same ground. We surrender and try to feel our way forward on that ground because the infinite complexities of the universe cannot be univocalised with our minds. Instead of trying to *solve* the problem of evil as Richard does, Aisling reaches into the *immanent beyond* and *dissolves* the problem by actualising her prereflective faith that the universe somehow makes sense. Aisling is not duped into abandoning spirituality simply because the image of God she learned about as a child turns out to be inadequate. Instead, she moves forward in a theopraxical sense into a deeper spiritual life.

Richard, Aisling, Malachowski and Fuentes faced the perplexities of everyday life, and did so with the help of God as the source of order leading them away from evil and suffering. Therefore wherever they met evil and suffering in their co-creation, they were not heeding the ever-present divine guidance—they were not surrendering to God. Evil is ubiquitous, yet it need not be. Opening ourselves via surrender to the divine lure, feeling and acting upon the will of God is, indeed, the fundamental human enquiry and can only be answered with the quest that comprises an entire human life from birth to death. Surrendering to a God who lures creatures, even in the midst of suffering, and occupying that seemingly impossible "middle" space between activity and passivity, is the way to actualise a co-creation that brings God's harmonious atemporal vision into the temporal world. This is the path to overcoming evil. This is the crux of the process theodicy, as well as the hope of those who ask, as does Dr Fuentes, "What kind of God can we continue to believe in, given the presence of so much undeserved suffering?"

UACHTARÁN NA hÉIREANN
PRESIDENT OF IRELAND

MESSAGE FROM PRESIDENT McALEESE

I am delighted to convey my good wishes to Professor Santiago Sia on his upcoming retirement. As Dean of Philosophy at Milltown he has been a tower of inspiration to countless students, just as he always been during such a distinguished academic career. But, of course, as well as being a fine teacher, Santiago has never put down the pen - or the keyboard! - of the researcher and the writer and his legacy also includes such an impressive corpus of writing and wise scholarship. Given his great energy and enthusiasm, I have no doubt that retirement day will be for Santiago merely another milestone along the journey of such a full and active life and no doubt we can look forward to several more interesting publications in the future. Martin joins with me in sending Santiago and his family our warmest best wishes for a happy, healthy and fulfilled retirement.

Mary McAleese

MARY McALEESE
PRESIDENT

16 FEBRUARY, 2010

SELECTED BIBLIOGRAPHY

Alpers, Paul J., ed. 1967, *Elizabethan Poetry: Modern Reflections in Criticism*, Oxford University Press

Anderson, Bernhard. W. 1971, 2nd ed. *The Living World of the Old Testament*, London: Longman

Aquinas, Thomas. 1981 repr., *Summa Theologica*, Christian Classics

Aristotle, trans. with introduction and notes by Martin Oswald. 1989, *Nicomachean Ethics*, N.Y.: Macmillan Publishing Co.

Beck, Hubert. 1970, *The Age of Technology*, St. Louis: Concordia Publishing House

Bloch, Chana. 1985, *Spelling the Word: George Herbert and the Bible*, University of California Press

Bloom, Harold, ed. 1987. *William Shakespeare's Sonnets: Modern Critical Interpretation*, Chelsea House Publishers

Booth, Stephen.1969, *A Reflection on Shakespeare's Sonnets*, New Haven and London: Yale University Press

Bowker, John. 1991, *The Meanings of Death*, Cambridge University Press

Buber, Martin. 1957, *Eclipse of God: Studies in the Relation between Religion and Philosophy*, N.Y.: Harper and Row Publishers

—. ed. and trans. M. Friedman. 1963, *Pointing the Way: Collected Essays*, N.Y.: Harper and Row Publishers

—. trans. R. Gregor Smith (2nd ed.). 1966, *I and Thou*, Edinburgh: T. & T. Clark

—. ed. M. Friedman. trans. M. Friedman and R.G. Smith. 1965, *The Knowledge of Man*, N.Y.: Harper and Row

—.trans. M. Friedman, 1967, *A Believing Humanism: 1902-1965*, NY: Simon and Shuster

—. 1971, *Between Man and Man*, Collins

Calderwood, James L. 1987, *Shakespeare and the Denial of Death*. University of Massachusetts Press

Cloots, André and Santiago Sia, eds. 1999, *Framing a Vision of the World: Essays in Philosophy, Science and Religion* Louvain Philosophical Studies 14, Leuven University Press

Cobb, John B. Jr. and David Ray Griffin, 1976, *Process Theology: an Introductory Exposition*, Philadelphia: The Westminster Press

Cocking, J.M. 1991, *Imagination: a Study in the History of Ideas*, London & N.Y.: Routledge

Cruttwell, Patrick. 1955. *The Shakespearean Moment and its Place in the Poetry of the 17th Century,* Columbia University Press

Di Cesare, Mario A., ed. 1978, *George Herbert and the Seventeenth-Century Religious Poets,* N.Y.: W.W. Norton & Co.

Dubrow, Heather. 1987. *Captive Victors: Shakespeare's Narrative Poems and Sonnets.* Cornell University Press

Ellis, Peter. 1963, *The Men and Message of the Old Testament,* Minnesota: The Liturgical Press

Erickson, Peter and Coppelia Kahn, eds. 1985, *Shakespeare's Rough Magic,* University of Delaware Press

Ferry, Anne. 1975, *All in War with Time: Love Poetry of Shakespeare, Donne, Jonson and Marvell,* Harvard University Press

Fineman, Joel. 1986, *Shakespeare's Perjured Eye: The Invention of Poetic Subjectivity in the Sonnets,* University of California Press

Fowler, James. 1981, *Stages of Faith,* Harper and Row

Fromm. Eric. 1972, *The Art of Loving,* London: Unwin Books

Gardner, Helen. 1970, *The Metaphysical Poets,* Penguin

Gardner, W.H. 1949, *Gerard Manley Hopkins (1844-1889): A Study of Poetic Idiosyncracy in Relation to Poetic Tradition,* Vol. II, London: Martin Lecker & Warburg

Gilligan, Carol. 1982. *In a Different Voice.* Cambridge, Mass.: Harvard University Press.

Griffin, David Ray. 1976, *God, Power and Evil: a Process Theodicy,* Philadelphia: Westminster Press

—. 1991, *Evil Revisited: Responses and Reconsiderations,* N.Y.: SUNY Press.

Gutierrez, Gustavo. 1987, *On Job: God-Talk and the Suffering of the Innocent,* Maryknoll, N.Y.: Orbis Books.

—. 1991, *The God of Life,* Maryknoll, N.Y.: Orbis Books

Harbage, Alfred. 1983, *A Reader's Guide to William Shakespeare,* New York: Octagon Books

Hartshorne, 1953, *Reality as Social Process: Studies in Metaphysics and Religion,* Glencoe: The Free Press, and Boston: the Beacon Press

—. (with William Reese). 1953, *Philosophers Speak of God,* University of Chicago Press

—. 1962, *The Logic of Perfection and Other Reflections in Neoclassical Metaphysics,* La Salle: Open Court

—. 1967, *A Natural Theology for our Time,* La Salle: Open Court

—. 1970, *Creative Synthesis and Philosophical Method,* London: SCM

—. 1984, *Omnipotence and Other Theological Mistakes,* SUNY Press

—. 1987, *Wisdom as Moderation: a Philosophy of the Middle Way,* SUNY Press

—. ed. Mohammad Valady, 1997, *The Zero Fallacy and Other Reflections in Neoclassical Philosophy,* Open Court, 1997

Heidegger, Martin, trans. Albert Hofstadter. 1971, *Poetry, Language and Thought,* N.Y.: Harper & Row

Hetzler, Florence M. and Austin H. Kutscher, eds. 1978, *Philosophical Aspects of Thanatology,* Vol.1, N.Y.: MSS Information Corporation

Holzapfel, Rudolf Melander. 1961, *Shakespeare's Secret,* Dolmes Press

Hubler, Edward. 1976, *The Sense of Shakespeare's Sonnets,* Westport, Conn.: Greenwood Press

James, William, with an Introduction by Martin E. Marty. 1985, *The Varieties of Religious Experience: the Study in Human Nature,* N.Y.: Penguin Books

Jasper, David. 1989, *The Study of Literature and Religion: an Introduction.* Studies in Literature and Religion, London: Macmillan

—. 2004. *The Sacred Desert: Religion, Literature, Art and Culture,* Blackwell Publishing

Kneller, George F. 1917. *Foundations of Education,* N.Y.: John Wiley

Knights, L.C. 1959, *Some Shakespearean Themes,* London: Chatto and Windus

Landry, Hilton. 1965, *Interpretations in Shakespeare's Sonnets,* University of California Press

Lao Tzu, trans. by John C.H. Wu and ed. by Paul K. T Sih. 1961, *Tao Te Ching,,* N.Y.: St. John's University Press

Lever, J. 1978, *The Elizabethan Love Sonnet,* London: Menthuen & Co. Ltd.

Levinas, Emmanuel, trans. Bettina Bergo, ed. and annotated by Jacques Rolland. 2000, *God, Death, and Time,* Stanford University Press

Loomis, Jeffrey B. 1988, *Dayspring in Darkness: Sacrament in Hopkins,* Lewisburg: Bucknell University Press

Low, Anthony. 1978, *Love's Architecture: Devotional Modes in Seventeenth-Century English Poetry,* New York University Press

MacKenzie, Norman H. 1981, *A Reader's Guide to Gerard Manley Hopkins,* Ithaca, N.Y.: Cornell University Press

Mariani, Paul L 1970, *A Commentary on the Complete Poems of Gerard Manley Hopkins,* Ithaca & London: Cornell University Press

Martin, Philip. 1972, *Shakespeare's Sonnets: Self, Love and Art,* Cambridge University Press

Martz, Louis L., ed. 1969, *English Seventeenth-Century Verse,* Vol. I, New York: W. W. Norton & Co.

Middleton, Darren J. N., ed. 2002, *God, Literature and Process Thought,* Ashgate

Milward, Peter. 1975, *Landscape and Inscape: Vision and Inspiration in Hopkins' Poetry,* Grand Rapids, Michigan: William B. Eerdmans Publishing Co.

Morris, Van Cleve. 1966, *Existentialism in Education.* N.Y.: Harper and Row

Murdoch, Iris. 1997, *Existentialist and Mystics: Writings on Philosophy and Literature,* London: Chatto & Windus

Nussbaum, Martha. 1990, *Love's Knowledge,* N.Y.: Oxford University Press

—. 2001, *Upheavals of Thought: the Intelligence of Emotions,* Cambridge University Press.

Parfitt, George. 1985, *English Poetry of the 17th Century,* London and New York: Longman

Partridge, A.C. 1978, *John Donne—Language and Style,* Andre Deutsch

Pequigney, Joseph. 1985, *Such is My Love: A Study of Shakespeare's Sonnets,* The University of Chicago Press

Peterson, Douglas L. 1973, *Time, Tide and Tempest,* San Marino, Calif.: The Huntington Library

Pettet, E.D. 1960, *Of Paradise and Light: a Study of Vaughan's Silex Scintillans,* Cambridge University Press

Pick, John. 1943, *Gerard Manley Hopkins: Priest and Poet,* London: Oxford University Press

Pittenger, Norman. 1980, *After Death: Life in God,* SCM Press

Plantinga, Alvin. 1975, *God, Freedom and Evil,* London: George Allen & Unwin Ltd.

Polkinghorne, John. 1998, *Belief in God in an Age of Science,* New Haven and London: Yale University Press

Robertson, J.M. 1926, *The Problems of the Shakespeare's Sonnets,* Billing & Sons, Ltd.

Robinson, John. 1978, *In Extremity: a Study of Gerard Manley Hopkins,* Cambridge University Press

Rosenstand, Nina. 2002, *The Human Condition: an Introduction to Philosophy of Human Nature.* McGraw Hill

—. 2003, *The Moral of the Story: An Introduction to Ethics,* 4th ed., McGraw Hill

Roston, Murray. 1974, *The Soul of Wit: A Study of John Donne,* Oxford: Clarendon Press

Rudrum, Alan, ed. 1987, *Essential Articles for the Study of Henry Vaughan*, Archon Books

Santos, Ferdinand and Santiago Sia. 2007, *Personal Identity, the Self and Ethics*, Palgrave Macmillan, 2007

Sia, M.S. 1997, *The Fountain Arethuse: a Novel set in the University Town of Leuven*, Lewes, U.K.: The Book Guild, Ltd.

Sia, Marian F. and Santiago Sia. 1994, *From Suffering to God: Exploring our Images of God in the Light of Suffering*, London: the Macmillan Press

Sia, Santiago. 1985, *God in Process Thought: a Study in Charles Hartshorne's Conception of God*, Martinus Nijhoff

—. 2004, *Religion, Reason and God: Essays in the Philosophies of Charles Hartshorne and A.N. Whitehead*, Peter Lang

Simmonds, James D. 1972, *Masques of God: Form and Theme in the Poetry of Henry Vaughan*, University of Pittsburgh Press

Skulsky, Harold. 1992, *Language Recreated: Seventeenth-Century Metaphorists and the Act of Metaphor*, Athens: University of Georgia Press

Smith, Hallett. 1952, *Elizabethan Poetry: A Study in Conventions, Meaning and Expression*, Harvard University Press

Smith, Marion Bodwell. 1966, *Dualities in Shakespeare,* University of Toronto Press

Sobrino, Jon. 1983, *The Idols of Death and the God of Life: A Theology,* Maryknoll, N.Y.: Orbis Books

Strier, Richard. 1983, *Love Known: Theology and Experience in George Herbert's Poetry,* Chicago & London: University of Chicago Press

Truss, Lynne. 2003, *Eats, Shoots & Leaves: The Zero Tolerance Approach to Punctuation.* Profile Books

Tugwell, Simon. 1990, *Human Immortality and the Redemption of Death,* London: Darton Longman and Todd

von Rad, Gerhard. 1972, *Wisdom in Israel,* London: SCM Press

Wall, John. 1981, *George Herbert: The Country Parson and the Temple,* Paulist Press

Weiser, David K. 1987, *Mind in Character: Shakespeare's Speaker in the Sonnets,* University of Missouri Press

Wheeler, Michael. 1990, *Death and the Future Life in Victorian Literature and Theology*, Cambridge University Press

Whitehead, A.N. 1926, *Science in the Modern World*, Cambridge University Press

—. 1928, *Symbolism: its Meaning and Effect,* Cambridge University Press

—. 1929, *The Function of Reason*, Oxford University Press

—. 1938, *Modes of Thought*, Cambridge University Press

—. 1942, *Adventures of Ideas.* Cambridge University Press

—. 1961, *Adventures of Ideas,* N.Y.: Macmillan

— 1967, *The Aims of Education and Other Reflection,*. The Free Press Paperback Edition

—. corr. and ed. by David Ray Griffin and Donald W. Sherburne. 1978, *Process and Reality: Essay in Cosmology,* N.Y. The Free Press.

Whitney, Barry L. 1985, *Evil and the Process God,* Toronto Studies in Theology, volume 10, N.Y.: The Edwin Mellen Press

Willen, Gerald and Victor B. Reed, eds. 1964, *A Casebook on Shakespeare's Sonnets.* New York: Thomas Y. Crowell Company

Wilson, Katherine M. 1974, *Shakespeare's Sugared Sonnets,* Barnes & Noble

Winny,James. 1968, *The Master-Mistress: A Study of Shakespeare's Sonnets.* New York: Barnes & Noble

Wright, Louis B., ed. 1966, *Shakespeare Celebrated,* Cornell University Press